Wild Words

ESSAYS ON ALBERTA LITERATURE

Edited by Donna Coates
and George Melnyk

Wild Words

ESSAYS ON ALBERTA LITERATURE

Edited by Donna Coates
and George Melnyk

AU PRESS

Published by AU Press, Athabasca University
1200, 10011 – 109 Street
Edmonton, AB T5J 3S8

Library and Archives Canada Cataloguing in Publication

Wild words: essays on Alberta literature/edited by Donna Coates and George Melnyk.

Includes bibliographical references and index.
Issued also in electronic format (ISBN 978-1-897425-31-2).
ISBN 978-1-897425-30-5

1. Canadian literature – Alberta – History and criticism.
I. Coates, Donna, 1944- II. Melnyk, George III. Title.

PS8131.A43W54 2009 C810.9'97123 C2008-908001-7

Cover design by Kris Twyman
Cover painting by Marion Twyman
Book layout and design by Infoscan Collette, Québec

Printed and bound in Canada by Marquis Book Printing

This book was funded in part by the Alberta Historical Resources Foundation.

TABLE OF CONTENTS

PREFACE

THE STRUGGLE FOR AN ALBERTA LITERATURE

DONNA COATES AND GEORGE MELNYK

In October 2005, the University of Calgary hosted the "Wild Words" conference, which aimed to bring a critical perspective to Alberta writing on the occasion of the province's centenary. Admittedly, a one-hundred-year literary tradition is brief as literary traditions go, but Alberta's literary roots are much older. They reach back to the orature of First Nations peoples and the colonizing exploration and travel literature of the eighteenth and nineteenth centuries. In this tradition, one also finds various European cultural and linguistic streams associated with waves of immigration and settlement. The existence of historical depth is one thing; the matter of literary quality is another. Even the very concept of an "Alberta literature" is an issue. The Wild Words conference dealt with these matters in a wide-ranging and provocative examination of the work of prominent Alberta writers and so served as the starting point for this book project.

The idea of a distinct Alberta literary identity is a recent one, first formulated in George Melnyk's two-volume *Literary History of Alberta* (1998,1999). But the concept has deeper roots. It began in an embryonic form in anthologies of Alberta writing published in 1955, 1967, and 1979, all of which were associated with political landmarks such as Canada's centenary.[1] These three celebratory collections were then followed by literary anthologies of Alberta fiction – *Alberta Bound* (1986) edited by Fred Stenson, *Alberta Rebound* (1990) and *Boundless Alberta* (1993) both edited by Aritha van Herk, and *Threshold: An Anthology of Contemporary Alberta Writing* (1999) edited by Srja Pavlovic. More recently we have *The Wild Rose Anthology of Alberta Prose* (2003), a historical collection edited by George Melnyk and Tamara Seiler and *Writing the Terrain: Travelling Through Alberta with the Poets* (2005) edited by Robert Stamp. This fifty-year span of anthologies suggests that Alberta literature is a reality, and yet there has been no critical literary study of Alberta writers as *Alberta* writers other than the *Literary History*. The concept of Alberta writing as a distinct literature includes within it the evolution of a cultural framework that defines that literature. A cultural framework is both grounding and a context out of which literary production occurs. This volume applies contemporary literary theory to Alberta writing in support of the concept of a meaningful Alberta literature. But it does so in a preliminary way because the essays in this book deal with only a small portion of Alberta's literary reality. It is our hope to produce further volumes that bring scholarly attention to the work of numerous writers not dealt with in *Wild Words* as part of a continuing exploration of what it means to be an Alberta writer.

The idea that a province in Canada, other than Quebec, could have a distinct literary identity is novel and debatable, just as 80 years ago the idea that Canada itself had a distinct literary identity was novel and debatable. By the 1970s, Canadian literature as a concept had become commonplace. In the same decade, the concept of Prairie literature also became an accepted label to distinguish regional writing in Canada. The idea had been first articulated by Edward McCourt in *The Canadian West in Fiction* (1949) and was reiterated by Laurie Ricou in *Vertical Man/Horizontal World* (1973) and Dick Harrison in *Unnamed Country: The Struggle for Canadian Prairie Fiction* (1977).

A special Prairie Poetry Issue of *Essays on Canadian Writing* (1980) edited by Dennis Cooley of the University of Manitoba, who spoke at the 2005 Wild Words conference twenty-five years later, confirmed the validity and viability of the Prairie Literature concept. It was based on a regional division of Canadian literature. Once the concept of Canadian literature had been accepted, its diverse content was acknowledged. The PrairieLit concept had grown out of an era in Canadian history that linked the provinces of Alberta, Saskatchewan, and Manitoba into a single agrarian political economy with a common cultural base. This unity began to unravel after World War II, when Alberta became the centre of Canada's energy industry. The resulting urbanization, industrialization, and new wealth distinguished Alberta from its two sister "Prairie" provinces, which remained, until the twenty-first century, have-not provinces. With a population in 2008 that was almost triple each of the other provinces and with an oil and gas economy (extraction, processing, and transportation) that was booming, Alberta evolved into a different kind of entity. The term "Prairie" made little sense when applied to post-1980 Alberta because the geographic designation was at odds with the economic and social realities of the province. But what could the replacement term, Alberta, mean?

Regarding literature produced in Alberta, one can first look at the measure of provincial self-consciousness that critics find in creative works by asking, how expressive of its origins is a literary product? What do these origins mean? What should be made of the Alberta-centric contexts that inspire, inform, and transform that creative work in distinctive ways – ways that link it to other creative works produced by writers from Alberta? Second, one can examine how a particular narrative or body of narratives by a writer fits into a literary past, a heritage of writing that is the province's literary history. By positioning a work or a writer in the continuum of a literary tradition, one augments and expands that tradition. The discursive associations in the texts define the Albertan literary ethos, whether one is relating them to earlier texts or one is drawing distinctive parallels with contemporary works. Third, one can group literary works from Alberta into various categories of cultural grammar based on gender, class, ethnicity/nationality, language, generation, sexual orientation, and genres of writing. By doing so, one removes any sense of the monolithic or exclusive from the concept of an Alberta literature. The term cannot be considered a simple container of straightforward or obvious labels. If anything, this volume is inclusive of all genres and all backgrounds. This, in fact, may be the distinguishing characteristic of Alberta literature in the twenty-first century – its political, social, and cultural diversity. Finally, there is the unifying goal of creating a literary canon that captures that diversity. The formation of an Alberta canon awaits an acknowledgement from the writing, reading, and critical communities in the province, the region, and the country. The growth of scholarly analysis and discussion of Alberta writing can lead to the articulation of such a canon. However, we are too early in the process to do that.

Because the study of Alberta writing is not a regular feature of academe, though Alberta writers are studied in other contexts and under different rubrics, acceptance of the concept of Alberta literature as a valid field of study remains an uphill struggle. The weight of historical prejudice and conventional negativity toward provincial identity in literature is a significant barrier. So the concept of Alberta literature remains contested by other boundary concepts and so becomes a work in progress. This volume is a step on the long road of legitimization.

Writers themselves prefer various terms of self-identification that suit their interests, with "Albertan" not high on the list. Likewise, their works of art are always open to numerous overlapping labels, depending on what aspect literary critics are keen on. In an era when poststructuralist, postmodern, and postcolonial thinking continues to be in vogue, though its influence is beginning to wane, the term "Alberta" may seem irrelevant to mainstream criticism. But it is, we would argue, no less "irrelevant" than terms such as "Canadian" and "Prairie" or even "Quebec" literature. Each of these terms needs to be understood as a general context framing numerous cultural grammars and influences that inform a writer's identity. Alberta's contemporary literary house is as dependent on global literary trends, the evolving political economy of the province, and the formative influences of linguistic change and developing critical theories as is any Canadian literature.

In the struggle for an Alberta literature, this volume is not blind to the challenges facing the concept. The philosopher Wolfgang Iser, in *The Range of Interpretation* (2000), states: "The task of interpretation is thus twofold: it has to constitute its subject matter, and it has to furnish understanding of what has been constituted."[2] This volume attempts to do both. Future volumes will add to this body of criticism and thereby enhance the validity and viability of the concept of Alberta literature as a field of study.

We would like to thank our fellow organisers of the Wild Words conference – poet Tom Wayman, novelist Suzette Mayr, and Harry Vandervlist of the Department of English at the University of Calgary, playwright Clem Martini of the Faculty of Fine Arts, Special Collections librarian Apollonia Steele and Anne Green (Director of WordFest: Calgary-Banff International Writers Festival) for their participation in this task. While not a proceedings, this volume was inspired by the conference and the papers given at the conference. The combination of scholarly and creative energy that went into the conference by both organisers and presenters became the foundation for this book.

NOTES

1. The first was *The Alberta Golden Jubilee Anthology,* ed. W. G. Hardy (Toronto: McClelland and Stewart, 1955); the second was *Chinook Arch: A Centennial Anthology of Alberta Writing,* ed. John Patrick Gillese (Edmonton: Government of Alberta, 1967); and the third was *The Alberta Diamond Jubilee Anthology: A Collection from Alberta's Best Writers,* ed. by John W. Chalmers (Edmonton: Hurtig, 1979).
2. Wolfgang Iser, *The Range of Interpretation* (New York: Columbia University Press, 2000), 59.

INTRODUCTION

WRESTLING IMPOSSIBILITY: WILD WORDS IN ALBERTA

ARITHA VAN HERK

Attempts to essentialize Alberta's literary tradition are about as permanent as snow before a chinook. The writing aligned with Alberta (whether by accident or location) is a chiaroscuro, swatches of light and shade that dazzle and surprise, conceal and reveal. We're identified as young, unformed, the literary school (well, kindergarten) without a tradition or an encapsulating definition. Not for us the solemn blessing of Ontario Gothic or hip Toronto urbanism. Not for us the racy stripes of Montreal translative transgression. No, if anything, Alberta writing earns a dollop of good old "prairie realism" (which I have proven elsewhere does not exist) and then quizzical incomprehension. The books that erupt from Alberta are too unpredictable, too wide-ranging and varied to be summarized and contained. Alberta writing is a mystery, a tangent, a shock, unexpected and vigorous.

Three books are essential to anyone wishing to understand Alberta writing. Actually, they are two books, if one considers that George Melnyk's *The Literary History of Alberta* is a two-volume affair, altogether 540 pages. But were I required to frame a bookshelf that declared the nature of Alberta's Wild Words, I would put at one end Melnyk's as-close-to-comprehensive-as-possible-under-the-circumstances literary history, and at the other end Robert Kroetsch's elusive evocation of absence, *The Hornbooks of Rita K.*

Already, I know, I am in trouble. Alberta writing, as I have learned to my own greedy delight, is a sprawling lovely monster. When I tried to include a bibliography of essential Alberta literature at the end of my idiosyncratic and unreliable history of Alberta, *Mavericks: An Incorrigible History of Alberta,* I knew the list to be terminally incomplete, remarkably inadequate. I included it anyway, determined to assert that Alberta, for all its reputation, has a literate culture and a complex literary life, one that embraces immigrants and newcomers, exiles and diasporic settlers, original peoples and carpetbaggers.

An Alberta writer is one of those strange designations that some say contains its own contradiction, like Alberta culture or military intelligence. What does an Alberta writer encompass? Someone who lives in Alberta and who writes about elsewhere, all the many elsewheres that tempt a global citizen? Someone who writes about Alberta even if they do not live here? Someone who frequents the buffet tables of the Banff Centre, but who literally can't figure out how to get there without a guide and who complains bitterly about the elk rutting on the grounds? Someone who drew a mark on this place even though she was here for the briefest of periods? As George Melnyk so eloquently argues, this is a place of "multiple and contradictory narratives" (Melnyk, Vol. 1 xvii), and there is simply no essential set of measures that can delineate an Alberta writer, unless that measure is itself multiple and contradictory.

Alberta is an evocative site for writing because it occupies a landscape that wears its metamorphosis proudly. Here presides a geography that has undergone movements and erosions, upheavals and glaciations that resonate still, however we might imagine the physical ground as a static or exhausted medium. It is impossible and, I would contend, it will always be impossible to ignore Alberta's spatial effect, unless one is truly insensate, aesthetically numb. What we see, whether lifting our eyes west to the mountains or east to the plains is a reminder of the world as beauty. What we see looking north is the imaginative future, and looking south, an early subversion of conterminal division. Our writing cannot help but be influenced, positively or adversely, by this spectacular space and our specular gaze. Even hidden in the *cul de sac* of a suburb it is impossible to ignore the intensity of the light.

Even hunkered away from an obliterating blizzard, it is impossible to remain unaffected. The very changes in barometric pressure will insist on prescribing a migraine.

This Alberta practices a version of disorderly inclusion, a peripheral and careless acceptance that frees the writing writer to focus, to fall in love with what words can do out here. Not what words mean – that is for the thematic interests of a Canada that shaped its trajectory and project long before Alberta became a distinct cultural entity. We have a different sense of literary engagement here, one impossible to define. Except that its effect is remarkable, as seductive as warm days and cool nights.

Let me cite an example. Out of fourteen Canadian writers who have been Markin-Flanagan writer-in-residence holders at the University of Calgary, six who came from elsewhere decided to stay in Alberta. Three more who could not stay (the tyranny of having a job) expressed open longing to stay. Four were already Albertans. Only one fled after what was clearly an experience determinedly unhappy. Now why this seeming conversion? Isn't Calgary the heart of Alberta's economic crassness? Isn't the literary energy percolating to the east or west more telling? Certainly, Alberta writing struggles against the old clichés that see us writing only about cowboys, nature, and isometric conservativism. Although that is not the issue at all.

In truth, Alberta's literary world is inclusive and inspiring. It's even kind to buffalo hunters, those writers who move here when the economy is good, and who bag every grant and prize in sight, even if they care nothing about this place and contribute little to the writing community. It's quietly protective of its gentle sinners, those writers who have lived here forever, and who slowly grow more bent with time as they work away at tilling this sometimes-infertile soil. And it can be angry too, at writers who characterize this place as reductive or simple, those who visit and dismiss. Alberta has been home to or alienated enough writers to cause a modernist period, if we wanted something like that. Although we'd have to call it something else. Wild Words is a good description.

So why then do I insist on the bookends that I have chosen? Inclusive, comprehensive, and objective in its required compression, given the number of writers and texts that he apprehends, George Melnyk's *Literary History of Alberta* makes obvious sense. Melnyk provides a powerfully engaged sweep of this literature, from Writing-on-Stone and the messages recorded in the cliffs there to his closing with Thomas King and Richard Wagamese, both First Nations writers. That he leaves his history at the end of the twentieth century and cannot engage with the most up to the minute contemporary writing is simply reflective of the time when he completed the project; the present cacophony of voices argues that there are more tentacles and offshoots than were even imaginable ten years ago. Melnyk does what he sets out to do, articulating three fundamental claims: “that Alberta has a literary history that is definable and worth knowing; that Alberta’s literary identity is multicultural and polyphonic; and that Alberta’s literary history is now moving toward a global synthesis” (Melnyk, Vol. 1 xx). For that reason, his is a reassuring and solid guidebook to our writerly inheritance.

But the other bookend, a strangely inconclusive poetic text published just after the turn of the century, by Robert Kroetsch, a man who might be called Mr. Alberta (along with having once been identified by Linda Hutcheon as Mr. Canadian Post-modern) except that he has not lived in Alberta since 1980, is a more arbitrary choice. And yet, it is exactly its bizarre “translation of strangeness” (Melnyk, Vol. 2 231) that argues for its synergy and its metaphorical positioning as writing that could be deemed “ur-Alberta.”

The very construction of *The Hornbooks of Rita K* declares the provisional nature of writing out here, the process of trying to piece together fragments into some kind of literary history.

> Each line of the poem is a provisional exactness.
> We write by waiting for the mind to dispossess. (3)

So declares Hornbook #10, as if to persuade the reader that there is order to be found within the pages of this meditation, just so long as it knows enough to divest itself of possessiveness. Alberta is poem, poet, narrative, journalist, critique, critic, and archivist, and yet, always more. Claiming to be “intimate friends” with Rita K, the archivist (or whatever he is, perhaps even a literary historian in some way related to George Melnyk) pretends to serve as an interpreter for the bewildered reader, proposing to gloss Rita Kleinhart’s “dense poems” (7). Of course, her poems are not dense, and the reader is not bewildered. It is Raymond who is both dense and bewildered, he the johnny-come-lately to Alberta writing. Raymond pretending to be an expert on Rita (Rita the writer who exists and yet has vanished; the writer who has written enough to have a reputation, yet left almost no trace), is a gloss on those who would parse Alberta writing, those who would reduce it to its marginalia and location.

Raymond is careful to explain Rita’s provenance, thereby identifying her as a literary work:

> Kleinhart was invited, during the late spring of 1992, to visit Germany and lecture briefly to the Canadianists at Trier University. On her way back from Trier she paid a visit to the Museum of Modern Art in Frankfurt and while at the museum mailed a number of postcards to friends. She was not seen alive thereafter.
>
> Her ranch in Central Alberta – her house overlooking the coulees and the valley of the Battle River – contained at the time of her disappearance neat stacks of scrawled notes, manuscripts, partially filled notebooks and, yes, unfinished (or unfinishable?) poems. (8)

Here then is the model for the Alberta writer: a person of some international renown who when she leaves Alberta manages to vanish, although her "ranch" home (and the tongue-in-cheek irony encoded in that designation is beautiful considering the dread brand of ranching that all Alberta writing must resist) contains a huge repository of words, poems "unfinished (or unfinishable?)" as well as the story of who and where she is. Part poetics, part documentary, part fiction, Rita collects all genres into her writerly presence and then refuses their designation by leaving that category empty.

Raymond happily and lavishly interprets the absent writer for a would-be reader. She was intrigued with back doors and escape (10); she worked from photographs (11); she admires snow (19); she is fascinated by prairie cemeteries (12) – all claims that Raymond makes on Rita's behalf. Rita herself speaks only through a few Hornbook fragments, enigmatic as inspiration and elusive as the metaphorical effect of literature itself. But I am dwelling on minutiae, taking up the cudgels that Raymond so assiduously beats. Let me get straight to the point. I suspect that Rita *is* Alberta writing.

This textual anthropomorphism speaks to the numinous nature of Alberta writing. "Her disappearance ... had everything to do with entrance into the world. Only by disappearing could she escape the bonded ghost she had become to her readers" (27). The playful conundrum of appearing by disappearing is indeed the template for Alberta writing. Alberta writing occupies that fugitive category of doubt that inscribes by vanishing, that articulates its existence by an act of erasure. So different from the declarative trumpets of "national" writing, this text is a "bonded ghost," haunting and yet geographically determined, a writer of and from Alberta and yet impossible to identify, let alone lay eyes on.

Raymond tells us that Rita "was at work on a huge – and I would say bizarre – work that ultimately... caused her disappearance. She held to the conviction that... she would leave each object or place or person that fell under her attention undisturbed" (16). The Alberta writer is indeed an ethical thief, estranged from her own material or at least shy with that material, shading in a few words to delineate this bizarre and eccentric world, careful not to damage its integrity, almost afraid to recite its distinctiveness. And the open question of creativity vibrates through *The Hornbooks of Rita K*, as if it were a tuning fork for Alberta writing. "One of the considerable and neglected art forms is the stack of papers" (75). This then, is the essence of Alberta writing. A stack of papers, unsifted and disorderly, intent on what they have not yet booked. Wild Words.

The writer and the written engage in a dance that must exhaust the writing, which, even as it persists, endures. By disappearing, claims Raymond, Rita gives freedom to her writing. And yet, around the corner of Raymond's obsessive tabulations, snooping, discussion, and analysis, Rita's words remain, endure. Enigmatic, almost aphoristic, the Alberta writer defines home and its hold over us.

> Home is a door that opens inward only.
> So how will you get out, stranger? I say
> to myself. (33)

It may be that Alberta writing does not "get out" at all, but circles its own secret knowledge of its own discomfort, its own one-page brevity. In fact, there is the rub. Alberta writing is stealthy, attributive, mysterious. Hornbook #55 declares, "We turn to speak and confront an absence" (55), yearning to say what we want to say but at a loss for audience. The result then can only be writing as a dance with words that cannot quite define a place, and yet eternally engages with the infinite variety of this place.

Writerly influences – the literary history that the writer circles and lies down with – cannot be neglected either, and here Melnyk's *Literary History* echoes Rita K. Rita confesses, "Sometimes I hear in my speech traces of languages I don't remember knowing" (14). All the different backgrounds and inheritances that inflect Alberta's character speak through those who try to write, whether they know it or not. And so, the essays in this volume, *Wild Words,* their careful reading paying attention to both sides of the phrase, Alberta writing, can be read in two directions, through George Melnyk's survey, and through Rita Kleinhart's transience.

My name is Rita Kleinhart. My heart is tough, a clenched and patient fist, determined to beat. Wild Words hum in my bones. Here is my summary of these essays that demarcate a few renditions of my Alberta.

Successful mourning, as Christian Riegel declares in his gentle admonition of Robert Kroetsch's *Stone Hammer Poem*, requires attention. We need practice in elegy and monument, the work of writing that incites the paradox of loss, a respect for what has gone before. Raspberry baskets hold more than harvest; they invest in the scent of the future.

How can we defend ourselves with poems, asks Douglas Barbour, and who is an Alberta poet? All of us, he answers, Watson and Wah, Mandel and Markotic, Whyte and Noble and Barbour himself, intimate immigrations of image. Those we miss show up in these pages, complete with words, the distinct energy of their outpourings, linguistic constructions. The poems work hard, the waitresses work hard, the service has aching feet. We can, Barbour asserts, defend ourselves with outriders, whose poetic "prologue lines" are intent on longing more than chronicle.

Tongue steeped in its childhood tea, I have stepped off the train at Strathcona, fought my way through the crowds in Edmonton to search for the settlement office. Being multilingual is both gift and limitation, as Jars Balan gently unpacks the trunk of Michael Gowda's voice, how to speak, when having just arrived here, your own voice must adapt to the needs of others. The question is repeated over and over: how do you write in Alberta, complete with the prescribed order, the limitations of ideology and economy?

If Alberta theatre can exhort the paradox, unpack destructive consequences, and shine the flashlight into dark corners, it will. Anne Nothof recites a diverse and diasporic staging, subliminal reaches toward cultural diversity, with neither prairie realism nor cowboy iconography in sight. No frustrated creativity, but a graceful acupuncture in the dramatists she identifies. Together with Sherrill Grace's clear-eyed examination of Sharon Pollock's theatre, changing names and changing places to take on the role of Alberta. Pollock proclaims a place where the self can reinvent the self and still shape the locale that shapes writing. With the land as a character, not landscape but character, she questions the inheritance that the generations await. Here in Alberta, the reinvention of a self is not only possible but probable.

Helen Hoy takes up the contradictory narratives of self in Suzette Mayr's *Moon Honey*, cacophonous race, gender, and sexual orientation. Hoy shows how those categories dissolve in an Alberta no longer monochromatic but hybrid, how parodic intervention and infused refusals of realism implicate bland liberal racism, and juxtapose power with social chemistry. This is, says Hoy, "the site where the imagination meets the skin." Both come away naked.

Rudy Wiebe's restless kinaesthesia, tracked by Malin Sigvardson, declares that home is always many steps away. In this migration, Alberta becomes destination but never quite location, a worship of what may never be, as opposed to what is present. You get what you settle for with memory and the future both, but the mergence of religious and geographical movement can propose a stasis too, travel-suffering another name for perambulatory virtuousness.

Frances W. Kaye retribalizes Alberta with the Ojibway presence of Richard Wagamese taking to the pages with polemic and passion in equal measure. Seeking explanation, learning lessons, questing for understanding, the First Nations writer negotiates this space. Defying the binaries of non-white and white, these wounded nomads must grapple with the truth of dispossession and its affect, wounds that must be reconciled to a place and its peoples.

Animals too in their speaking reject the mapped borders of "civilization" and occupy an entirely different site, one that does not recognize Alberta at all. In the grizzly world of the Russells, Andy and Charlie, a new language begins to take shape, claims Pamela Banting. In fact, the Alberta writer who carries a gun smells different, cannot embrace the metaphor of ethics, etiquette, and protocol.

Lisa Grekul takes extinction one step farther, in her examination of Myrna Kostash's wrestling match with genre. "The crisis of non-fiction" argues an Alberta bloodline that includes life writing, witness, analysis, and debate. Chronology and cause and effect contribute to a travelogue of the world larger than Alberta and yet historically and socially rooted in the horizon of Alberta. The imaginary coherence of this unpredictable – and yes, even doomed – place still argues that we come from the same village, even after we invent that village.

In this Alberta, then, reading these essays in the generous spirit they were written, I confess that my name is Rita Kleinhart. My heart is tough, a clenched and patient fist, determined to beat. Wild Words hum in my bones. The community that Fred Stenson describes in "Writing in Alberta – Up, Down, or Sideways" is my community, replete with memoir-writing, wispy-haired men who went to one-room schoolhouses, and with recalcitrant lyric poets. Fred Stenson's useful degree in Economics is the same degree I have;

I too remember when Culture was a proper ministry and not just a word at the end of tourism, recreation, and et cetera. I too taught in penitentiaries and shuffled my feet at meetings in rude and sophisticated Toronto. And yes, I too ran off to Europe with a backpack and managed to vanish in the Frankfurt Museum of Modern Art even while I remain, scribbling lines in a ranch house, there overlooking the valley of the Battle River. I am what is called an Alberta writer. I practice wild words.

And still, "somewhere out there, the fence is down" (Kroetsch 56). Escape is possible, indeed encouraged. The open door beguiles. Write and disappear. And yet, it is not so easy to vanish, or to stop being an Alberta writer. Hornbook #43 confesses to such a writer's irrepressible and unquenchable desire. "We write as a way of inviting love. Each text is a request that says, please, love me a little" (Kroetsch 19). Yes, this is the truth. Disappearance or not, from or within an elusive and illusory and contested Alberta, our writing is asking for exactly that.

Please, love our words a little.

WORKS CITED

KROETSCH, Robert. *The Hornbooks of Rita K.* Edmonton: University of Alberta Press, 2001.

MELNYK, George. *The Literary History of Alberta.* Vol. 1. Edmonton: University of Alberta Press, 1998.

———. *The Literary History of Alberta.* Vol. 2. Edmonton: University of Alberta Press, 1999.

VAN HERK, Aritha. *Mavericks: An Incorrigible History of Alberta.* Toronto: Penguin Books, 2001.

PART ONE
POETRY

1

THE "WILD BODY" OF ALBERTA POETRY

DOUGLAS BARBOUR, UNIVERSITY OF CALGARY

"How do you grow a poet?"

This question, asked a number of times in the most famous poem by Alberta's most famous poet, certainly stands as a central one for anybody attempting to write about poetry in Alberta, or Alberta poetry. Poets can grow anywhere, of course – Heisler, Alberta, or Estevan, Saskatchewan, for example. And move through many other sites on their way to and from Alberta: Europe in World War II and Montreal before coming to Edmonton; or the Mackenzie River up north, and SUNY Binghampton on the way to Winnipeg. Or from the West Coast to Edmonton to be published nevertheless by T. S. Eliot in Britain. It won't be easy to pin down the Alberta poet, nor how s/he has grown.

Robert Kroetsch himself offers a number of illuminating (and/but maybe not) responses. His father has no doubt that the question is useless:

Son, this is a crowbar.
This is a willow fencepost.
This is a sledge.
This is a roll of barbed wire.
This is a bag of staples.
This is a claw hammer.

. . . .

First off I want you to take that
crowbar and driver [sic] 1,156 holes
in that gumbo.
And the next time you want to
write a poem
we'll start the haying.

(Kroetsch, *Field Notes* 38)

The poet (implied) has a number of other answers, although they tend to cancel each other out, as is the way with so many of Kroetsch's poetic statements. Here are two:

As for the poet himself
we can find no record
of his having traversed
the land/in either direction

no trace of his coming
or going/only a scarred
page, a spoor of wording
a reduction to mere black

and white/a pile of rabbit
turds that tells us
all spring long
where the track was

poet… say uncle

(Kroetsch, *Field Notes* 38)

We silence words
by writing them down.

(Kroetsch, *Field Notes* 42)

So, are these the choices for a prairie poet in the second half of the twentieth century or the beginning of the twenty-first: some kind of offbeat pastoral or the paradoxes of language itself? That Kroetsch has managed to play both with such subtlety, as well as riff off almost every other kind of discourse only signals his essential mastery, a mastery few others have even attempted, let alone achieved.

Who is an Alberta poet? That's a tough question, but I'd like to keep any possible answer as open as possible, as open perhaps as the parkland stretching from flat prairie to the highest mountains. From the perspective of the early twenty-first century, there aren't many to point to before the general rise of new writers in the sixties. Of course, we can always mention the fact that Earle Birney was born in Calgary and spent his earliest years in Banff, but it's clear that he spent most of his writing life elsewhere. If his most famous poem is set in the Rockies, its mountain could be in either Alberta or British Columbia. That he was a great mentor and a significant figure for younger poets, including some in Alberta, does not really make him an Alberta poet. Far more likely to fit such a description are later immigrants, rather than this important emigrant.[1]

Two poets Albertans can, I think, claim, who originally shared an interest in mythological and highly symbolic lyrics: Eli Mandel, born in Estevan, Saskatchewan, and Wilfred Watson, born in Rochester, England, and raised in British Columbia. Both eventually ended up teaching at the University of Alberta, Mandel for a significant period, during which his poetry shifted toward a more late modernist stance, and Watson for his whole career, during which he shifted to drama and then to a highly individual experimentation in poetry. Sheila Watson sent the manuscript of Wilfred Watson's first book of poetry, *Friday's Child* (1955), to T. S. Eliot, who took it for Faber & Faber; it then won both the British Council and the Governor General's awards that year. The poems are densely lyrical in their mythological, religious, and literary allusions. Much the same can be said of Mandel's early work although, in his poems, his Jewish heritage also plays a strong part. That both of them slowly turned away from their early poetics toward different kinds of experimentation with voice, tone, and open form suggests they felt a shift in the Canadian poetic zeitgeist to which they responded in their individual ways. Their responses, the new poetry they each created in their own ways, are uniquely their own, and, although both knew or knew of Kroetsch, owe little if anything to his poetics. Nevertheless, because Kroetsch's work has become the foremost sign of a new Alberta poetry, one can argue that their work, like that of many younger writers to follow, appears "under the sign of Kroetsch," even when any sign of more direct influence is missing.

As time passed, many other poets would move to Alberta, and younger poets would be born and able to find their way to writing and publication in the province of their birth. But, as with so much of the workforce here, many are immigrants who have chosen to stay, for a long time, or for life.

❦

During Eli Mandel's time at the University of Alberta, he influenced many students with his energy, engagement, and excitement at the changes taking place in the writing of the period, many of which he incorporated into his own poetry. The young Mandel argued poetically that he came from a place where "the farmer's chorus, a Greek harbinger,/Forecasts by frost or rings about the moon/How ill and black the seeds will grow" (Mandel 15). In Alberta, as he shifted toward a stance much closer to where his slightly younger poetic comrade Kroetsch would begin – more open, more contingent, more what at the time writers came to identify as postmodern – he would remember that place differently, in "Estevan, 1934":

> remembering the family we
> called breeds   the Roques
> their house smelling of urine
> my mother's prayers before
> the dried fish she cursed
> them for their dirtiness their
> women I remember too
>   how
> seldom they spoke and
> they touched one another
> even when the sun killed
> cattle and rabbis
>   even
> in the poisoned slow air
> like hunters
>   like lizards

they touched stone
they touched

earth

(Mandel 159)

That memory could be so altered by the new possibilities of lyric intervention introduced by the New American Poetry speaks to the way formal innovation also forces innovation in content. Mandel found in the new freedom of verse possibilities for a subversive political poetry that would not simply be a rhetorically charged gesture. He could slide from comic/satiric political harangues like "The Mayor's Papers" (93) or "Messages" (134), through sharply etched images of the new powers at work in Alberta in "At Wabamun the Calgary Power Station" (163), "Lake Wabamun: Summer 68" (165), and "Oil Refineries: Edmonton" (166), to the spare beauty of the imagistic sequence, "Wabamun" (160–62). Whereas the former poems speak directly to power, often trying to demonstrate its comic emptiness, the latter enters a different kind of spiritual emptiness, one that attains a deeply poetic grace:

to have come to this
simplicity
to know
only
the absolute
calm
lake

before

night

(Mandel 162)

Mandel's changing poetic can be seen in terms of precisely a "wild" poetics of an Alberta open to all contemporary influences in ways that perhaps academic Toronto, under the influence of Northrop Frye, would not.

When we turn to Wilfred Watson, we find a writer who, even in his most mythopoeic writing, has always been unique. And although *Friday's Child* (1955) won both the Governor General's Award and a major British prize, his work has, on the whole, been ignored, which is too bad given its stark power and incredibly wide-ranging concerns. Certainly, the poems in *Friday's Child*, which caught T. S. Eliot's attention, belong, like Mandel's early work, "to the body of mythopoeic poetry which dominated Canada in the 1950s, and which is so closely associated with the influence of Northrop Frye" (Scobie 282). But Watson had no interest in repeating himself, nor in being part of any "school," and so he did not publish much poetry for the next two decades while exploring, partly in terms of the theories of Marshall McLuhan, new possibilities of poetic theatre. Because he published almost nothing until 1972, it appeared that he had given up poetry; the reality seems to be that he was experimenting with new forms, hints of which could be found in the few poems he did publish, like "A Manifesto for Beast Poetry" (1960) and "I Shot a Trumpet into my Brain" (1966), in which the concept of manifesto played as important a part as the looping free verse. There was also the unpublished sequence of "poems by Jenny Blake," written in the voice of a wild, virginal woman. These read like updated versions of Yeats's "Crazy Jane" poems, although they mix a near free verse with traditional rhyme.

Nevertheless, for those few who read it, *the sorrowful Canadians* (1972) was a revelation. Taking full advantage of the then new technology of the IBM electric typewriter with its various balls of different typefaces, Watson created poems full of different and often antagonistic voices, chanting in a highly politicized manner. Sometimes they explore the sexual politics of the time, as in "poem 1970," with its refrain of "**MY WILD BODY IS A CORPSE**," and its insistence that that body will not be buried but rather "sits up,/and sings, man is a noble potato" (163). In many of the longer poems, the politics emerges from the wars of the time and the new imperialism driving them, as in "lines 1967":

> they flew across our borders at the speed
> of light.
> **HANOI IS HERE**
> dropping images which fell alike on women
> children and infants.
> **HANOI IS HERE**
> we had only a few poems to defend ourselves
> with.
> **HANOI IS HERE**
> and no strong men like Thoreau, Whitman or
> Lincoln

> **HANOI IS HERE**
> they criss-crossed over our houses, dropping
> vowels that were block-busters
> **HANOI IS HERE**
> they set up bazookas which lopped novels into
> our roofs
> **HANOI IS HERE**
> they raked our streets with plays.
> they sent in lowflying jets armed with
> recordings.
> they blew us to bits just as we were saying
> they seemed such nice people
> **HANOI IS HERE**
>
> (Watson 172)

By this point, Watson reveals himself as one of our most protean poets, always changing, always new. And he is happy to take on icons, usually with a savage wit:

> 17 ways of not looking at the face of margaret atwood on the dust
> jacket of survival.
> the first is, not through the eyes of the west coast halibut.
> the west coast halibut will not survive.
> 17 ways of not looking at the face of margaret atwood on the dust
> jacket of survival.
> & the second is, not through the eyes of jack shadbolt.
> jack shadbolt will not survive.
> [etc.]
>
> (Watson 211)

Despite their highly "political" content, it seems to me that the poems of this period carry a heavy weight of anti-ideology, as well as a concentrated satiric contempt that cannot be called comic, exactly, but does have a certain sardonic heft.

Watson continued to write plays, and turned toward a new "metric" in them and his later poems, what he called "number-grid" poetics. In *I begin with counting* (1978) and later works, he achieved a new straightforwardness that nevertheless kept readers off balance by the simple presence of numbers in the middle of each line. Unlike his early poems, which paraded his high intelligence and wide vocabulary, these new poems appear to speak "naturally" and directly to the reader (and the addressees of so many of them), but the grid format and the numbers interrupting each line de-naturalize that speech and those poems. Take these lines from "re Phyllis Webb & Wilson's Bowl": "their real **1** essence/is a tombstone **2** with/the **3** inscription, I/was. **4** tiny worms eat/my bone, his **5** bones/consume her flesh. **6** their/flesh **7** chaws up/our minds, our mind **8** devours/**9** their/soul. her **1** mind/feeds on his **2** words…." (Watson 320). No doubt the sardonic awareness of mortality and its relation to art remains, but the poem seems to move forward with grammatical inevitability, sentence after sentence jarred into fragmentation by the simple presence of the numbers on the grid format of the page. Something new, which no other poet seems to have tried, has been made.

Wilfred Watson has few readers, far fewer than he deserves, but his work remains, for those who seek it out, as a signal example of other possibilities of form in contemporary poetry. It's important to remember that he wrote all these poems while teaching early modern and modern literature at the University of Alberta, demonstrating in them the ways such an outpost could nevertheless maintain contact with all the avant-gardes in the so-called centres of civilization. And to recall that, like Eli Mandel, he had great influence as a teacher, certainly on a few of the poets of the next generation, such as Jon Whyte and Charles Noble.

Jon Whyte, even more than his friend Charles Noble, is an exemplar of both the poet of place and the poet as experimenter, even as he also argued against experimentation as such and against any form of typecasting (such as "postmodernism," a term he apparently hated; it "was nice while it lasted, I believe. Thank goodness it's over" [Whyte, 113]). To cast him and Noble simply as students of Mandel and Watson is to underestimate their originality and breadth of study. Nevertheless, I think the work and presence of those two certainly helped to give them the sense of possibility that their own work carried forward (sadly, in Whyte's case only to his tragically early death in 1991). Born in Banff, Whyte spent some time in his late teens and early twenties in Edmonton as a student at the University of Alberta, and in California as a student at Stanford, but he soon returned to Banff, which remained his home base for the rest of his life. A close friend, and also a student at the University of Alberta, Noble spent his winters in Banff (as carefully notated in *Banff/Breaking* [1984]) and his summers working his old family farm near Nobleford. Both these writers brought their deeply learned poetics to bear upon their home places, seeking in their various ways to construct some part of the wild body of Alberta itself.

Jon Whyte's poetry is incredibly wide-ranging, but the posthumous *Mind Over Mountains* (2000) offers a good introduction to its variety and breadth, with its selection of shorter work, much of *Homage, Henry Kelsey* (1981), and large parts of *The Fells of Brightness: Some fittes and starts* (1983) and *The Fells of Brightness: Wenkchemna* (1985). Whyte liked to point back to both the riches of English poetry from at least the Middle Ages (he did his MA thesis on *The Pearl*) and to the high modernists (he liked to hold up the poetry of Marianne Moore against those who tended to revere the Pound-Williams tradition), but he was certainly aware of what was happening in poetry and poetics in the sixties and beyond. As Harry Vandervlist points out in his Introduction to *Mind Over Mountains*, however, he had also "been immersed in visual culture from birth. His aunt and uncle, Peter and Catherine Whyte... both painters, had enormous influence on their nephew, and it's clear he looked at pictures and printed pages as carefully as he listened to words" (Whyte vi). Many of his shorter poems, and all his longer works, demonstrate his desire "to treat the page as a canvas" (vi). He also wanted to avoid the personal in his poetry, and so chose large themes – Henry Kelsey's journey, or the history of the mountains around Banff. But many have done so; it's his ability to build huge linguistic constructions out of the pre-texts and history of these that sets his poems apart.

If he can play across the page in a painterly manner, as page after page of the long poems show, he also has a strong sense of the play of sound and sense through the line, as well as a painter's eye for the complex image of nature:

Fell: the darkness

And in: my dreams

Summing up: it adows me

Brevity: succinct summering

Alpenglow: and after stillness

At its shadowed edge
the frayed shore of the dark forest
beside the lake shored

looking at the lake
its farside scene reflected
noting

in the darker parts in nearness
through the surface of the water
toward that which is thither
but the water nearer
the darker, clear bottom of the
lake

the branch-strewn bottom
of the lake
on which a scene is etched
a sketchy scene
and

for a shimmering moment   hold both

(Whyte 117–18)

This is but one example of the kind of rhetoric of the page Whyte could pull off with equipoise. There are, of course long sections of the poems that read as highly informational modern narrative poetry, and others where a highly specified knowledge, and the vocabulary thereof, is brought to bear. And there are the flashes of intellectual punning that draw tentative conclusions before the poem carries on, regardless:

The Earth's intelligible because we share
with annelids, cyclops, elephants, bacteria
a tumor on the spine we call a brain?

The Earth intelligible before
intelligence sensed it,
before sensing all the world's bounty,
making sense of it,

it provided sense
sensation
the sensational

(Whyte 152)

It's hard to judge Whyte's influence; he was not part of the Banff Writing School, yet he was a presence in the town and a formative figure in its culture. His poetry, too, awaits a more complex and complete critical response.

As does that of Charles Noble, whose early work ventured into poetic sequences while his more recent work engages the long poem, as such. Like one of the characters in "Banff/Breaking," Noble's poems "ride the discrepancy train" (Noble, *Banff* 56) of thoughts meandering across home place and the world at large engaged in a complex dance of motive and meaning, as in "Scatterbrain Gathers," where

> the fields on the table
> are next to my heart
> and the list of machinery
> is growing into the world
> where the gentle lawyer, a minister's son
> my mother remembers from high school,
> is unfolding the law
> into our hands
>
> (Noble, *Afternoon* 11)

Such poems, full of intimate knowledge filtered through an intellectual screen, set Noble's poems apart from the usual prairie anecdotal lyric. But he was also interested in what length could do, as *Banff/Breaking*, with its two longer poems, full of characters caught in moments of attention and intention, demonstrates. Banff emerges as "this jagged edge that stays" (Noble, *Banff* 34), while almost all the people come and go. Noble's ear for the punning and rhyming edge of language sounds in lines like the following, about a hardworking waitress:

> Car lights move blandly
> through the atmosphere,
> a day in a moment,
> against her silently furious quickstep
> between tables
>
> her head above drowning.
> Her aching feet,
> a measure for pleasure
> to dawn.
>
> (Noble, *Banff* 13)

These qualities, plus a growing philosophical distancing, have continued to operate in his many books since, including his most recent, *Doubt's Boots* (2003), which he calls "a long poem that gathers itself as it scatters to chance, to pre-conditions, indices of how the times themselves are guilty" (9). Such comments indicate that, like his friend Jon Whyte, Noble has carried on the modernist project of constructing the long poem out of collage, bricolage, intertexts, and what he calls in an interview, "a wild, free play of language" (MacKintosh n.p.).

Our politicians talk up Alberta's immigration these days – how it's where everyone wants to come. This has been true of poets for a long time now. Some came to stay (how long do you have to live here to become a "real Albertan," at least according to the prevailing ideology?), some to return eventually to other places. Of course, in art, the importance of place can be overdone. And how do we locate that sense anyway? We still call Kroetsch an Albertan poet, although he has spent much of his life away. I think we now call people like Bert Almon and E. D. Blodgett Albertans, although they immigrated here in the 1960s (I assume four decades counts for something). Today, there are so many poets in Alberta, some born here, some who moved here; like all artists, their sense of inheritance, their poetic ideals, and their poetic mentors are scattered across the planet and through history. I'd call them Albertan, but that's not the most important aspect of their self-image as poets, I suspect: what they write counts most.

In 1988, Fred Wah came to Alberta as writer-in-residence at the University of Alberta; the following year he moved to Calgary where he became a major influence and mentor in the writing program at the University of Calgary. Already recognized as one of Canada's most innovative poets, a founding member of the West Coast TISH group, Wah brought all his energy, invention, dedication, and delight in language-play and experimental poetics to his teaching, and helped found a poetic community in Calgary, which continues to expand today, after his retirement in 2003. While in Alberta, he continued one of his most fascinating series, *Music at the Heart of Thinking*, in *Alley Alley Home Free* (1992), while writing other kinds of poetry, a poetic biotext, *Diamond Grill* (1996), and a number of important essays, collected in the award-winning *Faking It: Poetics & Hybridity* (2000). This kind of thinking at the heart of things – "If this is the edge of of, that's skating. If those/words aren't full of an ankle then nobody'll read them." (Wah 40) – others could and would read as a challenge to think poetry differently.

During a few summers in the mid-eighties, bpNichol taught at a writing summer school in Red Deer, where he too influenced a number of young writers from all over the country. Among his students there, Nicole Markotic, who later studied with Fred Wah, stands out as a major innovative writer in the Calgary scene of the nineties. But there are also Suzette Mayr, Hiromi Goto, Susan Holbrook, and many others who began to publish little magazines, run reading series, and create poems, stories, and novels, exploring modern genres and the interpenetration. Mayr and Goto are best known for their fiction (they also studied under Aritha van Herk, who was one of those responsible for hiring Fred Wah at the University of Calgary), but both have published poetry in various journals, and Mayr has two poetry chapbooks, *Zebra Talk* (1991) and *Tale* (2001). Holbrook published a very funny and subversive first book, *misled* (1999).

Although she is best known as a novelist and historian, Aritha van Herk has also written poetry, and has published one long poem, "Calgary, this growing graveyard," a work that certainly shows itself under the sign of Kroetsch. Van Herk studied writing at the University of Alberta, and wrote her first novel as an MA thesis, under the supervision of Rudy Wiebe, and on the whole seems to have mostly agreed with him that, as quoted by Robert Kroetsch, "You must lay great black steel lines of fiction, break up that space with huge design and, like the fiction of the Russian steppes, build a giant artifact" (Kroetsch, *Field Notes* 39) in order to satisfactorily represent the prairies. And even in her long poem, the lines spin out, more like the prose verses of the Bible than contemporary free verse, as it uncovers the lives and inevitable deaths and their memories in the four quadrants of Calgary.

Nicole Markotic[2] has published a novel, criticism, and two books of innovative poetry, *Connect the Dots* (1994) and *minotaurs & other alphabets* (1998). In these, she explores various forms of lyric deconstruction and the possibilities of a postmodern and feminist prose poem, with an eye for savagely ironic intertexts, as in the sequence, "In Turn," each piece of which begins with a quote from a woman writer:

Lovers desire and seduce only to murder and create.
Aritha van Herk *Places Far from Ellesmere*

> mythic hands transform from birds to fish and back again. just in time to pull up the reins. just in time to be cut off by the evil twin brother who has trained his snakes to swallow birds whole to slit fish with their tongues. the cross on your eyelids etched with tapwater
>
> trauma begins at the level of the sentence
>
> evil brothers are heroes gone mad
>
> the hero is a brother gone too too sane. a perfectly good alphabet, trembling at the level of sound. his fingertips drip blood as he strokes her frozen skin. his newly adopted snakes slither into his iron sable hair
>
> (Markotic 39)

As she plays across contemporary fiction, ancient myth, and textual/sexual critique, Markotic demonstrates a subtle mastery of all.

In years since, under the influence of such elders as Wah and van Herk (and Tom Wayman in the early 2000s), as well as younger teachers like Markotic, Mayr, and the recently hired Christian Bök at the University of Calgary, not to mention Ashok Mathur, Yasmin Ladha, and others who were such an important part of the burgeoning scene in Calgary, its writing community has become one of the liveliest in the country, with far too many younger writers to name them all.

As the reference to van Herk's studies at the University of Alberta suggests, the writing program in the English Department there has also been an important literary impetus. Back in the late sixties, Margaret Atwood and Dorothy Livesay taught there; Bert Almon has been teaching poetry for four decades. The presence of such important poets as E. D. Blodgett and Stephen Scobie on campus, as well as the many fine poets who have served as writer-in residence since 1975, has helped to produce a lively writing scene in the capital. Monty Reid, who left the university to work around the province – finally settling in Drumheller, where he worked at the Royal Tyrrell Museum and edited *The Dinosaur Review*, before moving to Ottawa – has published a number of volumes of innovative and delightful poetry. Recently, Andy Weaver, a visitor perhaps, as he has moved to Toronto to teach at York University, with his poet friend Adam Dickinson, helped start the Olive Reading Series in downtown Edmonton. His first book, *Were the*

Bees (2005), certainly reflected his studies and life in Alberta, even as its many intertextual allusions demonstrated his commitment to a postmodern poetry and poetics that knows no borders.

Such an ongoing list of names reveals an Alberta poetry scene all too rich and varied for any chronicler to cover. I have left out far too many fine and interesting poets, partly because my gaze has generally been directed at poetry I define as innovative. It is not enough simply to acknowledge such fine poets as Almon, Blodgett, Olga Costopoulos, Shawna Lemay, Scobie, not to mention many others, whose varied poems achieve a wide range of lyric possibilities. Yet that is what I must do in an essay that turned out to be a glance backward at important beginnings, as well as a quick overview of the present.

So, is the past truly prologue? I would tend to argue that it is, and that those three elder poets, Mandel, Watson, and Kroetsch, made in their work a complex of possibilities that later poets could build on. Indeed, in the case of the latter, it's a prologue that keeps expanding, as his recent books, especially *The Hornbooks of Rita K* (2001) demonstrate. *The Hornbooks of Rita*, like all his longer poems, asserts a novelist's rights in the middle of a poem, tells and untells a possible story, and argues itself into a reason for Alberta being – absent-ly – poetic. Its narrator is all too aware of the ironies and negations involved. His abstractions on the matter in Hornbook # 8 provide a fitting conclusion to these peregrinations:

> Rita is painfully absent when I let myself in at the back door of her richly modest home.
>
> ......
>
> Is not poetry a questing after place, a will to locate?
>
> ......
>
> I was stuck for words.
>
> (30–31)

NOTES

1. It is interesting that Birney became "younger and younger" as a poet in his later years, under the influence of such youthful experimenters as bpNichol. Nevertheless, he was not really an Alberta poet, nor should we call him one.
2. She was a graduate student, and then a member of the University of Calgary faculty, thus coming to influence other younger writers.

WORKS CITED

KROETSCH, Robert. *Completed Field Notes: The Long Poems of Robert Kroetsch.* Introduced by Fred Wah. Edmonton: University of Alberta Press, 2000.

———. *The Hornbooks of Rita K.* Edmonton: University of Alberta Press, 2001.

MACKINTOSH, Lachlan. "The Farmer-Poet Laurete [sic] of Banff." *Ffwd* 8:47. 30 October 2003 <www.ffwdweekly.com/Issues/2003/1030/book1.htm>.

MANDEL, Eli. *The Other Harmony: The Collected Poetry of Eli Mandel,* Vol. 1. Eds. Andrew Stubbs and Judy Chapman. Regina: Canadian Plains Research Center, 2000.

MARKOTIC, Nicole. *minotaurs & other alphabets.* Toronto: Wolsak and Wynn, 1998.

NOBLE, Charles. *Banff/Breaking.* Edmonton: Longspoon Press, 1984.

———. *Afternoon Starlight.* Saskatoon: Thistledown Press, 1984.

———. *Doubt's Boots.* Calgary: University of Calgary Press, 2003.

SCOBIE, Stephen. "Love in the Burning City: The Poetry of Wilfred Watson." *RePlacing.* Ed. Dennis Cooley. Downsview: ECW Press, 1980. 281–303.

VAN HERK, Aritha. "Calgary, This Growing Graveyard." *A/long Prairie Lines: An Anthology of Long Prairie Poems.* Ed. Daniel S. Lenoski. Winnipeg: Turnstone Press, 1989.

WAH, Fred. *Alley Alley Home Free.* Red Deer: Red Deer College Press, 1992.

WATSON, Wilfred. *Poems: Collected/Unpublished/New.* Edmonton: Longspoon Press/NeWest Press, 1986.

WHYTE, Jon. 2000. *Mind Over Mountains: Selected and Collected Poems.* Ed. Harry Vandervlist. Calgary: Red Deer Press, 2000.

2

"TO CANADA": MICHAEL GOWDA'S UNIQUE CONTRIBUTION TO THE LITERARY HISTORY OF ALBERTA

JARS BALAN

Michael Gowda (1874–1953) was a trailblazing pioneer who played a key role in the early history of Ukrainians in Alberta. The second of ten children born to a tailor and seamstress in the village of Vetlyn in Austro-Hungarian Galicia,[1] he immigrated to Canada as a twenty-three-year-old in June 1897 to avoid having to complete his military service in the Imperial Army. By the time he reached Strathcona Station on May 18, 1898, Gowda had picked up enough English to find work as a sales interpreter with the Bellamy Agricultural Implement Company on Jasper Avenue. In the process, he became the first permanent Ukrainian resident of Edmonton, since the settlers who preceded him had simply passed through town on their way to homesteads in the surrounding countryside.

A former schoolteacher, Gowda was fluent in Ukrainian, Polish, and German and could communicate in several other Slavic languages. As part of his job, he would assist both in-coming colonists as well as farmers in Edmonton on business, becoming a familiar figure to thousands of newcomers.

These activities soon brought him to the attention of local merchants and civic leaders, who began turning to Michael Gowda not only for his services as an interpreter but also for his firsthand knowledge about the customs and ways of the exotic-looking foreigners in sheepskin coats. Thanks to his linguistic abilities Gowda quickly got to know such prominent individuals as *Edmonton Bulletin* editor Frank Oliver (subsequently a federal Minister of the Interior in the government of Wilfred Laurier), and the future city mayor, William Griesbach.

Given his high profile, it is not surprising that Michael Gowda was at the centre of many landmark events in the formation of the Ukrainian community in Alberta. In March 1899, he began submitting occasional reports from Edmonton to the Pennsylvania-based newspaper, *Svoboda* [Liberty], both describing and commenting on how his countrymen were faring in their efforts to make new homes in the Canadian West. His accounts, which were followed with great interest by *Svoboda* subscribers across North America and in Western Ukraine, remain an invaluable source on the evolution of Ukrainian life in Alberta at the turn of the twentieth century.

In 1901, Michael Gowda became one of the initiators of the Taras Shevchenko *Chytalnia*, or Reading Society, the first Ukrainian organization to be established in Edmonton. Named after Ukraine's greatest poet, the association's small library of Ukrainian-language books and periodicals was located at the home of John Kilar on 101A Avenue east of 96 Street. Although short-lived, the reading room served as an important early gathering place for farmers visiting town as well as for the Ukrainians who were starting to find jobs in the city.

Inevitably, Michael Gowda also became embroiled in the religious controversies that erupted in the Ukrainian community as soon as missionaries began competing for the confessional allegiances of the immigrants. Despite being raised in a devout Greek Catholic family and having an older brother who was a priest, Gowda was fiercely critical of both the Ukrainian Catholic clergy and their Latin Rite counterparts, often airing his grievances in the press. Gradually acquiring a reputation as a "troublemaker," his uneasy relationship with Catholic authorities deteriorated even further with his 1903 marriage in an Orthodox Church to the daughter of Bukovynian settlers who had homesteaded near Willingdon. After briefly joining the Protestant-backed Independent Church and for a time assisting the Russian Orthodox Mission in its work – setting aside his strong opposition to the latter's imperialistic, often chauvinistic character – he eventually became a member of the Ukrainian Greek Orthodox Church of Canada organized by *narodovtsi*, or national populists, like himself.

In 1907, Michael Gowda directed the first Ukrainian-language play staged in Edmonton – the popular classic, *Natalka Poltavka*. Fittingly, it was written by Ivan Kotliarevsky (1769–1838), the celebrated founder of modern Ukrainian literature. In 1908, Gowda got a job as an interpreter with the city's Dominion Lands Office, where he helped many homesteaders to register title to their farms. The following year, he spearheaded an ambitious campaign to form a "Ruthenian Regiment" in the Canadian Army in the belief that it was the best means by which his fellow immigrants could demonstrate their loyalty to their new land.[2] To support his initiative Gowda circulated through the Ukrainian press a sample petition to the "Ministry of War in Ottawa," which he urged everyone who wanted to join such a regiment to sign. The petition explained the motivation behind the drive to create a Ruthenian corps along the lines of the Scots, Irish, and French-Canadian units already in existence:

> The signatories' desire to take part as a nation in the defence of the administration of this empire primarily because all of the signatories as foreigners and former citizens of foreign countries essentially desire the status of loyal citizens of this land, and at the same time the British Empire, of which Canada is a part. (qtd. in Marunchak 337)

Even though Gowda won the backing of cavalry Captain William A. Griesbach and the *Edmonton Journal*, as well as several influential Ukrainian leaders in Alberta, his proposal was vigorously opposed by Ukrainian socialists and failed to win the approval of Canadian military officials in Ottawa.[3] In retrospect, one can only wonder if the unhappy fate experienced by the Ukrainian Canadians who were interned as "enemy aliens" during the Great War might have been avoided if such a regiment had been in existence before the outbreak of hostilities in Europe.

In early 1910, Michael Gowda was enlisted as one of the Alberta shareholders and directors of the Ukrainian Publishing Company in Winnipeg, set up by the emerging Ukrainian Canadian intelligentsia to publish a weekly newspaper, *Ukrains'kyi holos* [Ukrainian Voice].[4] Although initially billing itself as the organ of the Federation of Ukrainian Social Democrats and Anarchists, *Holos* quickly dropped its left-wing identification to become the chief vehicle of the pioneer era Ukrainian nationalist movement.

Around the same time, Michael Gowda joined the Federation of Ukrainian Social Democrats of Canada (FUSD) at its inaugural convention held in Edmonton in August 1910. However, Gowda's membership in the socialist camp was short-lived, as he was first and foremost a Ukrainian patriot in the populist tradition and his politics were always closer to those of the Liberal Party of Canada. Often employed as an interpreter by politicians when they were campaigning among Ukrainians, in the 1913 provincial elections Michael Gowda finally became a candidate himself in the heavily Ukrainian Victoria constituency northeast of Edmonton. Along with three other community activists, Gowda ran as an Independent when the provincial Liberals failed to support Ukrainian demands for bilingual Ukrainian-English schools or to have riding boundaries redrawn in a way that would improve the chances of an immigrant getting elected to the legislature. Lacking the financial and administrative resources of an established political party, all four Independents were roundly defeated. Meanwhile a Russophile, Andrew Shandro, nominated under the Liberal banner, became the first Ukrainian elected to provincial office, much to the chagrin of national populist community leaders.

Upset by what he regarded to be a betrayal by the Ukrainians who had voted against him, Gowda wrote a stinging rebuke that he had printed and put up in post offices throughout the Victoria district. The language of his diatribe, titled "Thanks to All the Real Turncoats," not only showed how bitterly disappointed Gowda was by his defeat, but at the same time revealed his poetic gift for invective:

> For all the swines with long piggish snouts = sell-outs = traitors, abject wretches and scoundrels, reptiles, honeyed serpents, scorpions, moneygrubbers, Judases, and those who allegedly speak the word of God, but who sold themselves like that Judas Iscariot – I wish them many, many, many long years, may they not fall ill but languish in poverty and never die, and may they wallow about this world like stinking fetters and look upon their vile work every step of the way, so that the black spectre of betrayal always stands before their eyes, and may their conscience be so heavy and gnaw at them the way it gnawed at Judas, who nevertheless stood higher than they did because he understood his treachery, understood that he conducted himself dishonourably and he finished his miserable life at the end of piece of rope on a withered aspen-tree.

> And as for the betrayers of the national cause like those who essentially behaved like swine in the Victoria district and are not ashamed of their baseness, but even pray to a righteous God, may He prolong their abominable lives. This is unbridled baseness. (Michael Gowda Papers, PAA)[5]

This unhappy episode brought to an end Gowda's only attempt to win elected office. Afterwards, he established a successful farm implements dealership in Mundare and still later worked as a Dominion Lands administrator and a representative of the Canada Pacific Steamships Company, for a time relocating to Saskatchewan while his family stayed behind in Edmonton. However, by the 1920s it was becoming increasingly difficult for Gowda to find a steady job, since many of his former patrons and employers were no longer able to help him and his multilingual skills were not as necessary as they once had been. As the 1920s wore on Gowda also experienced marital difficulties that compelled him to move from the family home. In his later years, he became dependent on the support of his adult children, one of whom, Faust, graduated in 1928 with a degree in dentistry from the University of Alberta. By the time that Gowda wrote a letter to the editor of the *Edmonton Bulletin* identifying himself as the city's "First Ukrainian Citizen" – published in the paper's "Mail Bag" on November 17, 1933 under the heading "Money-Mad Maladministration" – he was already a somewhat marginalized figure whose groundbreaking achievements were mostly remembered by other "old-timers" like himself. Always a passionate Ukrainian-Canadian who was equally comfortable in both of his identities – the Ukrainian one he was born with, and the Canadian one that he chose as an immigrant – Michael Gowda died in 1953 at the age of 79, and was buried at Edmonton Cemetery.

In many respects, Michael Gowda was an atypical member of the first major wave of Ukrainians to immigrate to Canada. Much better educated than most and endowed with a self-confident nature, he possessed a degree of charisma and drive that made him a natural leader among his fellow Ukrainian pioneers. Furthermore, like many *hromadski diachi*, or community activists of his generation, Gowda was inspired by the example set by such revered Ukrainian writers as Taras Shevchenko and Ivan Franko. Gifted authors as well as visionaries, they were at the forefront of mobilizing the Ukrainian people against their economic, political, and national oppression. Thus, it is not surprising that in addition to being a grassroots organizer Gowda also entertained literary aspirations, or that he turned to poetry to goad and cajole his Galician and Bukovynian kinsmen into action.

Because of Ukraine's long and painful history as a battleground of rival empires, in the nineteenth century poets were the heroes of the Ukrainian nation, keeping alive the memories of Ukraine's storied past while inciting resistance to foreign domination. As a stateless people, Ukrainians looked to their literary champions as their "unacknowledged legislators" and torchbearers for the cause of Ukrainian self-determination. Indeed, simply writing poetry in the Ukrainian language was in itself a political act – a tradition that continued through the defeat of the Ukrainian national movement in the early twentieth century, through the persecutions of the communist era to the collapse of the Soviet Union.

Viewed in this context, Michael Gowda's poetic and literary efforts during his heyday in pioneer era Alberta can best be understood as an extension of his work as a community activist. How both were inextricably intertwined is evident in the very first article that Michael Gowda contributed to the newspaper *Svoboda,* which dealt with the growing religious discord among Ukrainian immigrants. Published on March 16, 1899, under the heading "News from Canada," the article concluded with the following three stanzas of didactic verse urging Ukrainians to stay united:

Best of luck to you, brethren of good will,
May God grant you strength!
Take up harmony in your free life
Because that is what the Supreme Being demands.

Clasp your hands together,
And love each other like brothers,
Let us pay no heed to those who sow discord,
And let us not follow after them.

Stand, brethren, together in one line,
Always try to look ahead,
And be sure to pay heed
As to what kind of traces you leave after yourself!

This untitled twelve-line composition earned Gowda the distinction of becoming the third Ukrainian-Canadian immigrant to have an original work of poetry appear in print. Just one month earlier, an 111-line poem by a Star-area farmer named Ivan Zbura had been published in the same newspaper under the title "*Kanadiis'ki emigranty*" [Canadian Emigrants], and it may well have been responsible for prodding Michael Gowda to try his own hand at composing verses.[6]

Gowda's next submission to *Svoboda* on August 31 of the same year was a twenty-four line poem titled "*Rus'komu narodu!*" [To the Ruthenian People!]. Like Ivan Zbura's piece, it lamented the plight of the *muzhiks* languishing in Europe, the opening lines painting an especially bleak picture of the harsh conditions in the old country:

> They are writing from the homeland: We're being tormented so cruelly,
> That we don't have the strength to breathe.
> Everywhere you turn it has now become so corrupt,
> That even food isn't appetizing anymore.[7]

The poem went on to complain about police harassment as well as electoral treachery and deception by local authorities. However, it concluded with an optimistic prediction about Ukraine's coming liberation through the efforts of its "slender young fighters." What is perhaps most striking about Gowda's composition is its strongly nationalistic sense of a *Ukrainian* identity (notwithstanding its title), since most immigrants at the turn of the century still primarily thought of themselves as Ruthenians, Austro-Hungarians, Galicians, or Bukovynians.

Gowda again included some original verse in his third submission to *Svoboda*, which appeared on September 27, 1900, under the heading, "Several words to the Ruthenians in Canada." In it, Gowda pointed out that the 30,000 Ukrainians in Canada – almost 12,000 of whom had reportedly settled in Alberta – represented "real strength," and he therefore offered the following advice to his countrymen: "As quickly as possible we ... have to familiarize ourselves with the workings of the country that we are living in, love our faith and language, but above all else learn the local language." He then summoned his Ruthenian brethren to overcome their legacy of abuse and oppression at the hands of old country lords, with these words of exhortation:

> For the might and the glory of the Ruthenian people
> I sing you this song,
> Awake from your deep slumber to the great task
> I implore you today.
> Arise, get ready, the star is now shining,
> The eagle of freedom has already awakened
> The fields overgrown with forests await you,

It is time for you to seize upon the opportunity,
In the name of the Father put a cross on yourself,
Jesus His Son will help you,
Ask for enlightenment from the Holy Spirit
Because with faith your strength will multiply.

Paraphrasing the famous New Testament passage that begins, "Ask and it shall be given you," Gowda consciously tried to stir national pride among his kinsmen, describing them as "brothers and sons of our glorious Mother Rus'-Ukraine."

Gowda continued to be an occasional contributor to *Svoboda* in the following years, holding forth on various issues and using the paper to educate and to rally his fellow immigrants behind causes that he was either leading or working to promote. However, with the founding of three newspapers in Winnipeg in short succession in 1904–1905, *Svoboda* lost its journalistic monopoly among readers in Ukrainian settlements across Canada. Competition came in the form of the Liberal Party-backed *Kanadiis'kyi farmer* (Canadian Farmer), the Conservative-subsidized *Slovo* [The Word], and the Presbyterian-sponsored *Ranok* [The Dawn], all of which were issued from Winnipeg. Together, they provided for a range of perspectives on how organized Ukrainian life was beginning to develop in Canada. Besides serving as platforms for lively debate and discussion, the new periodicals also offered immigrant authors a choice of outlets for expressing their ideas and feelings. Michael Gowda was quick to take advantage of these opportunities, and on November 2, 1905, he had a lengthy poem published in *Kanadiis'kyi farmer.* Titled "In Memory of Our Emigrants," the poem began on the following dramatic note:

Like prisoners from captivity
Their faces damp, oppressed, sickly
Creatures enveloped in grief
For some reason their eyes redden
Is it from anger or from crying?
If you ask or don't ask
They won't tell you anything
And seemingly lost they look for the road
As if they were waiting for someone or something

Signed "M. Gowda, Edmonton, 10 October 1905," the 149-line poem was steeped in a mixture of anger and pathos. In it, Gowda railed against everyone he regarded as being responsible for the unhappy plight of the Galician immigrants, including "Those age-old bloodsuckers / Depraved nobles and lords," Austrian authorities and Ruthenian leaders. Reflecting attitudes that were widespread in those days throughout much of Europe as well as North America, Gowda at the same time singled out Jews for condemnation, accusing them of profiting from the misery of the peasantry and describing them as having been responsible for Christ's crucifixion. While lacking technical polish, "In Memory of Our Emigrants" is forcefully expressive and filled with a heartfelt sense of grievance that still makes a powerful impression upon the reader, notwithstanding some of its dubious content.

In October 1905, Michael Gowda achieved yet another "first" when one of his poems became the earliest work by a Ukrainian immigrant writer to be translated and published in English. Produced and disseminated with the help of the renowned author, poet, and journalist, E. W. Thomson, "To Canada" initially appeared in the *Manitoba Free Press* and the *Boston Evening Transcript*, before being reprinted in the *Edmonton Bulletin*. In the *Boston Transcript* the poem served as the conclusion to the first instalment of a fascinating report that Thomson wrote about his late September visit to the Ukrainian colony east of Fort Saskatchewan. Entitled "Five Days in Galicia," the two-part story appeared on October 17 and 24, 1905, while the *Bulletin* only ran the small portion of the report that dealt with Michael Gowda on October 18 under the heading "Galician Poetry." In introducing Gowda to Canadian and American readers, Thomson offered the following observations about him:

> How the Galicians, whether they be German, Polish or Russian, feel toward their new country may best be told by their own poet. Edmonton and the surrounding region know him only as Michael Gowda, interpreter to the Bellamy Agricultural Implement Company, and a very keen, clever stump-speaker at election times. He was a school teacher in Galicia, and has been out here, after escaping from the Austrian army, some eight years.

Thomson goes on to mention that Gowda had translated "into Russian verse" [sic] "Snowbound" and twenty other poems by the American Quaker and abolitionist, John Greenleaf Whittier (1807–1892). However, these do not seem to have ever been published and are not preserved among Gowda's papers at the Provincial Archives of Alberta. Thomson's biographical introduction concluded with the explanation that "… he is, unless I mistake, a genuine poet himself. Here is a rough versification, made by myself, from his prose English translation of his poem to Canada:"

TO CANADA

O free and fresh-homed Canada, can we,
Born far o'erseas, call thee our country dear?
I know not whence nor how that right may be
Attained through sharing blessings year by year.

We were not reared within thy broad domains,
Our fathers' graves and corpses lie afar.
They did not fall for freedom on thy plains,
Nor we pour out our blood beneath thy star.

Yet we have Liberty from sea to sea,
Frankly and true you gave us manhood's share.
We who, like wandering birds, flew hopefully
To gather grain upon thy acres fair.

From ancient worlds by wrong opprest we swarmed
Many as ants, to scatter on thy land.
Each to the place you gave, aided, unharmed,
And here we fear not kings nor nobles grand.

And are you not, O Canada, our own?
Nay, we are still but holders of thy soil.
We have not bought by sacrifice and groan
The right to boast the country where we toil.

But, Canada, in Liberty we work till Death,
Our children shall be free to call thee theirs,
Their own dear land, where, gladly drawing breath,
Their parents found safe graves, and left strong heirs.

To Homes, and native freedom, and the heart
To live, and strive, and die if need there be,
In standing manfully by Honor's part
To save the country that has made us free.

> They shall be as brothers to all the rest,
> Unshamed to own the blood from whence they sprang,
> True to their Fathers' Church, and His behest
> For whom the bells of yester Christmas rang.[8]

Unfortunately, the Ukrainian original of this eight-stanza poem never made it into print and has not survived, so it is impossible to determine how faithful the English rendering is to the primary text. It seems fairly certain that "To Canada" was less a translation than an inspired collaboration, and that the metre, style, as well as much of the phrasing of the poem, owed more to Thomson than to Gowda. Nonetheless, knowing Gowda's feelings for his adopted land one can be confident that "To Canada" accurately captured his sentiments as well as his thoughts about how Ukrainian immigrants would ultimately need to earn their full citizenship through sacrifice on a battlefield. This may seem rather contradictory given the fact that Gowda had emigrated from Austria-Hungary partly to evade military service, but it is actually consistent with what is known about his political views and allegiances. Although Gowda felt no great love or loyalty to the Austro-Hungarian crown, he fully believed in many of the British ideals and institutions that formed the pillars of Canadian society in the early twentieth century. Furthermore, as demonstrated by his efforts to organize a Ruthenian infantry unit in the Canadian Army, he clearly was not a pacifist. Indeed, in 1907–1908 he enlisted in the 101st Regiment of the Canadian Home Guard, proudly serving it for four years around the same time that he was urging Ukrainian Canadians to support the creation of a Ruthenian detachment.

What is therefore perhaps most striking about "To Canada" is that it was composed just six years after Gowda landed in Halifax, as indicated in the *Bulletin* version, which carried the credit line, "Michael Gowda, Edmonton, 1903." It is evidence as to how quickly Gowda adapted to his new homeland, and how whole-heartedly he embraced mainstream Canadian values. Equally telling, however, is the last stanza, which unequivocally reaffirmed Gowda's sense of ancestral pride and commitment to preserving his Ukrainian heritage. Obviously, the notion of being a "hyphenated" Canadian was not problematic for the author of the poem, who wanted to keep the best of his old world identity while becoming a full-fledged citizen of Canada.

"To Canada" was the first and for a long time, the only Ukrainian-language literary work by an immigrant author accessible in English. Because of its uniqueness, it was reprinted in whole or part on several occasions over the span of many years. It was included in a book entitled *Our Fellow Slavic*

Citizens, published in New York in 1910, and a slightly revised portion of it was cited in an untitled and unattributed January 29, 1913 article on Gowda that appeared in the *Vegreville Observer.*[9] According to a news story that ran in the *Edmonton Journal* under the heading "Work for the Foreign-Born" on July 9, 1920 and reproduced five of its eight stanzas, the well-travelled poem was next reprinted in the 1920 *Handbook for New Canadians,* compiled by Alfred Kirkpatrick for The Frontier College. And it has been published in several Ukrainian-Canadian sources in recognition of Michael Gowda's singular contribution to Ukrainian-Canadian literature, which serves as an early benchmark of Ukrainian integration into Canadian society and culture.[10]

Michael Gowda and E. W. Thomson first became acquainted in the fall of 1905, when Thomson was touring the rapidly changing Northwest writing a series of articles prompted by the founding of the provinces of Alberta and Saskatchewan. Being the "point man" for the Ukrainian community in Alberta at that time, Gowda was undoubtedly introduced to Thomson soon after he arrived in Edmonton from Los Angeles with his wife. Gowda was henceforth to remain a trusted journalistic contact for Thomson on matters pertaining to Ukrainian immigrants in the Canadian West, their friendship being a reflection of the out-going characters of both men and the bond that they forged while travelling together through the burgeoning Slavic colony northeast of the city.[11]

Edward William Thomson (1849–1924) was a multi-talented individual who led a remarkable and adventure-filled life. Born and educated in southern Ontario, as a teenager he saw action with the Union Army in the American Civil War and afterwards fought with the Queen's Own Rifles against the Fenians. Subsequently employed for several years as a surveyor on the Prairies, he eventually pursued a successful career as a journalist, and from 1878 to 1891 was a member of the editorial staff of the Toronto newspaper, *The Globe.* In the following decade, he edited the Boston magazine *Youth's Companion,* where he published many adventure stories that were included in his 1897 book, *Between Earth and Sky and Other Strange Stories of Deliverance.* After briefly working for the *Montreal Star,* in 1902 he was named Canadian correspondent for the *Boston Transcript,* a position that he held until two years before his death (Bourinot).

Thomson's wide circle of friends included such celebrated political figures as Joseph Howe, Wilfred Laurier, and Henri Bourassa, and the Canadian poets Duncan Campbell Scott, Archibald Lampman, and W. H. Drummond. Besides being a poet and fiction writer of some distinction himself, he also produced a number of translations from French and German, including works by Victor Hugo, Sir George Etienne Cartier, and Heinrich Heine.[12] Thus, "To Canada" was not the only time that he tried his hand at literary translation, though unlike French and German, he undoubtedly did not know a word of Ukrainian before coming to Alberta.

Whereas E. W. Thomson obviously developed feelings of both sympathy and respect for Ukrainians during his brief encounters with them in the Canadian West, the same could not be said for some other important opinion-makers, most notably the well-known Winnipeg writer and Presbyterian minister, Ralph Connor – the pen name of the Rev. Charles W. Gordon (1860–1937). In his 1909 novel, *The Foreigner, A Tale of Saskatchewan*, Connor provided a largely unflattering and utterly confused depiction of the Galician immigrants in Canada, provoking howls of protest from the Ukrainian community. Among those to condemn his book was Michael Gowda, who gamely, if not altogether successfully, tried to express his criticisms in English in "An Open Letter to Ralph Connor" that was published in the *Edmonton Journal* on April 12, 1910. Struggling to control his anger after reading the book, Gowda lashed out at the author in a lengthy rant, part of which reads as follows:

> In my opinion and also in the opinion of over 100,000 people in Canada there is doubt whether you were conscious at the time you wrote the "Tale of Saskatchewan" or whether you were delirious in some hidden disease which is known only to people suffering by the prejudice of foreigners.
>
> In this respect I must tell you that you have done a great injustice to our nationality by bringing false facts before the people of the English speaking world....
>
> The history will tell in the future that you are wrong in this case; the history will mark you as the one who had strained the situation and the relation between the foreign class of people, especially the Ruthenian nationality and the Canadians and English class of people. Your name will rank in the memory of the future history of the people as one who had done great wrong to the national name of the people, as one who insulted the people at the very time that they should have been petted and learnt how to do better.

> The injustice you have done by writing the "Tale of Saskatchewan" is injustice that will never be forgotten, and I will not be responsible if the day will come that you will be called upon to explain yourself before the public.

Demanding that Gordon suspend publication of his book and to stop publicly describing it as a work of fact rather than "pure fiction," Gowda concluded his tirade by "kindly" requesting a reply to his letter in the near future and politely signing his complaint, "Your friend."[13]

It is worth noting that in Michael Gowda's extant papers there are a number of clippings on literary themes, many of them nondescript poems submitted to newspapers by would-be poets. Some of these homespun verses were included in a special page of the literary section of the *Boston Evening Transcript* for May 5, 1917, which was undoubtedly mailed to him by E. W. Thomson. The same issue contained an article about "The Literary World of Today," though Gowda was probably more interested in the feature story about Joseph Conrad and reviews of two recent books, *The Russians and Their Language* and *Something about the Revolution and Other Affairs.* Other clippings saved by Gowda were of obituaries for the Polish novelist Henryk Sienkiewicz (1846–1916) and for Ralph Connor (d. 31 October 1937), who appears to have never responded to Gowda's angry letter in the *Journal.* Equally noteworthy is the first page of the *Reader's Digest* version of Henry Kreisel's 1948 novel *The Rich Man,* as it reveals that Gowda continued to follow contemporary literature long after he abandoned his own creative ambitions.

Other materials of literary interest in the Gowda papers are two poems in typescript: one written about a return visit that he made to his native village in 1912, and another composed on the tenth anniversary of the 1898 death of his father. Handwritten documents include a poem called "To Mother" – penned on Dominion Lands Office stationery and dated May 10, 1912 – as well as a few poetic fragments and short texts that are difficult to decipher but appear to have some literary content. In 1912, Gowda also produced a 169-page draft manuscript of a scrawled autobiography in a notebook that similarly remains to be decoded.

Although this evidence points to the fact that Gowda never lost his enthusiasm for literature and poetry, his own authorial attempts seem to have ended sometime during his second decade in Canada. Notwithstanding E. W. Thomson's generous praise of him, Gowda was not really blessed with great natural talent and he lacked the discipline and determination required to hone his poetic style and technique. His handling of rhythm and phrasing were sometimes awkward, and it is clear that his emotions and prejudices occasionally got the better of him. Still, he was capable of giving vigorous and colourful expression to his ideas and passions, as is evident in his memorable condemnation of the Ukrainians who did not support him in the 1913 provincial elections. He also distinguished himself from other immigrant poets of his era by choosing to compose in free verse instead of the naïve and folkloric style that was typical of the earliest "songs" produced in Canada by Ukrainian pioneers. (Slavutych 12–13; Marunchak 299–300, 307, 310)

Michael Gowda may have only left a handful of modest poems to posterity, but he will always be remembered as the creator of "To Canada," which is his most significant literary achievement. That and being recognized as the "First Ukrainian Citizen in Edmonton" and the activist who broke ground for organized Ukrainian life in Alberta are worthy accomplishments for an immigrant who so quickly became an ardent Canadian while always staying true to his ancestral roots. Indeed, he can be said to have lived up to Taras Shevchenko's invocation in his famed "Friendly Epistle," whose words would have made an appropriate epitaph on Gowda's tombstone:

> Educate yourself, my brothers!
> Think, and read,
> And learn about others,
> But do not renounce your own.... (Shevchenko 193)

NOTES

1. Vetlyn is now in southeast Poland.

2. Gowda's original appeal to the "Ruthenians in Alberta and all of Canada" appeared in *Kanadiis'kyi farmer* in April 1910: "We are recruiting our own regiment in the army and we are turning to you, the youth of our nationality who are here in a foreign land, with these words: Anyone who has a sense of honour for his own nation, for whom it is pleasing to recall our glorious ancestors from Zaporozhian times, for whom it is important that other nations here give us more respect, who wants to leave some glory to the good residents of this, our new country, and renown to their children, should join our new regiment." (qtd. in Marunchak 337)

3. To help build support for the creation of the Ruthenian military unit, a public meeting was held to discuss the proposed regiment on 1 May 1910. One of the speakers at the gathering was Iwan Letawsky, who had been a co-founder of the Taras Shevchenko *Chytalnia* and along with Michael Gowda had previously joined the 101st infantry regiment. Among those who supported Gowda in his effort to establish a Ruthenian corps were such well-known figures as Peter Svarich, Paul Rudyk, and Gregory Krakiwsky (also spelled Kraikivsky, Krakiwski, and Krikevsky).

4. Other Albertans who were part of the company's board of directors or shareholders were Gowda's friends and frequent collaborators, Svarich, Rudyk, and Krakiwsky.

5. Translated from a broadsheet dated 1 May 1913, which is now found with the rest of the Gowda papers at the Provincial Archives of Alberta. All translations from Ukrainian sources used in this article are my own, and materials from the Gowda papers that were utilized in writing this article are from my personal collection, obtained from the Gowda family prior to their deposition in the PAA.

6. The first published poem by a Ukrainian-Canadian author was "*Do bratov halychan*" [To Brother Galicians], by Yuri Syrotiuk, printed in *Svoboda* on 27 May 1897. The second was the poem "*Kanadiis'ki emigranty*" [Canadian Emigrants] by Ivan Zbura of "Beaver Creek," Alberta, which appeared in the same paper on 2 Feb. 1899.

7. The poem was reprinted in Slavutych, Yar, comp. & ed. *Antolohiia ukrains'koi poezii v Kanadi, 1898–1973* [An Anthology of Ukrainian Poetry in Canada, 1898–1973]. Edmonton: *Ob'iednannia Ukrains'kykh pys'mennykiv u Kanadi*, 1975: 8; and Hay-Holowko, Oleksa. *Ukrains'ki pys'mennyky v*

Kanadi. Literaturno-krytychni narysy. Tom Pershyi [Ukrainian Writers in Canada: Literary-Critical Sketches. Volume One]. Winnipeg: Tovarystva "Volyn," 1980: 21–23.

8. The version of the poem that appeared in the *Transcript* had a couple of minor differences, such as "… free and fresh-home Canada!" in the first line, and "wrong" written with a capital in stanza four – the first likely being a typographic error and the second a stylistic preference on the part of Thomson's Boston editor.

9. The latter featured several revisions that do not improve on the original, such as "But Canada, our hearts are thine till death" in the sixth stanza, and "True to their Father's creed and His behest," in the penultimate line of the last stanza.

10. The version of the poem in the Balch anthology was reproduced in abridged form in Mandryka, Mykyta. *History of Ukrainian Literature in Canada.* Winnipeg-Ottawa: Ukrainian Free Academy of Sciences, 1968: 41–43. A complete Balch text then appeared in *Forum: A Ukrainian Review* 16 (Spring 1971): 29.

11. Thomson's *Boston Transcript* articles on his trip through the Ukrainian bloc settlement northeast of Fort Saskatchewan are datelined 23 and 28 September. Eight years later Thomson included a quote from Gowda in an article that he wrote in defence of Ukrainian efforts to get provincial recognition for bilingual schools, describing him as a former "… schoolteacher, an excellent poet in his own language, long an enthusiast for spreading English amongst and Canadianizing his own people…." See "Persecution of the Ruthenians" in Thomson's article, "Old King of Ottawa Vale," *Boston Evening Transcript,* 8 Oct. 1913.

12. In his biography of Thomson, Arthur S. Bourinot (13–14) judged him to be "…a competent but not an inspired translator."

13. Gowda's name was then misconstrued as "M. CJOWDA."

WORKS CITED

BALCH, Emily G., *Our Slavic Fellow Citizens.* New York: Charities Publication Committee, 1910: 449–50.

BOURINOT, Arthur. S. *Edward William Thomson (1849–1924). A Bibliography with Notes and Some Letters.* Ottawa: privately printed, 1955.

Govda, Mykhailo. "*Kil'ka sliv do Rusyniv v Kanadi*" [Several Words to the Ruthenians in Canada]. *Svoboda* 27 Dec. 1900: 2.

———. "*Rus'komu narodu!*" [To the Ruthenian People!] *Svoboda* 31 Aug. 1899: 2

———. "*Visti z Kanadi*" [News from Canada]. *Svoboda* 16 Mar. 1899: 1–2.

———. "*V pamiat' nashym emigrantam*" [In Memory of Our Emigrants] *Kanadiis'kyi farmer* 2 Nov. 1905: 2.

Gowda, Michael. "An Open Letter to Ralph Connor." *Edmonton Journal* 12 Apr. 1910: 8.

———. "Money-Mad Maladministration." *Edmonton Journal*, 17 Nov. 1933: 4.

Marunchak, Mykhailo. *Istoriia Ukraintsiv Kanady. Tom I* [The Ukrainian Canadians A History. Volume I]. Winnipeg: Ukrains'ka Vilna Akademiia Nauk, 1968.

Shevchenko, Taras. "*Do mertvykh i zhyvykh i nenarodzhennykh zemliakiv moikh v Ukraini i ne Ukrainy Sushykh, moie druzhneie poslaniie*" [To the Dead and the Living and as Yet Unborn Countrymen of Mine in Ukraine and Outside of Ukraine, My Friendly Epistle]. *Kobzar. Narodnie vydannia.* [Kobzar: Folk Edition]. With commentaries and annotations by Dr. Vasyl' Simovych. Katerynoslav-Kam'ianets'-Leipzig: Ukrains'ke Vydavnytstvo v Katerynoslav, 1921: 193.

Slavutych, Yar. *Ukrains'ka poeziia v Kanadi* [Ukrainian Poetry in Canada]. Edmonton: Slavuta, 1976.

Thomson, E. W. [misspelled Thompson in the *Bulletin*]. "Galician Poetry." *Edmonton Bulletin* 18 Oct. 1905: 8.

Untitled article. *Vegreville Observer* 29 Jan. 1913: 1. Published without attribution under a photograph of Michael Gowda.

"Work for the Foreign-Born." *Edmonton Journal* 9 July 1920: 4.

3

PASTORAL ELEGY, MEMORIAL, WRITING: ROBERT KROETSCH'S "STONE HAMMER POEM"

CHRISTIAN RIEGEL

I want to begin with endings – closures, and even enclosures. These are endings that are in some cases beginnings, as in the ending of Robert Kroetsch's "Stone Hammer Poem," prologue to his *Completed Field Notes.* To begin I need to reach back to John Milton and his monumental pastoral elegy "Lycidas,"[1] and to look to the ending of that poem, the ending of a song of mourning by Milton's speaker, the swain, for his drowned friend, Lycidas. The swain articulates his content consolation, "weep no more, woeful shepherds, weep no more," (165) as he sings his story of Lycidas's ascension to heaven – a happy apotheosis, to spend his days with singing saints in sweet and glorious societies, to paraphrase the poem. As the swain's song comes to an end, Milton employs another speaker-narrator to close out the poem. This speaker tells us that the swain's song is done and that he has accomplished his goal of mourning his dead friend, for when he awakens on the next day he will look ahead and not back: "At last he rose, and twitched his mantle blue:/Tomorrow to fresh woods, and pastures anew" (192–93). Successful mourning is achieved in the space of a day-long song, and within the space of the poem, and now it is time to move on. Within the bounds of the poem, from beginning to end, a movement of mourning is enacted and contained. The structures of text become the enclosures within which grief can be worked through and serve to enable but also to retain the emotions of loss, even to restrain them from superseding the bound of the grieving moment. Thus, grief is given its proper space but it is also made clear that grief is to remain within that space, enclosed and closed.

Similarly, for Robert Kroetsch in "Stone Hammer Poem," the text itself serves also as a space within which loss can be engaged in a grief-movement. However, for Kroetsch the poem is space where mourning occurs but loss is not closed off at poem's end, as it is in "Lycidas." For Milton, the end of the poem of mourning marks a beginning, a move forward and onwards (outwards even from the song of grief's boundaries), but for Kroetsch's speaker the end of his contemplation of past, place, and family is a circular move, a returning, to the material that has occupied his mind over the course of the poem. There is no closing off of his rumination but rather an articulation of the ongoing nature of his engagement with fundamental elements that inform his life, such as the home place, and the loss of that place, the loss of his father and grandfather and the complexity of the emotional relationship with them, and the role of writing and creativity in his life. Thus, in the last section of the poem the speaker-poet is still contemplating the stone of the title, which he relates overtly to his writing:

I keep it
on my desk
(the stone)

Sometimes I use it
in the (hot) wind
(to hold down paper)

smelling a little of cut
grass or maybe even of
ripening wheat or of
buffalo blood hot

in the dying sun.

Sometimes I write
my poems for that

stone hammer. (8)

The stone of the poem's title is the central object of the text, clearly, but is also the subject of poems outside the scope of the specific text; thus, the stone refers to a larger signifying structure that is returned to repeatedly by the speaker and that supersedes the bounds – the enclosure – of the text of "Stone Hammer Poem." This pattern of repeated return to the subject of loss is concomitant with a late twentieth-century understanding of patterns of rief and of the textual response to loss.[2]

The elegiac currents of Milton's poem and Kroetsch's practice of dealing with loss in "Stone Hammer Poem" employ the idea of a momentary articulation as an exploration of loss. In "Lycidas," the swain sings a song of mourning over the course of a day, beginning at sun up and ending with nightfall. In "Stone Hammer Poem," the movement of the poem is encompassed by the speaker's contemplation of the stone on his desk, which begins the poem as well as ends it. The lyric – and thus song – mode of Kroetsch's poem is clear enough. Further, Milton's poem is decidedly pastoral, set in the countryside within a Greek and mythological world. Kroetsch, in exploring his feelings of loss looks to a pastoral world that has its own mythical associations. But even more significant, both speakers in these poems are deeply interested in the relationship between work and mourning, how indeed a necessary work of mourning can be carried out, and what the relationship of song, of poem, is to the work that is required of a grieving individual. Furthermore, the notion of monument and memorial, of a poem as a physical object that can be a site of memory and mourning, is important to how both poems function. For Milton, the success of the poem and its mourning is indicated by the fact that the poem gives textual presence to the lost friend, echoing the Orpheus myth in asserting the power of art over death. Kroetsch, by contrast, finds that poetry has no such power: it can invoke memory of the dead but it can do nothing to contain that death by paradoxically giving it life within the structures of the poem. For Kroetsch, "Stone Hammer Poem" is but one of many poems of mourning, and art is ultimately shown to be nothing more than the vehicle for the attempt to repair loss.

I will begin to address these issues by looking to some recent commentary on mourning and work before returning to Kroetsch. Jacques Derrida has written significantly about loss and about the role that work has in mourning in the essays that comprise his book *The Work of Mourning*.[3] Derrida takes his cue from Sigmund Freud, particularly from his seminal essay "Mourning and Melancholia," published in 1917, where Freud argues that mourning is a form of mental labour or work that the grieving subject needs to slowly and determinedly work through in order to be freed from the loss. In German, the word for mourning is *Trauerarbeit,* which literally is mourning-work. For my purposes, it is useful to note that in the German the word operates as a noun and as a verb; thus the work of mourning is both an object – such as a poem that deals with grief – and the process that is carried out in response to loss. For Freud, there is a rather strong emphasis on the idea of working through and past grief, but for Derrida, the work of mourning is a multi-dimensional process that deeply involves and affects all aspects of the mourning subject's life and it is not particularly something that ever ends – and this is what will become important for my discussion of Kroetsch in a moment. Derrida writes:

> Work: that which makes for a work, for an *oeuvre,* indeed that which works – and works to open: *opus* and *opening, oeuvre,* and *ouverture*: the work or labor of the *oeuvre* insofar as it engenders, produces, and brings to light, but also labor or travail as suffering, as the engendering of force, as the pain of one who gives. Of the one who gives birth, who brings to the light of day and gives something to be seen, who enables or empowers, who gives the force to know and to be able to see – and all these are powers of the image, the pain of what is given and of the one who takes pains to help us see, read, and think. (142)

To sing a song as Milton's swain does, or to sit and contemplate a stone, and then to write as Kroetsch's speaker does, is a form of work, and in the context of these two poems this form of labour is mourning. The role of the poet of mourning, as Derrida cues us, is to communicate a feeling of grief, and to do so with the overt idea of an audience. The poet gives something, enables and empowers, gives a force, as Derrida notes. For Milton's swain, the context of his song is clearly stated: he sings to his fellow shepherds who then also share in his moment of consolation. For Kroetsch, the idea of audience is more elusive, but implied audience can be read in the range of loss that is engaged as he contemplates all the things that have come and gone that the stone has come into contact with. In this way, Kroetsch's force of mourning is to articulate loss and to engage self-consciously the emotions of loss, to create his oeuvre and to fashion a sense of *ouverture.*

Freud's idealization of mourning, that a work can be completed, that such labouring produces tangible results is shifted by Derrida. As R. Clifton

Spargo notes about Derrida: "From the standpoint of cultural utility, since all of mourning's language-acts fail to produce anything measurably effectual in the way of action, mourning must seem aberrant, characterized by nothing so much as its resistance to the cognitive and recuperative structures of identity that might gather the other into the self as a resource for symbolic meaning" (27). The act of mourning, of labouring – and more importantly for my purposes – of writing grief, is to be aware of the impossibility of mourning whilst still persisting in acting. As Spargo remarks, "For Derrida, as mourning fails even in the midst of its continued attachment, it seems.... the sign of a longing to preserve what is obviously impossible" (27). At the core of elegiac writing is the realization that the very thing that is wished for – the resurrection of the dead, the making concrete of the departed – is bound to failure: text can be no more than symbolic. It is in the gesture, in the action of writing, that a ghost of the lost one will be given a fraught presence.

The work of mourning of Kroetsch's speaker in "Stone Hammer Poem" is catalyzed by his contemplation of the stone as object on his desk. The object is no more than a mere thing, a piece of matter, until the speaker infuses the object with meaning generated by memory, and that memory is infused with loss. The opening line of the poem reinforces this idea, for "This stone" (3) is transformed in the next line as it "become[s] a hammer" (3) by knowledge of the stone's history that only the speaker can supply. The reader soon learns that the stone has multiplicitous associations, for in the second section of the poem it becomes "This paperweight on my desk" to the speaker. Each of the next sections, until the last one, features different associations that the stone has. It is "stone maul" (3), and then "a stone/old as the last/ Ice Age" (5) and it is the stone that his grandfather found in the field: "This stone maul/stopped the plough/ long enough for one/ *Gott im Himmel*" (5). In this repetition of the event of the stone's finding by his grandfather, the speaker indicates the range of the human life cycle, from the earth of the field that signals life itself to the notion of a heavenly afterlife in the German phrase. Though overtly religious as the reference to God asserts, the word "*Himmel*" also means sky and thus takes on a double meaning. The grandfather is situated between the earth and the sky, and therefore the greater cosmos that the speaker finds attaches to the stone: stone as symbol of history, family, place, and the relation of the self to these elements. At the end of Milton's elegy, the speaker imagines his dear lost friend ascending to heaven in a moment of apotheosis; resurrected in heaven, the friend will now be happier than he was on earth and thus the speaker can derive consolation from this fact. For Kroetsch's speaker, however, the German phrase appears in the text ultimately only to signal the impossibility of easy consolation. The grandfather is given presence in the poem through the passages that feature him, and his language is used to reinforce that sense of presence. However, the phrase "*Gott im Himmel*" appears archaic, from as different a time as the spoken German of an immigrant farmer. The grandfather is remembered only as having been in this particular place, handling the stone, and not as having ascended after death to the positive space of a Godly heaven.

Over the course of the poem, the stone is returned to repeatedly in new enactments of the stone's significance. For the speaker, this returning is a means through which to attempt to give presence to the memories of things lost. The returning by inscription – the very acts of writing that make up the whole of "Stone Hammer Poem" – is also a mode of attempting to make solid what is absent. But the repeated returnings fail ultimately, as they must, for the speaker can do no more than assert the presence he desires: he cannot make present the impossible, and hence the labour of mourning is a paradoxical work. A work can do nothing to bring back the dead; it can do no more than assert its own existence as the writing of a poem, the active working of grief, and text becomes memorial, even monument, but it does not and cannot become that which has been lost.

Another element of work that is carried out is one of ancestral history, the tracing of associations that detail the speaker's feelings of loss in relation to his family history. This is a history of settlement, farming, and ultimately of the speaker's conflicted abandonment of the family farm. And so we have the story of the stone's finding:

> This stone maul
> was found.
>
> In the field
> my grandfather
> thought
> was his
>
> my father
> thought was his. (4)

And we have the stone's association with a million years of history in this place, from the Ice Age to Native existence to the unsettling effects of European settlement. And we have the speaker's engagement with all of these elements as he feels compelled to work to understand and process the feelings of loss he has that are generated by contemplation of the stone on his desk, the paperweight that holds things down in a hot wind:

> ?what happened
> I have to/ I want
> to know (not know)
> ?WHAT HAPPENED (5)

The paradoxical movement of wanting to know and not to know simultaneously is indicative of the active labour of grief that is occurring, of an active process of engagement with loss and with working at mourning, for grief is a process attempting to make real that which has been lost. To carry out, in fact, the impossible, and such is then inherently a paradoxical process.

The speaker's awareness of his working at mourning through the composition of his poem becomes evident in the seventh section when he relates the stone to the poem that he is writing. For the poem, like the stone, has been worked at, has been part of a process of complex struggle rooted in history and time:

> The poem
> is the stone
> chipped and hammered
> until it is shaped
> like the stone
> hammer, the maul. (6)

Thus, the poem is an implement of struggle, of active work, and it is overtly a concrete tool to carry out a necessary psychic work. Similarly, Milton's swain begins his song to Lycidas by self-consciously reflecting upon the necessity of singing, of using language, as an implement to perform a work of mourning. As the swain notes: "[Lycidas] must not float upon his watery bier/Unwept, and welter to the parching wind,/Without the meed of some melodious tear" (12–14). The swain feels compelled to employ some "lucky words" (20) to "bid fair peace" (22) to his beloved Lycidas.

Kroetsch alludes to several key elements of pastoral elegy to provide context for the work he has his speaker carry out over the course of the poem. In the fifth section, for example, he uses the convention of comparing vegetative cycles to the finite human cycle to figure the passing of traditional Native life. The speaker notes "the retreating Indians" and links them to the vibrant growth of berries:

> (the saskatoons bloom
> white (infrequently
> the chokecherries the
> highbush cranberries the
> pincherries bloom
> white along the barbed
> wire fence (the
> pemmican   winter (5)

The growth is contrasted with the fence, a construct of the settlement that has caused the loss to the Indians. The berries here are also loosely allusive, elusively allusive I am tempted to say, to the "berries harsh and crude" that Milton's swain plucks for poetic inspiration when he begins his song of mourning.

Close to the end of the poem, the idea of vegetative cycles returns when Kroetsch notes that his father kept the stone "on the railing/ of the back porch in/ a raspberry basket" (7). And while the stone is decidedly unlike anything that grows, it metonymically takes on the status of a naturally growing, and cyclical, object that transcends the human life span. The stone in the basket has further figurative qualities, for the basket is the container for the stone just as the speaker's poem is the container, or enclosure, for the memories and stories associated with the stone. And so, a key element of work that occurs in the poem is a work of memory, a work of remembering and extrapolating the associations of the stone that originates the contemplation that is the poem. Another element here is that in the stone's multiplicitous symbolism, the work of memory broadens the spectre of loss. The stone is not a singular object that has a direct referent, and it becomes unclear ultimately what exactly is being made present. Kroetsch signals his own awareness of the paradoxes of loss and of writing loss: why try to fix meaning when the lost object can never be made present?

Kroetsch employs other elements from the tradition of pastoral elegy as well. The seasons and nature are used frequently in pastoral elegy to "reflect the changes in the dead person (autumn or winter, then spring) and in the mourner's grief" (99) as Jahan Ramazani states. The cycles of growth and harvest are noted by Kroetch's speaker in reference to the growing activities of the father and grandfather and to the abundant growth that occurs on the farm. His grandfather first finds the stone in the spring while he is ploughing – "This stone maul/stopped a plough" (5) – a clear reference to a springtime activity. The blooming berry bushes are indicative of the vibrant growth of spring, countered by the ironic reference to "pemmican winter" (5) that contrasts the loss of the parent and grandparent with the cyclical and ongoing growth of the bushes. When the speaker remembers his ancestors, he remembers them as being active during the growing season of summer, noting that his father "was lonesome for the/ hot wind on his face" (7); the speaker then connects this notion of growth to his own practice of writing, for the stone serves as paperweight "in the (hot) wind" (8) in section ten. Further, for the speaker the stone is associated strongly with growth as he imagines it "smelling a little of cut/grass or maybe of ripening wheat." (8). But this process of ripening also ironically refers to the notion of death, for things that are ripe are harvested (as the grass has been), and thus are no longer alive. The speaker acknowledges this connection when he references the dead buffalo blood and the death of the sun in the next lines: "buffalo blood hot/ in the dying sun" (8). The father is remembered in part by the association of the raspberry basket and the stone. The raspberry basket is used at harvest time, and thus in the autumn, to contain the growth – the raspberries – that has been plucked. Thus, the basket paradoxically indicates both life and death. Kroetsch's use of the seasons along with vegetative growth is a gesture to traditional pastoral elegy where, as Ramazani notes, the "seasonal tropes are anthropomorphic" (99). The raspberry basket takes on associations with death and thus is related to the dead father. That the stone contained in the basket later becomes an integral part of the speaker's writing desk, as is made apparent in the section that follows, reinforces the elegiac function of "Stone Hammer Poem," but also reflects the memorial status of the stone and of Kroetsch's poetry.

The stone, then, gains symbolic significance through its associations with memorial stones or grave markers. "Stone Hammer Poem" becomes a textual site of memory and memorial, where inscription can allow grief to be enacted and for the force of mourning to be borne. The significance of the notion of memorial is interesting as it applies to "Stone Hammer Poem," for Kroetsch's speaker associates the stone closely with the function of memory, and then links that memory with mourning. The stone thus is linked with grave markers and monuments and other signifiers of memory and death. James E. Young argues that monuments are the "material objects, sculptures, and installations used to memorialize a person or thing" (4). For Kroetsch's speaker, the stone becomes an object of memorial in the multiple, taking on what Young describes as the funereal function of a monument: "The traditional monument (the tombstone) can.... be used as a mourning site for a lost loved one" (3). For Kroetsch, the poem as a whole can be thought of as a *monumental text* for it stands as a memorial to the various elements of loss presented in the poem, and especially for the lost father and grandfather. A monument's meaning operates only, as Young notes, within the framework of what is brought to it: "As an inert piece of stone, the monument keeps its own past a tightly held secret, gesturing away from its own history to the events and meanings we bring to it in our visits" (14). Likewise, Kroetsch's stone takes on variable meaning, from a mere piece of rock to a historical artefact, to the focalizing object of the speaker's grief.

For Kroetsch the work of mourning is an open-ended process, where the poem is an enclosure that contains elements of his labour; it does not close out his grief-work as Milton's poem does for the swain. Kroetsch's work of mourning is akin to the late twentieth- and early twenty-first-century understanding of grief as an all-encompassing experience without closure. That is, loss cannot be compartmentalized, worked through and past in the Miltonic and Freudian sense; rather, loss becomes an intrinsic part of the experience of living, and for a writer it becomes an intrinsic part of his oeuvre and his opus, to echo Derrida. For Jacques Lacan, as Alessia Ricciardi remarks, loss takes on an "interminable, monotonous tempo.... a rhythm that flattens the singularity of the object and renders its historical circumstances irrelevant" (Ricciardi 43). Derrida effectively describes this idea in another passage from *The Work of Mourning*:

> This being at a loss says something, of course, about mourning and about its truth, the impossible mourning that nonetheless remains at work, endlessly hollowing out the depths of our memories, beneath their great beaches and beneath each grain of sand, beneath the phenomenal or public scope of our destiny and behind the fleeting, inapparent moments, those without archive and without words. (94–95)

And so, for Kroetsch we see in "Stone Hammer Poem" a sign of that hollowing out of the depths of memory, of the impossible work of mourning that remains, that labours on. And, we are reminded in this contemplation that "Stone Hammer Poem" is mere prologue to the collected poems he has published as *Completed Field Notes.*

NOTES

1. Milton's poem is generally acknowledged as foundational in the English tradition of elegy, as critics like Peter Sacks and Melissa F. Zeigler note. Zeigler remarks that "Lycidas" is "resonantly influential for most later English elegy" (7), and though allusions to Milton are not direct in "Stone Hammer Poem," it is clear that Kroetsch's poem employs elements from the English tradition begun by Milton, as well as from the Greek, Roman, and later pastoral elegy traditions that Milton also borrows from.
2. See especially John Bowlby's *Loss: Sadness and Depression*, where he writes about the cyclical nature of grief over the course of a lifetime, and Ronald Schleifer in *Rhetoric and Death: The Language of Modernism and Postmodern Discourse Theory* on the limits of language in articulating loss.
3. I discuss the notion of the work of mourning further in *Writing Grief: Margaret Laurence and the Work of Mourning*, and in my introduction to *Response to Death: The Literary Work of Mourning*.

WORKS CITED

BOWLBY, John. *Loss: Sadness and Depression.* London: Pimlico, 1980.

DERRIDA, Jacques. *The Work of Mourning.* Eds. Pascale-Anne Brault and Michael Naas. Chicago: University of Chicago Press, 2001.

KROETSCH, Robert. *Completed Field Notes: The Long Poems of Robert Kroetsch.* Edmonton: University of Alberta Press, 2000.

MILTON, John. "Lycidas." *The Norton Anthology of English Literature*, 5th ed. Gen. ed. M. H. Abrams. New York: W. W. Norton, 1987. 658–64.

RAMAZANI, Jahan. *Poetry of Mourning: The Modern Elegy from Hardy to Heaney.* Chicago: University of Chicago Press, 1994.

RICCIARDI, Alessia. *The Ends of Mourning: Psychoanalysis, Literature, Film.* Stanford: Stanford University Press, 2003.

RIEGEL, Christian, ed. *Response to Death: The Literary Work of Mourning.* Edmonton: University of Alberta Press, 2005.

———. *Writing Grief: Margaret Laurence and the Work of Mourning.* Winnipeg: University of Manitoba Press, 2003.

SACKS, Peter. *The English Elegy: Studies in the Genre from Spenser to Yeats.* Baltimore: Johns Hopkins University Press, 1985.

SCHLEIFER, Ronald. *Rhetoric and Death: The Language of Modernism and Postmodern Discourse Theory*. Urbana and Chicago: University of Illinois Press, 1990.

SPARGO, R. Clifton. *The Ethics of Mourning: Grief and Responsibility in Elegiac Literature*. Baltimore: Johns Hopkins University Press, 2004.

YOUNG, James E. *The Texture of Memory: Holocaust Memorials and Meaning*. New Haven: Yale University Press, 1993.

ZEIGER, Melissa F. *Beyond Consolation: Death, Sexuality, and the Changing Shapes of Elegy*. Ithaca: Cornell University Press, 1997.

PART TWO
DRAMA

4

NO COWPERSONS ON THIS RANGE: THE CULTURAL COMPLEXITY OF ALBERTA THEATRE

ANNE NOTHOF

Contemporary theatre in Alberta performs the cultural diversity of the province, playing against the stereotypes of prairie realism and cowboy iconography. Alberta playwrights reflect a wide multicultural spectrum, but their focus is rarely on a reification or validation of specific ethnic communities; they are not compelled to dramatize their distinctiveness, although their family and community histories inform the complex moral and cultural dynamics of their works. Their ethnicity is integral to their consideration of a broad range of subjects: from Canadian immigrant history, to the dialogic structure of Baroque music, to the tragic consequences of the political exploitation of science.

Their work has not been nurtured in ethnic community theatres, but through a network of theatre companies in the province all engaged in the development of new Canadian plays: Workshop West and Theatre Network in Edmonton, Alberta Theatre Projects in Calgary, and the Banff Centre for the Arts. Moreover, Alberta ethnic theatre has played across the country in the regional and national theatres. Alberta's playwrights create complex and diverse scenarios, performing the wide range of Canadian identity. As Stuart Hall posits in his essay, "Cultural Identity and Diaspora," identity is a performative process, continually being negotiated through a complex historical process of appropriation, compromise, subversion, masking, invention and revival" (401). This essay will consider several works by four Alberta playwrights whose recent plays both subvert and reinvent the cultural identity of their province: *Mom, Dad I'm Living with a White Girl* and *The Forbidden Phoenix* by Marty Chan, *Ribbon* by Pat Darbasie, *The Red Priest* and *The Blue Light* by Mieko Ouchi, and *Einstein's Gift* and *Blowfish* by Vern Thiessen.

Edmonton playwright Marty Chan resists a "Chinese-Canadian" tag. He has written plays in diverse subjects and styles, including a thriller called *The Bone House* (1999) for the Edmonton Fringe Festival, in which a killer stalks the audience; the text for a rock opera for teens entitled *The Seventh Circle* (2001), using Dante's *Inferno* as a metaphor for a high school hell; and a political satire – *The Old Boys Club* (1997), which takes aim at systemic corruption in the Alberta government. The enthusiastic audience response to *The Bone House* proved to him "that writing was an intellectual endeavour, not a cultural one. Race was neither a boon nor a burden." (Chan, "Ethnic" 13); and he wonders why "in Canada we want to practice literary segregation" (14). Yet his plays consistently challenge racial stereotypes, and in two of his major plays, the dynamics of ethnicity play a significant role in deconstructing family relationships and national mythologies.

Mom, Dad, I'm Living with a White Girl, which premiered at the Cahoots Theatre in Toronto in 1994 and has since been produced in a revised form across the country, questions the assumption of a tolerant Canadian multiculturalism by foregrounding implicit racism that can operate in both directions – against the white majority, as well as against a Chinese minority. The protagonist, Mark Gee, is a young second-generation Chinese male living in Vancouver, who resists the traditional expectations of his parents, and decides to live with his white girlfriend. His mother, Li Fen, reacts strongly against his relationship with a "*Gwai mui*," whom she considers little better than a prostitute, and his father, Kim, wants him to learn acupuncture so that he can take over the family business. Mark's psychological defence is to demonize his parents in terms of the 1930s B-movie characterizations of the "yellow peril" as a sinister dragon lady, "Yellow Claw," and her henchman who are seeking world domination. These Western constructions of personified evil express the racist stereotypes of the majority culture, but also Mark's denial of his own heritage.

The play works on two intersecting planes – the literal and the imagined. In the imagined world of the B-movie, Mark plays a secret service agent named Agent Banana; his girlfriend, Sally, assumes the identity of his partner, Snow Princess. In these roles, they enact the battle of "good versus evil" in the terms constructed by Western society, although Sally is also the voice of a liberalism that is shown to be disingenuous and naïve in its response to perceived racism. For example, Mark's reaction to a film script of "The Wrath of the Yellow Claw" that Sally is reviewing as part of her job is that "it's got potential," whereas Sally believes that Asian caricatures and racist jokes are not funny because they "make[s] everyone think Asians are villains and buffoons" (Chan, *Mom, Dad* 126). Mark's response to her assertion that "we've outgrown these kinds of stereotypes," is to ask her whether she has seen a Jackie Chan flick lately. He thinks that Sally herself is guilty of appropriation of voice in speaking on behalf of the Chinese and that "it's better to have everything in the open" (126). Through such "role reversals," the playwright holds a mirror up to his audience, so that it will clearly see its own racist assumptions, and the inadequacies of a "politically correct" response. But he also expresses his own right to make ethnic jokes in his plays, and to explore complex issues of ownership. He satirizes entrenched and unacknowledged racism and apathy, but also the tendency to exoticize difference; for example Sally identifies Mark's quest for "independence" in terms of "the right to speak [his] mind [a]nd the apathy to say nothing" as being distinctively Canadian (99). On the other hand, Mark exposes Sally's fascination with Chinese culture as limited to her knowledge of enough Cantonese to order Chinese food.

In *Mom, Dad, I'm Living with a White Girl* the tensions between past and present, between a traditional culture that exacts obedience and a Western culture that assumes a freedom of choice remain unresolved. Mark finally decides to leave his girlfriend, but for a variety of personal and cultural reasons. The "*shuriken*" (throwing star) that he wields in his persona as Agent Banana doing battle with his parents in their personas as forces of evil can cut both ways since, in erasing them from his life, he also destroys something of himself. Although he resists his parents' expectations, he also resists the assimilative pressures of Canadian society. His final three statements, which have the formality of Chinese aphorisms, testify to his "rite of passage":

> **Mark:** The panda lets go of her cubs.
> *Mark looks to where Kim left.*
> **Mark:** The butterfly climbs out of its cocoon.
> *Mark finally notices his shadows on the back wall.*
> *He turns around and looks to Li Fen.*
> *Then he looks out.*
> **Mark:** The young tree has deep roots (167).

Like Alberta playwright Sharon Pollock, Chan has also disinterred the buried history of exploitation and racism in Canada. *Best Left Buried* explores the reasons for the burning of Chinatown in Nanaimo in 1960 from the point of view of the Chinese who worked in the coalmines. In *The Forbidden Phoenix* (Catalyst Theatre 2003), Chan deconstructs imperialistic "national" symbols, such as the Canadian Pacific Railway, which has functioned as an image of Canadian unity. The route to the west coast was blasted through the mountains by Chinese labourers, many of whom died in the construction of the "National Dream." *The Forbidden Phoenix* is a political allegory about Chinese immigrant experience in the late nineteenth century. Deluded by the myth of the Gold Mountain – the expectation of riches that awaited them in Canada – Chinese men toiled on the railways and in the mines; they were forbidden to bring their families with them, and were denied citizenship. In Chan's fable, the hero/protagonist is the Monkey King, the archetypal Chinese trickster figure, who leaves the starving Kingdom of the East and the repressive regime of the Empress Dowager to find a prosperous future for his people in the Western land of plenty. He also leaves behind his beloved adopted son, a starving young peasant. In the West, however, he is co-opted by Tiger (the forces of the establishment and government) to dig a tunnel through Gold Mountain so that Tiger can join his lover, the fearsome Iron Dragon. His only hope for a new life in the West lies in the Phoenix (which symbolizes the immigrants' dreams), and together they defeat the Tiger and the Iron Dragon. In Chan's deconstruction of the East/West binary, the forces of the industrialized West are destructive of environment, culture, and social harmony, and defeated only by intellect and imagination. Once this is accomplished, Monkey King can rescue his peasant son from the Empress, and lead his people into the West. As a tamed Tiger explains, "Home is not a place. It is a state of mind. As long as the curtain of water flows, [the Monkey King's] home is both kingdoms" (74).

The Forbidden Phoenix was performed as a Chinese opera, with some modifications to accommodate the martial arts and singing skills of local actors, only one of whom was Chinese in the 2003 Edmonton production – actor and playwright Elyne Quan, who played the Monkey King. Chan believed that in order to tell his story of Chinese immigrants it was important to use the conventions of Chinese theatre. His main purpose, however, was to introduce Chinese theatre and stories to Canadian audiences, since they were not in the public consciousness. He inflects the style and the content to tell a Canadian "nation-building" story from the point of view of the Chinese immigrants, but the play does not express Chinese values, according to Chan; it tells a Canadian story to engage Canadian audiences (Chan Interview).[1]

In *Ribbon,* Edmonton actor and teacher Pat Darbasie also recreates history as contemporary testimony; she demonstrates the importance of family and community in challenging social marginalization and establishing a sense of belonging and purpose. She believes that "home" is what is familiar; identity is realized through the touchstones that connect people (Darbasie Interview). In telling the story of a Black pioneer family in Alberta, she brings into social consciousness the diverse cultural matrix of the province. The play has an important educational function: Black people in Canada have been represented primarily by immigrants from West India and/or Africa; until recently, the voices of Canadian Black residents of Alberta have not been heard.

Ribbon was written, enacted, and directed as Darbasie's MFA project at the University of Alberta and produced in September 2005 in collaboration with Ground Zero Productions, "as part of an initiative to reflect the social reality of culturally diverse communities" (Darbasie Program). It enacts the reconnection of a Black woman in her mid-forties with her great-grandmother, whose voice she hears in the family home she has come to dismantle and sell near the town of Athabasca. Darbasie plays both the younger woman, Paula, and older woman, Lilly, whose monologue imagines the experiences of the Black families who migrated from Oklahoma and settled in Pine Creek (Amber Valley) in the early twentieth century. This is not Darbasie's history, although there are intersections with her own experience as a Black immigrant from Trinidad: despite her origins, like her protagonist, Lilly, she feels "wholly Canadian" (Darbasie Interview). In one scene in *Ribbon,* Lilly is in the land claims office in Athabasca, and is asked by an immigrant where she is from. Her response is, "I'm from here." For Darbasie, "It's wonderful to be able to say that" (*Edmonton Journal* 5).

Darbasie integrated stories from two other Alberta plays in *Ribbon*: a monologue by Ground Zero director, Don Bouzek, which she performed in 1999, about a woman who loses her husband in the Hillcrest Mine disaster; and *Beloved Community* by Jane Heather, in which a mother and daughter, the descendants of Black pioneers in Alberta, respond to globalization issues. Darbasie began to speculate on a possible life for a Black woman in Alberta in the early twentieth century. She found the Black community very supportive, in particular the Black Pioneer Society of Alberta, which mounted a front-of-house display for the Studio Theatre premiere. She accessed stories collected over many years, some of which have been published in the two-volume anthology, *The Window of Our Memories*, and incorporated into her play historic details such as the fires near Athabasca that threatened the community, and the Amber Valley baseball team. She also drew on significant socio-political details such as White racial assumptions in respect to miscegenation, the reasons for Black immigration from the United States, and employment and relocation patterns. Through her stories, Lilly recalls her childhood, her first marriage to a miner, her early widowhood, and her remarriage of convenience to a C.N. railway porter. Her stories reveal a strong-willed and courageous woman with a sense of humour.

Paula only begins to understand the importance of the stories of her family when she finds a red ribbon that her great-grandmother tied in her hair when she was a child, and which she believed lost to a gust of wind. She realizes that the "junk" in the home embodies a precious legacy. The line Paula reads from Lilly's copy of *A Tale of Two Cities* resonates with her own experience: "For as I draw closer and closer to the end, I travel in the circle, nearer and nearer to the beginning" (quoted in *Ribbon* 2). However, although Lilly's stories are intended for Paula, they are directed at the theatre audience, and Paula only dimly begins to sense Lilly's presence in the house at the end of the play. The symbolic family detritus functions as a mnemonic for Lilly, not Paula, whose role is that of a convenient link to the present.

Director, actor, filmmaker, playwright Mieko Ouchi began to explore her heritage by making a documentary film based on her grandfather's life during the 1940s internment of Japanese Canadians. She is fourth-generation Japanese and her mother is Irish/Scottish, and she never thought of herself as Japanese as a child. She spoke no Japanese and attended a French immersion school in Calgary. However in the process of making the film she discovered that she was representing a collective Japanese-Canadian war experience; the Japanese community "gave [her] back her culture" (Ouchi Interview *Mote*). In effect, she had been part of this community her whole life, but never knew it (Ouchi Interview Nothof). Although Mieko has contacts with other Asian artists across the country, established primarily during her days as a touring actor, she has yet to collaborate with Asian theatres or groups in creating a play. She feels no obligation to speak for the Japanese-Canadian community, members of which have a range of perspectives depending on age and experience; nor that she should limit herself in respect to cultural representation. She believes that a unique cultural perspective may inform other stories than one's own. According to Ouchi, "a diversity of voices is what makes a community whole" (Interview Nothof). Her plays, *The Red Priest (Eight Ways to Say Goodbye)* (2003) and *The Blue Light* (2005), both distance themselves in time and place from the Canadian scene in order to explore the creative and destructive potential of the imagination – the ways in which art can function as an expression of freedom or a means of indoctrination and political control. In *The Red Priest*, Antonio Vivaldi debates the paradoxical nature of music with a reluctant pupil; in *The Blue Light*, Leni Riefenstahl defends her filmmaking for Hitler's Third Reich as an apolitical aesthetic enterprise.

The Red Priest is a duologue set in Paris in 1640 – one year before Vivaldi died in Vienna, impoverished and alone, despite his prodigious creative output of hundreds of instrumental and choral works. A French aristocrat has employed him to teach the violin to his wife in six weeks in order to win a bet with the king, Louis XV. Although teacher and pupil appear to be mismatched and out of tune when they first meet, Vivaldi and the "Woman" begin to appreciate their similarities and to work in harmony: both are powerless in terms of their social situation, dependent on the Count for their livelihood, and consequently obliged to be subservient; both speculate on the ways they can say goodbye to the patronage that enslaves them. They express intensely personal feelings indirectly through a conversation about music and gardens. Both have public and private faces and find ways to exercise a degree of imaginative freedom – Vivaldi through the making of music, the Woman through her love of gardens. Baroque music and French gardens are complex formal structures, characterized by repeated motifs, but which allow for elaboration and extemporization. The Woman resists her much older husband's concept of an ideal garden, "*Le Jardin de la*

Raison," because it is too controlled; it suggests "man's triumph over the slippery bits" with trees "twisted and trained into classical columns" (Ouchi, *The Red Priest* 3). She fully understands the beautiful yet ephemeral nature of gardens and of her own life – that "[t]wo hundred years from now, nothing will be left here but bones. The bones of a garden. No flowers. No order. No flesh. Just a skeleton of architectural remains and ruin" (9). Similarly, Vivaldi speculates on the nature of his musical creativity, which is not realized wholly through the extremes of punishing, disciplined effort, or emotional abandonment. It is both a gift and a curse: "Our ability to play a piece perfectly and with such ease unleashes its potential so completely, that our *own* feelings and connection to it are… irrelevant. The injustice of this is as malicious as it is heartbreaking" (8).

Vivaldi and the Woman extend their duet in a debate over the ways in which portraiture and statues can express women as trapped and caged, or as free. Vivaldi sees in a portrait of the Woman as "Flora" a personification of springtime, "Woman's connection to nature, fertility and the wild and untamed world" (38), but like Robert Browning's "My Last Duchess," it is a portrait commissioned and owned by her husband. He compares it to the portrait of Antea by the sixteenth century Italian painter, Parmigianino, whose restrained expression and formal attire are complicated by the pelt of a weasel draped over her shoulder, as an example of ambivalent and subversive art. Art may be used in many different ways, and may accomplish much or accomplish nothing; it may be demanding, even destructive. As Vivaldi explains to the Woman:

> Like the mother you describe, a good composition is not simple and one sided. And like the past, it should never be washed with the *colour of sentimental love* either. A piece of music is as multi-faced and dimensional as a … garden. It takes many viewings to truly appreciate and understand. It is alive and it is changing. (46)

Most importantly, as the Woman concludes in *The Red Priest,* it enables us to "see the world in a different way" (54).

Mieko Ouchi played the Woman in the Alberta Theatre Production's premiere at the playRites Festival in 2003, not as an exercise in "colour-blind" casting, but because it was impossible to find an actor who was skilled enough to play the violin solo at the end of the play – the symbolic expression of the Woman's triumph over her personal and social limitations. Ouchi learned the violin as a child, although reluctantly, and has come to appreciate the formative influences of musical structure, tone, and mood on her playwriting. Although she believes that her Japanese physiognomy should have no bearing on the role, at least one member of the ATP audience connected her performance with a vision of a Geisha in a garden setting. For Ouchi, however, "there are many connections between women who have been put in all kinds of cages all through history" (McLaughlin).

Ouchi's *The Blue Light*[2] also considers the role of a frustrated creative woman in a portrait of Leni Riefenstahl. The play celebrates her artistic achievement while questioning her ethical and political compromises. Like *Ribbon*, it is a memory play, cutting back and forth in time and place from a Los Angeles film studio office in 2002 to Leni's childhood in Berlin in order to focus on seminal scenes from her career as actor, director, and filmmaker. In effect, the play functions as an imaginative documentary: using a "filmic" style, Ouchi records the people and events that informed Leni's art. The play is unapologetic in its portrait, even as it reveals Leni's self-delusion. The blue light of the film image has only a partial relationship to reality: it illuminates, but can also be a romantic distortion. As Leni argues in the play, every film has a subliminal propagandist subtext, whether it is recognized or acknowledged.

In her early film, *The Blue Light* (1932), Leni played the heroine, Junta, a solitary woman considered to be a witch by her community, who discovers a cave of crystals in the mountains radiating a blue light. When she confides its location to a young man, he betrays her trust in order to take the crystals for himself. Her ideal world cannot sustain the intrusion of reality. The scenario of Leni's first film inspired her for the rest of her life, and also previsages her downfall, as she struggles to realize an ideal in art, but repeatedly finds that a price is exacted – by her mentor, the film director Arnold Frank; and by the Nazi Minister of Propaganda, Josef Goebbels, who solicits her skills as a filmmaker by pointing out that like her, Hitler "is dedicated and keen to make sure our German stories are told and remembered" (Ouchi, *The Blue Light* 39). Even though Hitler promises Leni the complete cooperation and support of the Nazi party, the blue light of her vision is subsumed by political fanaticism, and becomes a symbol of the "sacred shrine of Germany" (Ouchi, *The Blue Light* 53). Riefenstahl sees her 1934 documentary on the Nuremburg rally, *The Triumph of the Will*, as an ecstatic celebration of personified power: "On my knees, in the dirt, I shot [Hitler] against a sky set ablaze with light from the sacred shrine of Germany. Pious. Powerful. Invoking God himself" (53). Leni is driven to make unforgettable films, regardless of the consequences. She leaves personal and political judgements to others.

Ouchi's *The Blue Light* invokes Riefenstahl's life through the images of her films, and by scripting the infamous historical photographs of her meetings with Hitler and Goebbels. The men in her life function as variant influences and ideologies. Leni's first cameraman and lover initially supports her independent spirit and then disagrees with her decision to work for Hitler; he warns her about being "used" and offers an alternative response to the question of artistic integrity. The "father figures" represent the authorities in Leni's life with whom she negotiates some room to create her own vision, including Hitler and her own father. The "enabling" men, Josef Goebbels and Arnold Frank, have also exacted a personal price. Ouchi casts the same "father-figure" actor as the film icon, Walt Disney, a casting that suggests that American film empire is also heavily invested in political propaganda, although, ironically, its stories may be German: Disney's *The Sorcerer's Apprentice*, starring Mickey Mouse, is based on a tale by Goethe.

Questions of cultural representation are also raised in *The Blue Light*. The 1920s "Bergfilme," in which Riefenstahl starred as a romantic heroine saved from avalanches and crevasses by ski instructors, were a popular German national and cultural genre. In what sense, then, do Canadian or Albertan films and plays reflect national or local ideology or perspective? Does an artist have a responsibility to interrogate the politics and policies of her own society? In questioning the motives of other artists, is she also interrogating her own?

Vern Thiessen's plays are also engaged in ethical debates on a personal and political level. They range across cultures and histories to consider the possibility of exercising humanist values despite betrayals and compromises, and the possibility of faith and belief in a world bent on self-destruction. His plays also have a wide range of form and style: Theatre of the Absurd (*The Resurrection of John Frum*), domestic contemporary tragedy (*Apple*), an introspective monologue on love and marriage (*Shakespeare's Will*), and historical epic (*Einstein's Gift* and *Vimy*).

Raised in Winnipeg by Mennonite parents, Thiessen graduated from the MFA playwriting program at the University of Alberta in 1992, and has been based in Alberta for the past fifteen years, working as a playwright, actor, dramaturge, director, and theatre educator. In several of his plays, he explores the cultural contradictions and "outsider" status of his "German-speaking-Russian-Mennonite-turned-Canadian" heritage (quoted in DyckFehderau iii). His first play, *The Courier* (Theatre Centre, Toronto, 1988) is a monologue spoken by a young Mennonite from the Russian Ukraine as he reconsiders his moral responsibilities as a courier for the Nazi army in the Second World War. In *Back to Berlin* (Solo Collective, Vancouver 2005) a lapsed Mennonite son interrogates his elderly father about his complicity in Nazi atrocities during a trip to Berlin. And like Mieko Ouchi, Thiessen has explored the tragic consequences of a political expropriation of the creative imagination for nationalistic ends in his epic play, *Einstein's Gift* (2003).

In *Einstein's Gift,* Thiessen compares the philosophies and beliefs of physicist Albert Einstein and chemist Fritz Haber with respect to their scientific research, and the ironic and tragic consequences of their work. Haber proves to be a complex, paradoxical subject – a German Jew who converted to Christianity in order to retain his university position and advance in his career; a Nobel Prize winner and a war criminal; and an idealist who believes in the practical application of ideals. His life is framed as a memory play, beginning in 1945 with Einstein as narrator recalling his debates with Haber over a period of forty years, from their first meeting in Germany in 1905 to their final meeting in 1934. Both have engaged in scientific research that has resulted in the horrific destruction of human lives: Einstein's work on nuclear chain reactions fuelled the construction of the atomic bomb; Haber's work on nitrogen as a fertilizer was put to a more destructive application as chlorine gas in the First World War, and his work on the pesticide Zyklon B was exploited by the Nazis in the manufacture of gas for the death camps. In the play, Einstein extols the primacy of the intellect in research, and strives to be free of nationalistic and religious dogma while retaining his Jewish identity: "what man thinks and how he thinks, and *not* what he does or suffers... we must practice science and leave goodness to God" (46). Haber believes that his research should have a practical application, and serve the "greater good" of the state. Like Ouchi's *The Blue Light,* the play also underscores the importance of hope, belief, and freedom for imaginative creativity. In the words of Einstein, "[w]e require a new way of thinking if we are to survive" (91).

Einstein's exhortation is directed towards a contemporary Canadian audience as much as against Germany's National Socialism in the 1930s. It is also Einstein who poses the final question in the play: Should creativity be stifled or silenced when it can have destructive consequences? Einstein reaches a similar conclusion to the Woman in Ouchi's *The Red Priest:* science, like art, challenges perception and feeds the soul (13).

Thiessen rigorously researched the life and work of Haber in the Archiv zur Geschichte der Max-Planck-Gesellschaft in Berlin, and accessed previously unpublished material in German (*Einstein* 105). However, he also explains in his postscript to the published play that he is neither an historian nor a scientist, and has extemporized on events and characters in order to construct a story. In Act I, he covers events before and during the First World War. In Act II, he shows how Haber again makes tragic compromises the 1930s. Secondary characters perform functional and humanizing roles: Haber's two wives initially support and then challenge his decisions; and his research assistant is a confidante and friend in Act I, and an adversary aligned with the Nazis in Act II, ironically using Haber's own arguments against him.

The title of the play is ironically appropriate on several levels: the German word, *gift,* means "poison" in English; Einstein's legacy, even more so than Haber's, is a mixed one. His final gifts to Haber are a *kipa* [yarmulka] and a *tallis* [prayer shawl], for his journey to Palestine, where he hopes to find a place to die, having been betrayed by Germany, the nation for which he has sold his soul. According to Thiessen, their "gift" to the audience is their struggle to understand what they believe:

> I believe we are all like Einstein and Haber at some level. Even if we are not all brilliant physicists or ambitious chemists, I believe we all have hopes and dreams, and conversely, that we all wrestle with doubt. And if we follow Einstein and Haber's lead, we will see this doubt – and crises of faith – as a gift. (*Einstein* 105)

Like *The Blue Light, Einstein's Gift* is an ambitious play that interrogates history in terms of individual moral choices and compromises.

Thiessen's earlier play, *Blowfish* (1996), is also a moral and existential inquiry – a memory play in the form of a monologue with an Alberta setting. It explores the possibility of living humanist values through the philosophical ruminations and family memories of a caterer named Lumiere. He traces his life in Alberta from his experiences in the mortuary where he assisted his father, the death of his twin brother in a car accident, and the deaths of his parents in the Edmonton tornado of 1987. He describes his conversion to a right-wing political agenda, and finally enacts his own death as a ritualistic celebration. Lumiere's life unfolds as a series of disasters that test his beliefs, but which finally inform his beliefs. He formulates a philosophy of dying, which is integral to his philosophy of living, and he takes his cue from Socrates – whose dying provided the opportunity for one last symposium with his followers. A humanist philosophy that values rationality and self-determination is defined through interrogation and debate, not through fixed systems or ideologies. Thiessen's play employs a Socratic mode of inquiry that activates and energizes doubt and irony, pitting the chaotic, irrational forces of the Edmonton tornado against the positive cohesive elements of family as a microcosm of human society.

Alberta playwrights Marty Chan, Pat Darbasie, Mieko Ouchi, and Vern Thiessen all tell the stories that inform the culture and society of the people who live in the province – whether they are set here or elsewhere, in the past or in the present.[3] They also enable their audiences to see the world in different ways; through a wide range of perspectives. They explore the possibility and consequences of making moral, political, and personal choices, outlining the parameters and complexities, but assuming the necessary responsibilities attendant on choice.

NOTES

1. Marty Chan has also explored his Chinese heritage in the CBC radio play, *The Gift*, set in rural China during the Cultural Revolution, at a time when his own grandmother was persecuted by the Red Guard.
2. Vern Thiessen read an early draft of *The Blue Light*, and provided feedback from a German perspective.
3. In this respect, they share the moral imperatives of the plays of Sharon Pollock, who has mentored and encouraged many Alberta playwrights.

WORKS CITED

CHAN, Marty. *Mom, Dad, I'm Living with a White Girl. Ethnicities: Plays from the New West.* Ed. Anne Nothof. Edmonton: NeWest, 1999.

———. "The Ethnic Playwright's Challenge." *Canadian Theatre Review* 110 (Spring 2002): 12–14.

———. *The Forbidden Phoenix.* Unpublished MS/Catalyst Theatre, 2003.

———. "The Gift." *Where is Here? The Drama of Immigration,* Vol. 2. Ed. Damiano Pietropaolo. Winnipeg: Scirocco, 2005.

———. Interview with A. Nothof. 18 July 2003.

DARBASIE, Pat. Interview with A. Nothof, 19 December 2005.

———. Program for *Ribbon,* Studio Theatre, University of Alberta, Edmonton, Sept. 22–Oct. 1 2005.

———. *Ribbon.* Unpublished MS, 2006.

DYCKFEHDERAU, Ruth. "Introduction." *The Courier and Other Plays.* Toronto: Playwrights Canada Press, 2006.

Edmonton Journal. "Ribbon Ties Threads of Past to the Present," in "What's On," 23 September 2005: 5.

HALL, Stuart. "Cultural Identity and Diaspora." *Colonial Discourse and Post-Colonial Theory: A Reader.* Ed. Patrick Williams and Laura Williams. London: Harvester, 1993: 392–403.

MCLAUGHLIN, Gordon. "The Accidental Star." *Eye* 25 March 2004. <www.eye.net/eye/issue/print.asp?issue_03.25.04/arts.redpriest> 28 June 2006.

See Magazine. "On Stage Preview." Issue #436. 4 April 2002. seemagazine.com, <www.greatwest.ca/SEE/Issues/2002/0404/stage1.htm> June 18, 2003.

OUCHI, Mieko. *The Red Priest (Eight Ways to Say Goodbye).* Toronto: Playwrights Canada Press, 2003.

———. *The Blue Light. Mieko Ouchi: Two Plays; The Blue Light and The Red Priest.* Toronto: Playwrights Canada Press, 2006.

———. Interview. *Mote MGZN,* 2006. <www.moregoatthangoose.com/interviews.miekoOuchi.php> June 28, 2006.

———. Interview with A. Nothof, 2 August 2006.

THIESSEN, Vern. *Blowfish.* Toronto: Playwrights Canada Press, 1998.

———. *Einstein's Gift.* Toronto: Playwrights Canada Press, 2003.

5

PLAYING ALBERTA WITH SHARON POLLOCK

SHERRILL GRACE

> "I don't care if you understand it or not, I understand it! Sure I could go do some stupid job somewhere else, but when I'm standin' out there ... well ... there's just somethin' 'bout a person standin' there on the prairies, everything else stripped away. It makes things simple."

These words are spoken by David Nurlin in Sharon Pollock's play *Generations* and I want to return to them, to David's decision to stay on the family farm, and to this play because, of all her plays that deal in some way with Alberta, this one with this character in this speech strikes me as deeply resonant with the playwright herself. Over the years she has made it very clear that she belongs to the West, to Alberta, specifically to Calgary, and this is not simply because she does not know other parts of Canada. She has lived elsewhere for considerable periods of time; she was born in New Brunswick, grew up in Fredericton, and attended the University of New Brunswick, so she knew that place intimately, from the inside, as it were. She knew it, and she *chose*

Alberta, *not* Manitoba, *not* Saskatchewan, and most definitely *not* the West-beyond-the-West in Vancouver, where she found life in the early seventies to be maddeningly slow. In interviews she has often been downright fierce about where she comes from, and that place is where she has felt most at home: Calgary.

She first moved to the city early in 1966 at a time when it was just beginning to grow, when the theatre scene there was in its infancy, and she returned permanently in 1976, bought the house she still lives in, and began to play an active role in all aspects of theatre life in her hometown and, more widely, in the province. She was there in the early days of Theatre Calgary; *Walsh*, her first big stage success premiered with Theatre Calgary in 1973. In the eighties she would have a very brief stint as Artistic Director with Theatre Calgary, and she has acted in, directed, and premiered other plays with the company. Lunchbox Theatre, Alberta Theatre Projects, Alberta Playwrights Network, Vertigo Theatre, Theatre Junction, Calgary-based CBC radio, and local film and television – all these organizations have called on her for scripts or directing or dramaturgy or adjudication, and all have benefited from her leadership, mentoring, and artistic talent. Moreover, her connection with Banff and the Playwrights Colony, which she headed from 1977 to 1980, helped that organization develop and enhance its contribution to the theatre scene across Canada, not just in Alberta. And then there is the Garry Theatre, which she ran from 1993 to 1997, a small, independent, semi-professional company that came close to fulfilling her dreams for what theatre could be and could do for the community in which it lived.[1] In short, Sharon Pollock has been central to the Alberta theatre community for forty years. As well as winning numerous national and international awards, she has won provincial recognitions for her work, received honorary degrees from both of the province's major universities, and has been described as a local treasure. Five of her six children live in Calgary and her network of close friends and colleagues there is extensive. If all this does not make her a Calgarian, I cannot imagine what would.

However, as Pollock's biographer I have often asked myself why Alberta and why Calgary? What is it about this part of Canada that appealed to her in the first place and has continued to suit her so well? There are, of course, several answers to these questions, some of which are biographical: Sharon is a feisty individual, some would describe her as brash and aggressive, and she has small patience with stultifying social constraints or with the hierarchical advantages of class privilege, money, family name, and rigid traditions. For

Pollock, all this constraint and privilege, whatever decorous label we give it, spells Family Compact, and her critique of such power cliques is clear in her New Brunswick play *Fair Liberty's Call.* Indeed, Fredericton, the place of her birth, is the perfect antithesis to her chosen home because Calgary was, and is even more so today, a city of energy, enterprise, growth, and *comparative* freedom. Calgary and Alberta, then in the mid-sixties and still today, give her what Fredericton and New Brunswick never could: the freedom to be Sharon Pollock. Not, let me insist, Sharon Chalmers, daughter of Dr Everett Chalmers and Eloise Chalmers, but Sharon Pollock. Changing names and changing places, however accidental these changes may have been at the outset, have long since become the outward signs of a newly invented identity.

But it is not the biography that most interests me here, except insofar as being Sharon Pollock is inseparable from being a playwright. Her plays also provide answers to my questions – why Calgary, why Alberta? When I survey her work I am struck by how many of her plays for stage, radio, and television are in some way Alberta-based. *Walsh* (1973), "The Persons Case" (her 1981 ACCESS Alberta television play about Emily Murphy), *Whiskey Six Cadenza* (1987), and her new, as yet unproduced play, "Kabloona Talk" (2006), draw on people and events from Alberta's nineteenth- and twentieth-century history, whereas *Generations* (1980), the radio plays *Sweet Land of Liberty* (1979; 2005) and "Mary Beth Goes to Calgary" (1980), and the children's play *Prairie Dragons* (1989), are more personal and explore relationships between individuals or families and the land.[2] In these more personal plays, Alberta acquires a symbolic, at times, almost an allegorical or mythic significance. When I think of Pollock in terms of Alberta, I think first of this second group of plays, in part because the history plays, especially *Walsh* and *Whiskey Six Cadenza,* are dominated by (and, thus, are *about*) individual characters and in part because the more personal plays allow her imagination room to invoke place, to conjure up space, to suggest ways in which a physical locale can shape human beings. The titles alone of *Sweet Land of Liberty, Generations,* and *Prairie Dragons* indicate something of what I mean. I know, of course, that I am begging several questions by summarily classifying the plays in this way and by claiming that any work of art, let alone a play, can invent landscape, but bear with me while I demonstrate some of the distinctions, qualities, and symbolic impact of a few of these plays. My basic assumptions are that works of art can and do create places and landscapes that help us to understand where and who we are; that such works of art do, in fact, produce meaning that is emotional, psychological, and broadly cultural; and that audiences (readers, viewers) recognize not only the landscapes created in art but also invest these images with personal significance. The process of creation and reception is a dynamic one; it changes over time and becomes sedimented with associations and values.

Inevitably, any division of Pollock's work into categories – this is a history play, that is a family play – is arbitrary and fails to do full justice to the richness of a given play or, indeed, to the capacity of a designer and actors to reinvent the play each time it is produced. Nevertheless, I will use (*caveat lector*) such designations just as far as necessary to explore the various ways in which Pollock has scripted her home ground of Alberta. In the final analysis, her most public, history plays are deeply personal and intensely symbolic and her most allegorical plays are expressions of her own convictions about socio-political realities in a precise time and place. In the following discussion, I will mention the so-called history plays but I will focus more attention on these other plays. Where the history plays provide a wide-angle, or epic, view of Alberta, and give Pollock the appropriate scope to stage political, ethical, and judicial dramas about real people, the personal plays delve more deeply into how and why a place matters to ordinary people and communities. Novelists have always stressed the particular, the individual story when creating their fictional territories: think of Hardy's Wessex, Faulkner's Yoknapatawpha, Laurence's Manawaka. And so it is with Pollock. Mr Big in *Whiskey Six Cadenza* can tell us something about Prohibition and Major James Walsh can show us how isolated he was from the central government of the day, but if we want to touch the heart of the matter, of what it means to be Albertan in Pollock's vision, then we must listen to the Nurlins in *Generations*, believe in magic dragons and wise, buried mothers in *Prairie Dragons*, and walk with Tom in *Sweet Land of Liberty* into Writing-on-Stone Provincial Park, "down to the Milk River [where] the vegetation is lush and green, the water runs quickly, the hills rise sharply, and the Indian says this place is sacred" (Pollock, *Collected Works* I, 181).

Now that both *Prairie Dragons* and *Sweet Land of Liberty* have been published they will become better known and hopefully receive new productions. Certainly, the subjects of these plays have not dated and the moral issues faced by the protagonists in each play remain relevant. Of particular interest in my present context of Alberta landscapes, however, are the ways in which Pollock locates the stories and characters of these two otherwise so different works. *Prairie Dragons* is a play for children – a *Pollock* play for children in that it addresses serious questions of race and gender without the slightest touch of patronizing or talking down or merely entertaining kids – and *Sweet Land of Liberty* is a post-Vietnam tragedy about a young American veteran who has taken refuge first in Calgary and then in Lethbridge from where he can easily reach Writing-on-Stone Provincial Park. The first play focuses on two teenaged girls who must face down the men in their families and society in order to establish their own identities; this play ends happily because supernatural, yet *naturalized* forces come to their aid. The second play begins and ends in a death, a suicide to be precise, and the significance of this death is left for us to interpret, to come to terms with, or perhaps to learn from; all we are told is that the place of this death is sacred and that we must believe in this place if we are to find any meaning in the death. One of the girls in *Prairie Dragons* is Lily Kwong, the Canadian-born daughter in a Chinese immigrant family, and her father and brother both insist that Lily's role in life is to work in the family business, to become a wife and mother, and to obey the men of the family. Lily, however, is very intelligent and she wants to enter a spelling competition at school and win a prize; Lilly wants a good education; she wants to be her own person. The other girl is Sarah Whitherspoon whose mother died when she was just a baby, whose older brother has gone to fight in the Great War, and whose father dies in a farm accident at the beginning of the play. At sixteen, Sarah is left to manage the farm by herself until a greedy land speculator, one Mr Lowe (who is lower than low), turns up to pressure her into selling. The American veteran in *Sweet Land of Liberty* is called Tom, and he is a remittance man whose American father sends him money so that he will not return to the US and the family home because, in his father's eyes, he has become a shameful embarrassment; this father wishes his son had been killed in Vietnam, fighting for his country, so his name could go up on the local honour roll. Instead, Tom has become a conscientious objector, an ex-soldier who no longer endorses what his country is doing to another country.

From these basic situations of challenge and conflict, Pollock develops two stories about love, freedom, commitment, and community that are deeply rooted in Alberta prairie landscapes. Her characters seek to find themselves, albeit in very different ways, within and in terms of place. They are enabled, freed into a larger vision of life's virtues and possibilities, by being where they are. Alberta, in short, is transformed from an oil rich, cattle ranching province that loves to hate Ottawa into an almost mythic realm of opportunity, hope, and spiritual rebirth. In *Prairie Dragons* that sense of a mythic and magical landscape is established right from the start because the entire play is staged by, or comes from within, the Dragon; it is "A Dragon Tale. Tale of a Dragon!" But this dragon is neither a Wagnerian monster nor a silly stuffed toy. It is a "*gorgeous DRAGON whose colours are predominantly orange and red*" and it is a "Transformer," a "Magician" a "Giver of laws," but also a benevolent, wise, story-telling dragon who inhabits the underground paths of the province of "Alta" in the country of "Cannon" (II, 204–05). The characters in the play are called up by this dragon who introduces Sarah and Lily and turns the story over to them. More important still, it will advise them on how to overcome the men in their lives, like Mr Lowe and Mr Kwong, who want to stop them from realizing their dreams because they are only female. Not surprisingly this particular dragon has a special connection to Lily because Lily's family originally came from China and the year in which the story takes place is 1916 – the year of the Dragon – and the year in which Lily was born was 1904, the year of the Dragon, the same year of the Dragon in which Sarah's mother died. So Lily's Dragon and Sarah's mother are linked; they both inhabit the earth and from that place, in "Alta," they watch what unfolds for their daughters. Sarah has acquired the habit of going to her mother's grave for solace when she is beset by troubles, and at all times she wears a pearl necklace left to her by her mother, but when Lily explains her family problems and Sarah tries to help her by giving her especially difficult words to practice spelling, something very strange happens. By helping Lily, the Chinese-Canadian girl, Sarah has opened a pathway to the Prairie dragons, and the Dragon itself appears to assist and advise both girls. Amazed and inspired, Lily knows this is a sign that Feng Shui works in Canada, that the dragons too have emigrated and naturalized here, and she cries: "We'll find the path of the Dragon, and it will make everything clear" (221). And it does because this play is a play for children, especially for female children, and Lily and Sarah will prevail. Trusting in the Dragon and her mother's spirit, symbolized by the power of the pearl, Sarah will send Mr Lowe packing; strengthened in her resolve by the Prairie Dragon, Lily convinces her father that there are new rules in this new land and that the old guiding spirits are happy to be here now and to do things the Alta-way. But the play does not end until the Dragon reminds Sarah that she must "Speak to your Mama," and Sarah will speak for both herself and Lily when she says – "I got faith and hope and your pearl necklace. And … and Prairie Dragons" (226).

In this seemingly light-hearted, magical way, Pollock has deployed the resources of theatre to teach an important lesson: that prejudices can be overcome if we believe in ourselves and if we hold sacred the ground on which we live, if we recognize home as where we are and not where we once came from, if we put down roots of tradition, family, love, and community in this place, which for Pollock (like Lily and Sarah) is the prairie of Alberta.

By contrast, there is nothing light-hearted or even celebratory about *Sweet Land of Liberty* and yet some of the same ethical issues are confronted and a similar resolution is proffered. Like so many Pollock plays, this one has a dramatic frame. When the play opens, Tom is arriving at the entrance to Writing-on-Stone Provincial Park. As he talks, he walks into the park and he tells us where he, and we, are. He has a gun with him and he positions himself at a point where he can look "over the border to the Sweet Grass Hills of Montana" and down into the campsite where visitors to the park will spend vacations (I 181). He tells us that a black bird is following him and that an Indian appears to him; he wonders if everything he does and says and sees is only in his imagination. He has come to this place to die and the Indian, real or imagined, tells him that "it's a good day to die" (I 182). From this monologue, we cut to a legal interrogation and the past story leading up to the opening frame scene begins to unfold. At the end of the play we will be returned to the park, to Tom, and to his Indian guide/spirit, but in between we will hear (and see, if this piece is ever produced on stage) why the man called Tom has chosen to take his own life in Alberta's most sacred place.

Sweet Land of Liberty is in many ways a play of the late seventies, an anti-war play, and a play about Canada as a possible space of rescue, idealism, and safety. And yet, even then, even in 1979, Pollock doubted (perhaps *problematized* is the better term) these associations with her native land and the home ground of Alberta. It is interesting, therefore, to pause and reflect on the geography of this play. To date, this play has not received a stage production, but now that it has been published it can and should be produced for live theatre. However, no one can recreate on stage the physical spaces that must be imagined and would be created aurally on radio. To capture the movements and spaces demanded by the plot, a designer would have to work from the central scenes of interrogation, as the police investigation into Tom's death unfolds through flashback/imaginings, to establish Tom's presence in southern Alberta as he rides a bus from Calgary to Lethbridge, falls into conversation with a young boy, Stevie Harris, and his mother, Rena, who are returning to their home in Lethbridge, and then follow Tom after he moves in with Rena and Stevie because Rena is renting out a room in her house. From the moments on the bus to his later more intimate relationship with the family, Tom slowly comes to trust Rena and to develop a close bond with Stevie; for the first time in many years he finds a modicum of peace and happiness. But of course, all is not well: Rena's estranged husband has an ugly habit of showing up and threatening violence to Rena and Tom and, worse still, Tom is tormented by memories of the violent brutality he witnessed in Vietnam. He suffers from what today we call post-traumatic stress syndrome. But he had not come to Lethbridge in the first place because of Rena and Stevie; meeting them on the bus was a stroke of good luck for Tom. He comes to Lethbridge because it lies close to the southwest boundary of Writing-on-Stone Provincial Park, and although we are not told so, it seems that he has planned to kill himself in this sacred place from the moment he boarded the Calgary bus. Just as his head is filled with horrifying images of war, so also his imagination constantly relocates him to the park where he is when the play opens and when it ends. Staging *Sweet Land of Liberty* would entail finding ways to suggest the beauty, mystery, and spiritual power of a real landscape, a landscape famous for its coulees, hoodoos, and prairie habitat, its centuries-old rock paintings and rock carvings, a place sacred to the First Nations, a place controlled in more recent history by the Blackfoot Nation, and a space for warriors and shamans. But this park also borders to the south on the American state of Montana, and from a bluff in the park Tom imagines his small-town Montana home, that home he cannot return to.

While I can accept the necessity of allowing this aspect of landscape-as-home, which is evoked in the play, to remain an imagined place, the park itself is another matter. Several questions are begged by Pollock's use of a real Alberta park in this play. How to *stage* it is just one, but after that a director (like a reader) must decide exactly how to position Tom – a white American – in this place *in Canada* that is sacred to another race. Given the history of White/Native relations in the American and Canadian Wests, this is a delicate matter. And yet the play does suggest that Tom's presence and his suicide in the park are sanctioned by the Indian spirits who inhabit this sacred space. Of equal importance, I think, is the question of land and liberty: Where is this land? Whose land is it? And what makes it a "sweet land" of liberty? Is Pollock placing this symbolic weight south of the border, in Montana, and thus warning us that a United States at war has betrayed liberty and has no room left for a man with Tom's experiences and views? Or is she asking us to reflect on this small and unique place within our borders as the "sweet land of liberty"? Insofar as Tom finds peace in death there and appears to be welcomed and accepted by the Indian who guides him, I think it is safe to conclude that this symbolic place of freedom is indeed Alberta's famous, historic park. Or at least, until I can see this play on the boards, transformed from what Pollock always calls a "blueprint for performance" into a staged production, this will be my interpretation of her play.[3] Just as she found spiritual beauty and an emotional *home* in the real landscapes of southern Alberta, so she has created this place for her tormented character. The most diametrically opposite place she could imagine to the bloody, napalmed land of Vietnam was Writing-on-Stone Provincial Park, a land of sweet grass, spirits, liberty, and rest.

Generations is a very different play.[4] Where *Prairie Dragons* created an Alberta of magical powers under the prairie that could be called on to assist the living, and *Sweet Land of Liberty* imagines one special Alberta place as a real, yet symbolic, site of release from torment and violence (even for a white man), *Generations* is firmly rooted in a realistic setting and in the realities of contemporary farming life. The dramatic action of the play turns on the challenges facing the Nurlin family. One third-generation Nurlin son, David, still lives on the family farm with his parents, Alfred and Margaret, and his grandfather, Old Eddy Nurlin. But the other Nurlin son, Young Eddy, has left the farm to become a Calgary lawyer; he sees the future of Alberta farmers as dim indeed, and he is not willing to expend his life struggling to make a farm pay. As the play opens, Young Eddy has come home for a visit, but his underlying purpose is to ask his father to sell off a section of the farm that would one day be his share, so that he can have the money now to invest in his legal practice. To add to the complications, and to expand on the dilemma of whether to stay and farm or sell and move to the city, Pollock introduces a girlfriend, Bonnie, who is engaged to David but is not prepared to sink her life and education (she is a teacher) into the family farm by marrying him. Bonnie cannot understand, let alone share, David's passionate attachment to the farm; she sees matters more as Young Eddie does. This conflict between David and Bonnie finds its clearest formulation, not in the arguments between the two young people, but in a serious conversation between Bonnie and Margaret Nurlin. In this critical discussion between the two women, Pollock allows both sides of the argument to emerge forcefully: Bonnie is amazed at the older woman's capacity to lose herself – and loss of self is crucial for Pollock – in a mute subservience to the farm, the seasons, and the rhythms of nature and routines of an isolated life that is ruled by men who serve the land. For her part, the gentle, soft-spoken Margaret reveals her principles emphatically when she tells Bonnie that, in her eyes, this life as a farmer's wife has made her "part of something" that is bigger than one individual and worth being a part of, and she asks Bonnie if she is "so special, so fine, so wonderful" that she cannot imagine anything bigger to be part of (I 326).

Indeed, it seems to me that this is really the crux of the matter for Pollock and for the play. The immense question she poses is this: can we find something bigger and more significant to be part of, to dedicate our lives to, even if that commitment does entail self-sacrifice? To ground this question she has chosen a particular landscape in a specific late twentieth-century moment when men and women can, and must, make tough decisions. All around the edges of the action, like the farm surrounding the Nurlin house, lie the external, elemental forces of the prairie: earth, air, water, and fire. And present throughout the play is one other character – eighty-one-year-old Charlie Running Dog. These Alberta lands are his ancestral home, and he and his band are refusing to allow the local farmers (like the Nurlin family) access to water for irrigation because they believe the government has not provided adequate compensation for this precious resource. As the stage instructions make clear, Pollock intends Charlie to represent not just the issue of Native rights but, in fact, the land itself. She tells us that, "*time and the elements have so conditioned and eroded his skin that he looks less like a Native Canadian, and more like some outcropping of arid land*" (I 280). As tensions and tempers mount, the Indians will hold out, meetings will be convened, Young Eddy and David will clash, Bonnie and David will pull apart, and finally, in a moment of rage, David will set fire to the section of the farm that Young Eddy was hoping to persuade his father to sell. Check mate. Except that Pollock does not leave the play hanging on the brink of immediate disaster. Old Eddy, appalled at what his favourite grandson has done, strikes the younger man screaming "I'm gonna kill ya!!" (333). He built this farm; he stayed on it even when his beloved wife died. He had two boys, one of whom died as a child, while the other, Alfred, who fought in the Second World War and survived, was happy to settle down on the farm. But now that Alfred and Margaret are struggling to make the farm pay, to believe in this something bigger than themselves during hard times, this foolish grandson does something so careless and dangerous as to threaten the destruction of all that Old Eddy has worked for.

This overt, physical battle between the generations acts like a catalyst, at least on the symbolic level, because, as the old man tires, the rain suddenly starts to fall. The crisis brought on by drought, combined with the Indians' withholding of water, is over. The fire set by David is quenched; the farm is saved. The message is obvious: if one cares enough, believes deeply enough, gives enough of one's self to the land, then the land will respond. As the play ends, Bonnie and David will go their separate ways, Young Eddy will have to wait for his inheritance, and Charlie Running Dog and Old Eddy get the final words: "We're still here, Charlie. Hell, we'll always be here" (335). If there are winners and losers in this play, then the winners, at least for now, are those who belong to the prairie, to the land and the elements, to a way of life that is big and means something larger than a single individual self. Those who cannot identify themselves with the land, as Margaret, Old Eddy, and David do, should move out and on to other kinds of lives – in the city, in offices, away from the Alberta that is home to the Indians and the farmers.

Chief among my reasons for choosing to emphasize *Prairie Dragons, Sweet Land of Liberty,* and *Generations,* instead of *Walsh* and *Whiskey Six Cadenza,* in this consideration of Sharon Pollock's Alberta is my sense that in these three plays she has made room for the physical landscapes of Alberta to play a role in the drama. I would go so far as to say that, in each of these plays, the land becomes a character that impinges directly on the human characters to shape their lives, deaths, and choices. Skillful set designs, sound effects, and lighting should be able to capture this symbolic, magical, or mythic presence on stage. By contrast, the two historical plays centre on dilemmas created by and between human beings. James Walsh is the protagonist and agonist in his play, and his betrayal of others and of his best self could take place anywhere. Moreover, the play we watch is his memory play; it unfolds, expressionistically, on the stage of an older, drunken Walsh's tormented mind. The lessons of this play are personal, political, and historical, and they are explored through one man's (at most two men's because of Sitting Bull's role) story. *Whiskey Six Cadenza* uses the era of Prohibition and the story of a local bootlegger as a vehicle for exploring issues of power politics within families and communities. The historical record fixes this drama in Blairmore, in the Crownest Pass, and we hear about wild rides in those infamous McLaughlin six-cylinder cars favoured by rum-runners, but the moral and emotional core of the play is not outside in the mountains, country roads, or fields. The core of this play is set in the human soul and within the breast of the family, where mothers fight for control of sons and putative fathers exploit their so-called adopted daughters. This play is less about Alberta than it is about who has the right to do what to whom and, when a person abuses this power, what price should be paid and by whom. This play could easily be set in downtown Toronto, or in Calgary for that matter. Which raises another question in my mind: why has Sharon Pollock not yet written an urban play, a play set in her home city of Calgary? Calgary gets very oblique and passing mention in a few of the radio plays, but the only Pollock play I can think of to *use* a city setting is her unpublished 1976 television play *The Larsens,* which is set in Winnipeg.

Of course, I cannot begin to answer such a question. Only Pollock can do that and maybe she will write a Calgary, city-based play. But when I think of her in context with other major Canadian playwrights of her generation, or of the younger generation for that matter, I am struck by the absence of Calgary from her vision. Pollock has not done for her chosen city what Tremblay has done for Montreal's Main, what George F. Walker has done for Toronto (or North American urban life) in his *East End Plays,* or even what George Ryga did for Vancouver in *The Ecstasy of Rita Joe.* I cannot imagine a Judith Thompson play without thinking about city streets; even in a play like *Sled,* with its northerly woods setting, the streets of Toronto are omnipresent. Marie Clements' *The Unnatural and Accidental Women* is inconceivable without Vancouver's downtown east side, and I could multiply examples of urban plays from there. Whatever the reasons, whether for matters of timing, sensibility, or perhaps even locale, Sharon Pollock's Alberta is deeply rooted in the prairie land that is still visible beyond the sky-scrapers of her city. As her biographer I know that she constantly drives across the Prairies; she has done this almost from the January day in 1966 day when she arrived in Alberta from New Brunswick and soon began to tour nearby towns by bus with a small acting troupe called Prairie Players. She has driven back and forth between Calgary and Banff, between Calgary and Edmonton, and, with her goods and children, between Atlantic Canada and the Prairies. She has always loved to drive, and by driving she established, from the outset, an intimate personal connection with the Prairies, which she once described, in the moments it took to cross the Ontario–Manitoba border, as opening out before her to offer "a glimpse of infinity full of significance beyond the individual" and to promise a form of rebirth.[5] Sharon Pollock's Alberta, then, is the place of her reinvention of self, a reinvention that demanded all the amenities of a sophisticated city with an active theatre life, but that could only flourish in a Prairie landscape of the heart, soul, and imagination in which she could work and feel at home.

NOTES

1. I am only mentioning these organizations here because I discuss Pollock's work with them in detail in *Making Theatre: A Life of Sharon Pollock*, and I have devoted a chapter of this biography to her Garry Theatre, which was a major event in her life. For representative examples of Pollock's insistence in interviews that she defines home as Calgary, see Dunn or Hofsess.

2. Unless otherwise indicated, dates given are for first publication or for first production, when a play has not been published. All quotations from published plays, however, are from *Sharon Pollock: Collected Works*, volume I or II. In addition to the plays I have noted here, Pollock has written several other unpublished scripts for theatre, radio, and television that have an Alberta setting or story. These include "Mail versus Female" (Lunchbox Theatre, 1979), "Chautauqua Spelt E-N-E-R-G-Y" (Alberta Theatre Projects, 1979), "Mrs Yale and Jennifer" (Calgary, CBC, 1980), "Death in the Family" (Garry Theatre, 1993), "Highway #2: The Great Divide," co-written with Paul Gélineau and Janet Hinton-Mann (Garry Theatre, 1995), and episodes for CBC television series.

3. This idea that a written script is no more than a blueprint for performance is a frequently reiterated one for Pollock. She made this point most recently in her 2005 interview with Pat Demers.

4. *Generations* was originally performed as a CBC radio play on December 10, 1978 and produced as a stage play by Alberta Theatre Projects in 1980, under the direction of Mark Schoenberg. It received a production with Tarragon in 1981 and was directed by Robert Fothergill in Baroda, India, in 1981. In October 2004, Ted Price directed a new professional production of the play for Theatre North West in Prince George, British Columbia. Although this is not one of Pollock's best plays, it does work on stage and it does capture an aspect of her sense of place.

5. Pollock made this comment to Pat Quigley during a taped lecture, with question and answer session, that she gave at Stratford, in their Celebrated Writers Series, on July 11, 1993 in conjunction with the world premiere of *Fair Liberty's Call*. The cassette is held in the Stratford Festival Archives in Stratford, Ontario, and it has not, to my knowledge, been transcribed or published. I would like to thank the archivists for their generous assistance with Pollock materials during my fall 2005 research visit. It is worth noting that Pollock describes her arrival on the

Prairies in this way during a lecture about a play set in eighteenth-century New Brunswick; underlying her remark is the realization that her New Brunswick birthplace does not appeal to her as much as does her adopted home in the West.

WORKS CITED

CLEMENTS, Marie. *The Unnatural and Accidental Women.* Vancouver: Talonbooks, 2005.

DEMERS, Pat. "An Interview with Sharon Pollock and Jan Selman." *wwrMagazine* 2.1 (2005): 15–19.

DUNN, Margo. "Sharon Pollock: In the Centre Ring." *Makara* 1.5 (1976): 2–6.

GRACE, Sherrill. *Making Theatre: A Life of Sharon Pollock.* Vancouver: Talonbooks, 2008.

HOFSESS, John. "Playwright Sharon Pollock: Mother, Lover, Artist." *Calgary Albertan Magazine.* 9 March 1980: 10–12.

POLLOCK, Sharon. *Sharon Pollock: Collected Works,* Vol. I [*Walsh, Sweet Land of Liberty, Generations*]. Toronto: Playwrights Canada Press, 2005.

______. *Sharon Pollock: Collected Works,* Vol. II [*Whiskey Six Cadenza, Prairie Dragons, Fair Liberty's Call*]. Toronto: Playwrights Canada Press, 2006.

———. "Kabloona Talk." Unpublished play script. 2006.

———. "The Persons Case." Unpublished television script. 1981.

———. "Mary Beth Goes to Calgary." Unpublished radio script, 1980.

———. "The Larsens." Unpublished television script, 1976.

RYGA, George. *The Ecstacy of Rita Joe.* Vancouver: Talonbooks, 1970.

THOMPSON, Judith. *Sled.* Toronto: Playwrights Canada Press, 1997.

WALKER, George F. *The East End Plays,* 2 vols. Vancouver: Talonbooks, 1999.

PART THREE
FICTION

6

"NO WOMAN IS NATURAL": THE (RE)PRODUCTION OF RACE, GENDER, AND SEXUALITY IN SUZETTE MAYR'S *MOON HONEY*

HELEN HOY

> The oft-evoked contrast between the visibility of race and the invisibility of queer sexuality, then, hierarchizes queer sexuality over race by ignoring the cultural terrorism that maintains race as a stable category to contain its manifestations. (Dhairyam 32)

Prefaced by a quotation from Ovid's *Metamorphoses* and opening with a reference to the central character Carmen "back when she is still a white girl" (1), Suzette Mayr's *Moon Honey* pivots on transformations, of race, of sexual orientation, even of species. The 1995 Alberta novel is an investigation of the social and discursive production and reproduction of raced bodies and sexual identities – and ruptures of that process and lineage. So weddings as a synecdoche for marriage (and marriage as a synecdoche for heteropatriarchy) provide moments of parodic excess. The novel itself is a curious generic hybrid, a cross between comedy of manners[1] with its mordant, realist attentiveness to social and surface detail, on the one hand, and expressionism, with its distorted, symbolic representations or exaggerated projections of internal states, on the other. This allows Mayr to focus on the site where the imagination meets the skin.

The "still" in the opening description of Carmen denaturalizes race as a given identity, constant over time and place, producing it instead as a contingent feature of an evolving history. The nonchalance of this casual anticipation of race-change is startling. Its unexpectedness highlights the degree to which, for all the talk of social construction and pseudo-scientific categories, race continues to function, in everyday thinking, as an immutable, biological fact, a box to be ticked off once and for all. As opposed to the briefer, alternative wording "back when she is a white girl," the line "back when she is *still* a white girl" establishes Carmen's white identity as always already temporary, a phase or stage, a not-as-yet something else, hearkening towards a future outcome. The doubled and unstable perspective in time, simultaneously past and present – "*back when* she *is*" – reinforces the contradictoriness or doubling of a narrative that seems to ascribe incompatible racial identities to its protagonist, and, in so doing, stages the question of what and how race means.[2]

Race is not, after all, a fixed, physical feature like skin colour (nor, for that matter, is skin colour so very fixed, even in hue, let alone in perception).[3] The very categories of race themselves have revealing and self-defeating histories: Omi and Winant point to the presence, in much nineteenth-century US federal and state law, of only three legal categories – "white," "Negro," and "Indian" – and to the California Supreme Court ruling in *People v. Hall* (1854) that the Chinese should be considered "Indian" (75). Race then is a practice, a conjunction of performance and reception, negotiated and produced within geographically, historically, socially, politically, and economically specific constraints. Race is, in Omi and Winant's definition, "*an unstable and 'decentered' complex of social meanings constantly being transformed by political struggle*" (68). Why be surprised if Carmen fails to be or remain the white girl she appears to be, any more than if another character, such as Renata, fails to be or remain the heterosexual she appears to be?

> Identity politics can mean the politics of changing given identities. (Perreault 29)

> The meanings of the categories of identity change and with them the possibilities for thinking the self. (Scott 410)

Using examples – of Daphne, of Echo, of Lot's wife – from Ovid and the Bible, Mayr's narrator explains that women transform into birds, plants, voices, or pillars of salt, "at the moment of crisis" (25). (The explanation occurs in the first of the italicized passages of metamorphosis that temporarily lift the narrative out of the realistic.) Carmen's transformation into a "brown girl" (proffered as literal through the absence of italics) occurs at just such a moment of crisis. In the novel's sardonic rewriting of the myth, though, the "crisis" is a minor one, fear of losing her waitressing job over an ill-considered outburst to her South-Asian-Canadian employer, Rama. Carmen's escalating diatribe to Rama is a breathless compendium of the manoeuvres of common-sense racism[4]: othering ("Where do you come from Rama?"), power evasion[5] ("My boyfriend's Scottish from all the way back"), coding Canadian as white[6] ("You speak... just like you're Canadian"), appeal to exceptionalism ("You're not like other coloured people"), the discourse of deficit[7] ("A lot of the time I don't even notice"), token apology ("I'm sorry. But..."), downplaying ("I don't understand what the big deal is"), liberal humanist universalizing ("I mean we're all the same underneath"), appeal to intention not effect[8] ("I would never say anything racist intentionally," "People don't mean to be mean"), demand to be educated ("Why can't you just tell me"), reducing to the personal ("why it bugs you so much"), deflecting from cause to effect ("Why are you so angry all time?"), inverting the offence ("What d'you have against white people anyway?"), invoking extremist racism as the exculpatory paradigm ("it's not like the KKK goes galloping up and down the streets"), demanding accommodation ("Why try to stick out all the time?"), blaming the victim ("Don't set yourself up as a target"), and false or trivializing analogy ("Being called a Canuck may hurt my feelings") (19–21). The passage's comic and disturbing power comes not from the originality of its formulations – the individual phrases are all too familiar – but from the masterful concision of its consolidation. Everything you wanted to know about everyday liberal racism, in one efficient little package.

The formulaic predictability of Carmen's arguments is the point. She is disseminating cultural doxa, in almost automaton-like fashion: "the words that come from her mouth don't come from anyone she knows" (21). Her off-key voice, inebriated with power or daring, is figured as the product of violin strings wound too tight. It is Carmen, though, who is in a larger sense the instrument, played upon by ideological systems that she serves to further (and that serve to further her). Carmen's self-estrangement here – the words issue from "the other, another Carmen" – functions in multiple ways. It simultaneously signals the character's facile evasion of responsibility, gestures towards larger discursive and institutional forces, and proleptically disrupts the unitary, stable self, anticipating the production of a (racially) other self that is to come. "Show me the difference!" demands Carmen, and the novel does. Or does it? Through Rama's look, a gaze that flays Carmen's face and refashions her, from the bone outward, with the skin colour, hair texture, scar tissue, and history of a brown girl, Carmen's request is taken literally. The alteration is immediate, even retroactive: "Her history is etched out in negative." "[N]ow a brown girl," Carmen profits from Rama's resulting capacity to receive her diatribe differently, to appreciate it as insider irony, a parodic pastiche of racist clichés, and to reply in kind: "Yeah, some of my best friends are coloured people too" (23).

In Carmen's transformation, Mayr uses racial absolutes against themselves, while maintaining a "power cognizance" (Frankenberg 157) mindful of the real effects of these imagined racial categories. Engaged in enforcing (while denying) a system of racial difference and inequity, Carmen undergoes a change that, on the one hand, confounds a racial economy insisting on an irreducible divide between "white girl" and "brown girl." How or what can such a divide mean, when the same person can occupy both locations from one eye blink to the next? On the other hand, the change promises to expose her to the difference she has demanded, to unimagined, racialized new realities, beginning with the words she has just spoken, the same, yet transformed. The scene stages and heightens notions of a deeply biological permanence to race; Carmen's change requires a radical physical excision that "burrows through the layer of subcutaneous fat and splays out her veins and nerves… snaps apart Carmen's muscles and scrapes at Carmen's bones, digs and gouges away Carmen's life" (22). The scene stages this biological determinism, though, only in the very process of transgressing it, through the simple instance of instantaneous racial transfiguration. The novel presumes to think the unthinkable, that (biological signifiers notwithstanding) the gears of racialization can slip – or be sabotaged – that race-change can just happen, even over the course of a conversation. Simultaneously, it asserts graphically that such change, at least in a thoroughly racialized society, is, in its implications, profoundly bone-deep.

> Naturally, says Isabelle. Naturally you're joking I hope. (Mayr, *Moon Honey* 163)

In denaturalizing *sexual* identity, Mayr selects a different strategy from her handling of race, relying less on an instantaneous and thoroughgoing shift between ostensibly incompatible identities and more on an array of sexualities that confounds any simple taxonomy. *Moon Honey* also carefully situates fluidities of sexual identity in the context of racial instability and inversion to ensure that, as Sagri Dhairyam cautions, challenges to the naturalness of heterosexuality do not draw support from implicit contrast with the presumed, relatively greater immutability of racialized identities.

"'Two flats do not a note make, you hear me? You need a man because what are two women gonna do? ... they're gonna do nothing because no woman is natural without a man. No woman is natural!'" (108). So shouts Bedelia, in *Moon Honey*, to her fourteen-year-old daughter Fran who is burning with love and the memory of a kiss from a distant (engaged) relative Stephanie, at a cousin's wedding. So shouts Bedelia (herself "maybe even funny with her housekeeper the family thinks, until the arrival of Fran" [117]), for whom the heterosexual act producing her daughter is an isolated, fleeting, and anomalous one. By a quirk of her thinking, "[h]aving sex with the priest..." we are told, "is the next best thing to becoming the nun she wanted to be" (117). The Blessed Virgin Mary is, instructively, the model whom Vesta, the housekeeper, holds up for Bedelia, to hearten her at the prospect of abrupt and unanticipated single motherhood. Figured, then, as deviant, vestal, virgin, sexually suspect, and associated with figures of celibacy, Bedelia makes a queer proselytizer for heterosexuality.

Fran, after all, (like Heather in the Leslea Newman book that became a test case for lesbian juvenile literature in Canadian schools) has two mommies. In the mutuality of taking on the unborn Fran as "our" pride and joy, Vesta, the housekeeper, attains status as a full member of the household, as Bedelia's partner: "this baby in Bedelia's stomach is hers too, which makes Vesta a member of the family" (121). Biological reproduction, the ultimate signifier of heterosexuality, is here reconfigured ironically as enabler of homosocial/homoerotic legitimacy, entitling Vesta to claim a seat literally at Bedelia's family table. "Family values" takes its revenge.

Fran is the child not only of a female-female household ("No other girl Fran knows has two such loving mothers") but, as the reference to Vesta's "brown, wet face" implies, of a biracial one as well (123, 120). That this unconventional arrangement produces the homophobic and virulently racist Fran is not simply ironic, but one of the phenomena of social reproduction that Mayr sets out to investigate (in part through the evidence of Bedelia, whose ideology of sexual identity runs roughshod over her own practice). Two flats, Bedelia and Vesta, do and do not a note make here. They create and sustain a relationship and a social unit (susceptible to being read as lesbian), but not one that is socially legible, even apparently to themselves (or at least not to one of the participants, Bedelia).

> **Natural** sb. I. 7. Music. One of the white keys on a pianoforte or similar instrument. (*Oxford English Dictionary*)

"Two flats do not a note make" (108 [104, 105, 110]). An archaic, inverted syntax invests this saying with the authority of longevity and accumulated wisdom. Its import, though, is less obvious, the saying bewildering, even unintelligible. Every key on the piano keyboard produces a note or tone, and each has a note or musical symbol for that tone. Two flats would produce two (possibly simultaneous) aural notes or tones (and a richer sound) and would be represented by two written notes or symbols on the musical staff. At face value, the aphorism doesn't make sense, though it clearly wields considerable social force and communicates an interdiction powerfully: "Two flats do not a note make, says Bedelia. A phrase passed down from generation to generation so that it has barely any meaning, carries only a stench of confusion and panic" (110). Semantic or conceptual coherence is not necessary here for personal and social regulation, an indirect comment possibly on the broader sexual norms that Bedelia's sentence invokes.

The musical metaphor is a rich one, though. A piano key and the sound it produces signify as a flat only in relation to another piano key and sound (often, significantly, named the "natural"), and within a larger framework or key (such as the key of F flat). Configured otherwise, they might function as a sharp. To my rather uninitiated mind, flat (like sharp) conjures up black keys, as that is where these notes would be introduced for the simple, preliminary example of the scale of C major. And indeed, the natural keys on the piano are defined as the white keys. Race, reductively signalled by colour, and colour, reductively represented by polarities of black and white, begin to hover at the edges of Bedelia's maxim. The musical signs signifying flats and sharps are named "accidentals,"[9] with the scale of C major called "the natural scale" because of the absence of these accidentals. This language in music of "natural" and "accidental" (with connotations for the latter of inessential, subsidiary, even unfortunate), and their associations with white and black, do not only echo the notions of marked and unmarked locations, of norm and deviations from it, applied in Western culture to genders, sexual orientations, and racial identities. They also connotatively encode hierarchies of value, like those so crucial to the regulation of such identity systems.

Two flats, two women, two women wanting each other, two lesbians, (and subliminally perhaps, given the colour coding of flats and naturals, two women of colour[10]) do not a note make. "Flat," the potentially neutral designation of a key or tone, in Bedelia's contemptuous context accumulates its negative connotations of secondary, inflectional, deficient, below true pitch, or discordant, its association with the minor chord or key as less robust, more plaintive, or less consequential (and, in non-musical contexts, its implications of insipid, lacklustre, or deflated). "You keep those thoughts where they belong in the garbage with the rest of the trash" (108), Bedelia warns, of Fran's memories of her homoerotic kiss, assuming the insufficiency of women, as demonstrated and intensified by the insufficiency of women together without the male keynote.

> Woman is not a reaction to Man; she is not a response. She is her own first statement. Black is not a reaction to white; it is its own first statement. I am only Black and female, if you are white and male. (Philip 68).

Yet the musical analogy undermines Bedelia's position, and not simply through its incoherence. The metaphor of flats points to the arbitrariness of assigned identities, their functioning only within a system of agreed-upon and mutually defining relationships. The tones designated as flats exist as flats only within specific contexts and musical traditions. Even within conventional, Western notions of tonality, enharmonic notation recognizes that tones can have the same sound and be produced by the same piano key but be identified differently. So the white piano key known as B can also be evoked by the sign of C flat; the black key for E flat is also D sharp. Within different scales or key signatures, the flats that are Fran and the relative she is mooning over could well be sharps or naturals, capable presumably of producing (the same but now) quite recognizable and acceptable notes. Bedelia's "knotted and indecipherable bundle of words" (109) about flats that don't belong together, that aren't natural(s), that are unable to produce (or signify), dismantles itself. The truncated conclusion to her prescription of heterosexuality exposes the skeleton, the anxiety of the gender system: "no woman is natural without a man. No woman is natural!'" If no woman is natural without a man, then perhaps, no woman is natural. Full stop.[11] Perhaps gender itself is at stake. Bedelia's outburst illustrates Judith Butler's observations about heterosexuality's "panicked imitation of its own naturalized idealization" and her argument that "[t]he internal coherence or unity of either gender, man or woman, thereby requires both a stable and oppositional heterosexuality" ("Imitation" 23, *Gender* 30).

> **Natural** *a.* I. 1. Of law or justice: Based upon the innate moral feeling of mankind; instinctively felt to be right and fair, though not prescribed by any enactment or formal compact.
>
> **Natural** *a.* I. 3. b. Taking place in conformity with the ordinary course of nature; not unusual, marvellous, or miraculous. (*Oxford English Dictionary*)

Natural as a measure is itself under contention in *Moon Honey* here, as well. An array of women-desiring female characters displaces normative heterosexuality, challenging easy categories of straight and lesbian. Despite the insistent overlay of weddings and wedding talk, proto- and quasi-lesbian moments and characters proliferate (often, pointedly, in the context of weddings), even before the central lesbian union of the conclusion. The first, major, italicized transformation of the novel involves a marriage of social and economic convenience, intended to dispose of a contrary and unmanageable daughter, a marriage foiled when the brusque maid of honour moves from snickering to nickering, metamorphosing into a horse to carry off the bride. Fran, five-year-old flower girl at the wedding, lets out what I read as a celebratory whoop, one matching that of the bride Mabel herself, as Mabel jumps on the Maid's back and "[t]he two women gallop from the church" (40).[12] Years before her youthful passion for Stephanie, then, Fran is marked, in passing, as sympathetic to female attraction, although Bedelia's shaming ultimately proves conclusive: "So she meets God because who else is there to meet?" (110). With women eliminated as possibilities, Fran's options for a mate become indistinguishable, and the selection listless and perfunctory. God himself (and Mayr plays mercilessly, campily, on the diminutive of Fran's husband's name, Godfrey) proves to be an inadequate substitute for what Fran has desired.

Mabel and Honour's defection from marital and heterosexual compulsion prefigures Renata's flight with Mika, during Renata and Griffin's wedding reception, in the novel's closing action. Renata earlier has alternated between lesbian panic – "people think she's some kind of lez" – and nostalgic longing in response to her caressing of a girl's breast on a dare at age eighteen (145). "An expert at young men" for some time thereafter, she feels "all of one piece" for the first time ever only after bedding Mika, cashier at the liquor store, on cases of beer in the back room, on the eve of her own wedding (145, 155). This does not, however, immediately put an end to the wedding. Mika is in fact the novel's only unequivocal or classic lesbian, a fact that intensifies rather than diminishing the pervasiveness of the lavender menace. If Bedelia with her homophobic slurs, Fran relieved that her son Griffin is at least "sticking to girls, whorish and unmannered as Carmen may be" (3), Renata first glimpsed wiping Griffin's semen off her stomach, Mabel at the altar, if all these women are not reliably heterosexual, then what woman is? Lesbian desire colours the narrative, from five-year-old whoops to bridal mutinies, although sexual identity remains less easily defined.

I became a lesbian on December 6, 1990, at 11:30 in the morning. I can be precise about the date because it was one year, to the day, after the massacre of female engineering students at l'École Polytechnique in Montreal. That morning, back when I am still het, I attend, in a Minneapolis plaza, a public re-enactment of the massacre, in which fourteen costumed, female students mime accomplishments – as graduates, brides, lesbian lovers, athletes, artists – tearing off red, paper bull's-eyes pinned on their coat fronts, oblivious of the bull's-eyes remaining on their backs. After a laborious, slow-motion mime of attempting to climb makeshift stairs, they line up facing the spectators with placards of the murdered women's names around their necks and, as another woman impersonates the Montreal killer, drop to the ground as one. In a new country, with a new daughter and a new job, I am already suffering from various forms of loneliness and dislocation, and when I go to thank the organizers of the event, tiny maple-leaf pin in my lapel, I find myself unexpectedly bawling my head off, while identifying myself as a Canadian.

As I am cutting through Loring Park afterwards on my way to Amazon Bookstore nearby, head down, feet sinking so deep into untrampled snow that my coat hem is dusted with white, I look up, still swollen-eyed in the bright sunshine, to discover that I am unwittingly halfway across Loring Lake. Winter has been late this year, and the ice is a few weeks old at most, of unknown thickness or strength. I am literally on thin ice, debating the merits of spread-eagling my way across the pond on my stomach or taking chances with my dignity. I am on thin ice, as I will be twenty minutes later, in the Loring Park Café with lesbian theorist Marilyn Frye, whom I've run into at the bookstore and who is asking me if I am lesbian.

This is our first private conversation, Marilyn Frye and I, since she arrived at the University of Minnesota as a visiting scholar. She has been a guest at the lesbian-

feminist discussion group I attend (one needn't be lesbian, just interested) and has joked there about the Lavender Menace and herself as a lesbian recruiter making overtures to those hanging around waiting to be invited to the party. She knows about my partner, although I avoided the male pronoun for as long as conversation in English permitted. She tells me now that she and her research assistant (a raspy-voiced grad student who talks about baby dykes and about going to lesbian discussion groups just to get laid) have debated whether I'm lesbian. "I call myself a non-practising lesbian," I tell Marilyn.[13] *In Lethbridge I was pleased with my cleverness in inventing the term. In Minneapolis I haven't said it to anyone. In Minneapolis, women really are lesbians.*[14] *"I think of myself as pre-lesbian," I tell her, adding that I have decided that any future relationship of mine would be with a woman.*

Marilyn isn't taken with this "pre" talk. What about "premature birth," "pre-cancerous cells," "premenstrual syndrome," she asks. What about "the rights of the pre-born"? We talk about marriage resistance and anti-racist work and the concentration camps. She describes watching how painfully long it takes some women to come out, when their orientation is obvious to everyone but themselves. Clearly she doesn't see me as pre-lesbian. She sees me as a lesbian, a lesbian burrowed deep, deep in the back of the closet. Pre-lesbian has felt somehow bold, adventurous; a deeply closeted lesbian, well, I've had years of training on how to feel about that.

The first time that I taught *Moon Honey*, a British graduate student, exposed hitherto to a thoroughly heterosexual reality (finding even the book's critique of marriage eye opening), described the pervasiveness of its lavender brush strokes as among the "unrealistic" features of the novel. All the women in the book, she argued, seem to be somehow lesbian, and how representative is that? I, on the other hand, was inclined to see such characterizations as welcome evidence of a rarely represented lesbian sensibility, reflecting my own inclination (by then) to read for lost possibilities and muted tendencies in the women around me, even in the absence of overt lesbian identity. It was a world that felt familiar to me. We discussed the strategic normatizing of same-sex desire in the novel. The fantastic or expressionist nature of the book necessitated a distinction, in any event, between "realistic" and "realist," between the persuasiveness of the novel's vision and the verisimilitude of its representations. Certainly, the fantastic turns of the narrative advance its reframing of sexuality. In a novel where one bride, Demeter, can literally turn into an asshole during the hysterical preparations for her wedding day, requiring heavy veiling to conceal the anal puckers that have become her face,[15] a bride who runs off with another woman (even another woman transformed into a horse) is hardly shocking, at least by comparison. The rupturing both of identities and of the realist level of the narrative, through extraordinary metamorphoses, produces "unfinished space[s]" (156) for less confining narratives.[16]

But does *Moon Honey* construe lesbianism as natural? If Bedelia's challenge to the naturalness of lesbians is undone, does that make the inverse true, make lesbians natural? "'It's not like we're *seeing* each other, but of course she can't go through with this marriage crap now that she's slept with a *girl*.... Sleeping with me cancels out the wedding. Naturally.'" (163). So asserts Mika, after her rendezvous with Renata, only to be met with her sister Isabelle's scornful repetition of "naturally." Renata insists, instead, on the social and economic power of "the wedding business" to trump both infidelity and emotion. And the marriage crap/trap does proceed, albeit temporarily. My graduate students appreciated the contradictory echoing, in Mika's claim, of Bedelia's invocation of the natural. They welcomed Mayr's willingness to challenge conventional and progressive pieties alike. With both homophobes and lesbians having recourse to assumptions about what is "natural," with a "white girl turned brown girl" speculating about racialized traits existing "in her blood" (212, 49), *Moon Honey* opens up questions about the degree to which the body[17] – gendered, racialized, and desiring – carries its own meanings or has those meanings thrust upon it.

> Bodies and pleasure, she says. Foucault, Grrriffin. (Mayr, *Moon Honey* 44)

> The normalization of race – as with the normalization of gender and sex – as an obvious, visible, and predictive feature of the body is thus a discourse that gestures to the problem of how mechanisms of power produce proper and improper bodies. (Britzman 32)

On one level, with what Lisette Boily calls an "appropriate tone of superficiality and glibness" (165), *Moon Honey* sardonically represents characters who dwell less in possibilities than in externalities. And the narrative voice, with an ingenuous absence of analysis, echoes that value system: "When Carmen and Griffin are together they are so much in love. These are the kind of dishes we will buy, says Carmen" (8). Even late in the novel after her racial transformation might be expected to have initiated a process of self-awareness, Carmen, condemned to singleness by Griffin's wedding, rests resolutely on the surface: "Besides, she's not ready to go through the hell of looking for another wedding dress" (211). She considers getting a roommate – or, better yet, a satellite dish. The novel details the appropriate couture (black clothes), libations ("tiny cups of black coffee," followed by Maalox), décor ("dried mourning flowers"), and solace (Mocha Panther lipstick) that occupy the contemporary jilted lover (100).

On another level, more than one character is shown "commenting with her body" (39) – through fantastical transformations (into a rescuing horse, a fountain, a cactus, a basilisk, a magpie) – on personal desires or social constraints producing responses of flight or resistance. Figurative moments in the narrative – Fontana's body frightened to stone, Pascale growing eyes in the back of her head – become literal. As with the surfaces – of smell, hair, food, skin, makeup – so central to the text, such figurations, often in the form of cliché, are locations where understandings of race, gender, and sexuality are encoded, maintained, or proscribed.

> Bones, skulls, hair, lips, noses, eyes, feet, genitals, and other somatic markers of "race" have a special place in the discursive regimes that produced the truth of "race" and repeatedly discovered it lodged in and on the body. (Gilroy 35)

Moon Honey produces a thoroughly embodied (and simultaneously fantastical) narrative. The novel opens with Carmen's being accidentally knocked out during sex, both the blow to the head and the sex being forms of feeling through (and being vulnerable through), as well as being taken out of, the body. Using black comedy, the opening paragraph invokes the Freudian notion of biology as destiny, through Carmen's ability to time her unconsciousness by the length of Griffin's orgasm: "they've learned that orgasm speed relies on biology, the difference between men and women" (1). From the couple's mechanical clocking of their orgasms[18] to Griffin's oblivious humping of the woman he has knocked unconscious, the passage bristles with warning flags, suggesting that speed to orgasm (and gender differences more broadly) may be a product of much more than just physiology. In contrast, Carmen's racial transformation is triggered specifically by her Shylock-inspired appeal, with Rama, to shared human biology: "If I cut you you bleed, if I cut me I bleed, we're all the same underneath. Show me the difference" (21). By the time she is studying the colour contrasts of her naked limbs criss-crossed with Griffin's, she is already wondering, "The same underneath? Just bones? Maybe not" (44). Reductive uses of biological commonality, like reductive uses of biological difference, meet their come-uppance.

Certainly, Mayr's characters experience their gendered, racialized, and sexually oriented selves, and those of others, through their bodies. The question is what we are to make of this. Take smells. In othering Rama, still-white Carmen begins with her smell: "Rama even smells different." Although Rama uses an ordinary hand lotion, Carmen smells a distinctive, spicy, "strange brown-skin perfume" about her and speculates that skin chemistry can alter odour (13). This could be dismissed simply as racist invention. Later though, frustrated as a newly brown girl by the racial partiality of cosmetic counters, she recoils from the white-girl colours and from "that smell of foreign, unfamiliar bodies" (55). Even the "scent of her old self... from when her skin was pink," carried in Griffin's clothes, becomes tantalizingly strange (52). The smell of ferns links Renata, as a legacy of blood (along with her springy hair[19] and the calluses on her hands and soles), with her African-American great-great-grandmother (43, 149, 151, 177), and signals, to the hostile, her obscured racial heritage – "a smell Fran *knows*" (176). In each of these instances, the novel requires the reader to gauge carefully the degree to which white racism and racialized Black solidarity actually *produce* sensory data (olfactory markers of racial distance), the degree to which existent, neutral genetic traits acquire positive and negative significances, even the degree to which, in this expressionistic book, smell functions symbolically rather than literally. Or, take orgasms. Renata's sexual ability to come for the first time, with Mika, after considerable non-orgasmic heterosexual experience, registers as a physical fact in the novel. Filtered through dim, distasteful Griffin – "Generally, lesbians turn Griffin on" – though, the conclusion that this biologically confirms Renata's sexual orientation ("he should have guessed when he found out she was incapable of having an orgasm") becomes more suspect (185). Griffin's simplistic misreading of Renata's sexual unresponsiveness – this from a man who can overlook his sexual partner's unconsciousness – cautions against a similar misreading of her responsiveness. The body speaks, in *Moon Honey*, but what does it say? The body speaks, but where is its voice coming from?

> There is no raw, untrained perception dwelling in the body. The human sensorium has had to be educated to the appreciation of racial differences. (Gilroy 42)
>
> Contexts, then and what I am calling readers of gender fiction, as much as bodies, create sexuality and gender and their transitivities.... [O]ccupying a gender or fictionalizing a gender for

> some people requires an other, or others, witnesses or readers who will... confirm the gender performance, who will read the gender fiction. (Halberstam 220)

Much of Carmen's attempt to make her way as a person of colour in the world is represented through the challenges she faces to find a workable hairstyle and suitable makeup. Symbolically this is a fine instance of Mayr's imbrication of race and gender. The paucity of makeup for brown faces and lips, makeup that doesn't make Carmen feel like a clown or a "dark brown ogre," that makes the mirror her friend, reflects a larger cultural context contrived so that, rendered anomalous, "she looks WRONG" (56). Simultaneously, the frantic compulsion to find makeup in the first place reflects the gendered inadequacy of the female body: "You have beautiful eyes, says Kevin, and she knows this is because she's put on a lot of mascara, Smoked Ebony, and Black Onyx eyeliner which make her eyes..." dada dada dada (60). Mayr shows the gendered, racialized body both as product of and as exquisite seismograph registering the social vibrations acting upon it. Renata, whose wiry, red curls speak to her of "her great-great-grandmother's blood winding through her and bursting out her scalp," listens urgently, "with her hair poised like antennae," to blues singer Billie Holiday, seeking out her racial connections (177, 147). Even more dramatically, now-brown Carmen, assaulted by images of piccaninnies and Aunt Jemimas of which she's previously been oblivious, feels as though "[s]he's been fitted out with some kind of radar over the past year, her skin sensitive to stereotype" (169).

This brings us to the biological crux of the book. How is one to read Carmen's new body? What is the nature of the dramatic racial change that "scrapes at Carmen's bones ... gouges away Carmen's life" (22)? For me the critical, and risky, scene is the one in which Carmen is confronted with Griffin's reassurances about her new "pelt" and his long-standing interest in "having" a Black woman. Enraged – and irritated by her own touchiness – Carmen wonders, "Maybe her skin has something to do with this, making her want to be more violent, making her feel downright raw, maybe she *isn't* the same inside. The difference is more fundamental than pelt. Maybe it's in her blood. Like some sort of virus" (49). The passage seems to invite an essentialist reading of race. Carmen's change of skin colour, her race change more broadly, has, it seems, changed her identity, her very nature, transformed her more than just physically. And that new character is rooted in her body, her race, her skin, her blood. Biology is indeed destiny, it would seem.

> To claim that discourse is formative is not to claim that it originates, causes, or exhaustively composes that which it concedes; rather, it is to claim that there is no reference to a pure body which is not at the same time a further formation of that body. (Butler, *Bodies* 19)

> It is not individuals who have experience, but subjects who are constituted through experience. Experience in this definition then becomes not the origin of our explanation... but rather that which we seek to explain, that about which knowledge is produced. (Scott 401)

Besides the dehumanizing of "pelt" (the long-standing, racist association of people of colour with animals), which Carmen takes into her lexicon even as she challenges Griffin's language of ownership, my students noted the pejorative connotations of the virus simile. At the same time as Carmen is shown drawing on her "experience," sensing her responses as biologically innate, her own language insidiously betrays the social construction that confines her to her (devalued) body and simultaneously delegitimizes her observations and responses.[20] Through her expressionist strategy, Mayr conveys the experience of being transported, not so much – or simply – into a new body, as into a new – or newly perceived – world, an environment impinging upon the racially marked body so insistently that its tainted messages come to feel visceral, blood-borne. (We should note that, even before her metamorphosis and her awakening to some plausible causes, Carmen has recorded the media message of excessive Black rage: "All the coloured women Carmen meets seem so *angry*... She's seen them on television at demonstrations and riots and things in the United States" [14]). Most damagingly, the objects of racism experience its insinuations as their own and read themselves into existence, as subjects, in its terms.

Carmen is shown living the experience of race quite physically, in her body, through her very skin. Concurrently, Mayr implies, but only implies, (in part through the defamiliarizing speed with which a transformed Carmen acquires drastically new perspectives) how thoroughly such ostensibly intrinsic perceptions are mediated through social practice. Yes, Carmen experiences her anger as emanating from her skin, but it is this same skin we later learn that is so *responsive* (like "radar") to external stimuli. Yes, her skin does "have something to do" with her anger, but as recipient of provocation, not as arbitrary, genetic determinant. Carmen, through the magic of Mayr's narrative, takes on instantaneously the effects of years, even generations, of racial injury.[21] By that abruptness, Mayr highlights the contingency of a rancour that might otherwise arise so imperceptibly as to seem a given. Here today, but absent yesterday, Carmen's chronic hypersensitivity raises the question of whence it might be emanating, what might be generating it. Where did *that* come from? The socially staged visibility of her "race" – by contrast with the insidiousness of its staging – makes that the easy explanation, but not the only possible one. As Teresa de Lauretis observes, in a different context, about experience producing subjectivity, Carmen "perceives and comprehends as subjective (referring to, originating in, oneself) those relations – material, economic, and interpersonal – which are in fact social and, in a larger perspective, historical" (159).

What is original here is less Mayr's excavation of how culture constructs race (and gender and sexuality) than her representation of how those significations can occupy even the most fundamental avenues of physical perception and response (which might otherwise be used to counter them) and come to be embraced as immanent. "Internalized oppression," Mayr shows us, colonizes not only the mind, but also the body, so that Carmen can indeed be said to have some sort of virus in her blood. Yet even this intimate formulation might spuriously differentiate between Carmen's pre-existing self and a foreign infection. More disturbingly, the virus can be said to be part of the constituting process through whose noxious terms the subject who is Carmen, including her self-alienated body, comes to be known, even to herself.

In a sense, *Moon Honey* is Mayr's answer to the impertinence of John Howard Griffin's *Black Like Me*.[22] (Griffin's name, in Mayr's novel, is presumably a deliberate allusion to that text.) John Howard Griffin, in his 1961 documentation of his experiences of racism, as a white man turned Black man (by darkening his skin) in Jim Crow America, makes a number of assumptions that Mayr plays with. *Black Like Me* assumes (and the book's success with whites at the time would seem to substantiate the assumption) that the authority of a white voice is required to convey the injustice of racial discrimination and mid-century segregation, already experienced so fully by millions of Black Americans.[23] It assumes that two months permit an assimilation of the lived experience of being Black. It assumes, because a mere change in pigmentation utterly alters social perception and reception, that, in a segregated, thoroughly racialized and racist society, racial difference is only skin deep. It assumes – this is indeed the crux of the exposé – that, no matter the colour of his skin, John Howard Griffin is/will be the same person underneath.

Like the paired subjects – straight/gay, white/visible minority, male/female – used to test discrimination in housing or hiring, Griffin's experiment did serve a useful liberal purpose in exposing inequity and the superficiality of criteria bearing profoundly life-altering effects. What it couldn't address was the incommensurability of black and Black, the difference between a black(ened) Griffin and his Black counterpart. Mayr goes much further in complicating Griffin's scenario, simultaneously undermining and reinstating racial difference. The product of meanings projected upon the body, race can – and does – shift in a moment, at the behest of performer and audience, *Moon Honey* declares, through Carmen's metamorphosis. Race is that transient. Contrariwise, that new performance,[24] that new reading constitutes a new self, which goes far beyond blackface. To have a race, as Mayr shows, is not simply to have a particular colour, or even a particular genetics,[25] physiognomy, and physical morphology. To acquire a race, especially for the racialized Other, is to be (the "same" and yet) very much not the "same" underneath any more, for the occupier – as much as for the readers – of that fiction.

> As biographers and autobiographers know, every identity is retroactive. Identity comes to us from the future, rather than the past, and is *what will have been*, a defensive editing of the past (even the past of the body in transsexual and cosmetic surgeries) to make it all come out right, with the proper ending – for the moment. (Tyler 121)

What Marilyn Frye sees, in that Loring Park Café, splays out my veins and nerves, snaps apart my muscles and scrapes at my bone, digs and gouges away my life. I discover that sexual orientation can change just like that, even over the course of a conversation. I don't know what I'm going to do about it (and in fact, more than a dozen years later, as I write this, I am still with my male partner), but the difference is immediate. Thoroughgoing. I can no longer, for example, pick up a book, watch a movie, or turn on the television, without seeing from another place, without feeling frustration at the resolutely heterosexist world created. I experience my desire. The self who walks into the Loring Park Café on December 6, 1990 isn't the self who walks out.

My history is etched out in negative. I turn over my past, spadeful by spadeful, memories of playing doctor and confessing innocent impurities committed with my next-door neighbour Karen, of exquisite crushes on female teachers. I recall the eventual, occasional dances and dates that I undertook to develop the well-rounded personality required by the era. Carrying my purse on his side to thwart handholding, turning my head from kisses. I recognize my consistent homosociality, seeking out the women in a room (except as necessitated by professional considerations). Above all I return to the day Kathleen, grad-school friend and weekly lunch companion for years, about to marry the man she'd been living with, turned to me and kissed me, on the cushions in my Toronto flat. And the hours that followed. (Never mind the eight-year marriage to Christopher that preceded that moment. The many years, after, that I've shared with Thomas.)

Of course I know that I am reconstructing myself, retrospectively piecing together a coherent (and selective) narrative of myself as the lesbian subject. Moreover, Toni McNaron, a senior lesbian faculty member at the University of Minneapolis, has already reported, in the lesbian-feminist discussion group, her informal survey of feminist colleagues, which discovered the same accounts of bookish isolation, female crushes, and tomboy non-conformity among hets and lesbians alike. I know that I am putting pressure on my history (as we do routinely, remedially, in less dramatic circumstances) to produce the self I have, it seems, suddenly always been.

> How am I inside this problem? (Verdeccia)

> It is the aspect of "identification" and how it is used by my students that concerns me the most... It is crucial for these students not to weave their narratives together with their inner city counterparts in a blanket of shared victimization, which obscures the ways that racist domination impacts on the lives of marginalized groups in our society. (Rosenberg 83)

When I taught *Moon Honey* in an advanced seminar on women's writing, I referred early in the course to a student evaluation I'd received in a second-year Women in Literature course. "Most of the books," the student commented, "concentrated on lesbians, and being a different colour – which I do not have a problem with and at times found interesting, but I felt I could not relate to what was being studied. 'Women in Literature – Growing up Female' – how is it that I can't relate to this??" I quoted the evaluation not to mock the student or encourage a smug superiority in the new class. Rather I named it as evidence of a failure of teaching on my part and tried to use it to frame the problematics of the advanced course, since the focus in this case was fiction by lesbians of colour, and the majority of students were (at least overtly) white and straight. Discussing how we all become gendered, sexually oriented, and racialized (those who form the unmarked norm, as much as those marked "different"), and using Verdeccia's formulation, I asked students to consider the questions, "in what sense am I inside this problem?" and "how do I function inside this problem?"

I quoted Chandra Mohanty's idea of "co-implication," of power-laden, contentious, but mutually constitutive histories, relationships, and responsibilities (194), pairing it with Himani Bannerji's reminder that "a whole social organization is needed to create each unique experience, and what constitutes someone's power is precisely another's powerlessness" (74). I discussed Kathleen Martindale's concern that racism and sexism not be treated as effects of an already existing difference (but as producing that difference) and her lament, "My colleague and I had successfully taught our students how to 'read for the absence' of gays and lesbians in a way that did not implicate themselves and therefore did not teach them 'how to recognize heterosexuality' either" (159). I was explicit that I wasn't arguing for universalizing readings and clarified the risks of a liberal humanism that would argue we are all the same, while framing that sameness in dominant terms. The course was intended, I indicated, not to teach about some Others, but to use a particular constellation of texts to look at larger material, social, and discursive structures, at systems of power, operating on us all in diverse, but interlocking ways. How are *you* implicated in what you are reading here? I asked my students.

At the beginning of the next class, on *Moon Honey*, the first student who spoke had clearly taken my lecture to heart. She spoke of how she connected with the character of Carmen. "I don't know if I have some Black in me," she said, "I'm just as mixed as people of colour are. How do I know that I'm straight, and not lesbian?" The student who spoke after her echoed the sentiment. Evidently, for these students, implication meant identification (and the focus was specifically on individuals). I had thought I'd done a good job. (And my students *had* made difficult stretches, challenging familiar boundaries and identities.) So, later in the course, I made a point of exploring the "politics of empathy" (Rosenberg 83). Referring back to the *Moon Honey* discussion, I quoted Regenia Gagnier on middle-class students' desire to identify – and to identify with characters whose reflective, self-occupied subjectivities resemble their own – and Ron Scaap on the liberal need to re-describe the Other as oneself before being able to sympathize (Gagnier 136; Scaap, qtd. in hooks 13). We discussed possible textual efforts to create aesthetic distance, including Bertolt Brecht's alienation effects. Much in this novel, I argued, beginning with its non-realist narrative, suggests that identification with the characters is not the appropriate form of engagement.

Reviewer Eva Tihanyi remains unsure whether the novel's constant "flavour of parody" is intentional and deplores the failure of the women characters to inspire "the slightest bit of empathy" (35). Yet the wry distance *Moon Honey* maintains from its narrative, supplely varied though that distance may be, is central to its strategy. Lisette Boily refers, with more perceptive appreciation – and Mayr has been graced with this intelligent, lengthy, early review – to the "vacuity of so many of the characters" (165). A comedy of manners in the third person, the novel uses free indirect discourse ironically to let the characters' inanities speak for themselves. Exposition in the vapid voice of fashion magazines – "She never realized how vital make-up is to making a girl feel good about herself" (28–29) – cautions readers against being guided by the surface level of the narrative. Forestalling identification, Mayr bitingly juxtaposes self-presentation and action, to expose the characters' self-deceptions: "She has never cried so much [over Griffin's departure], never been so much in love. So that when she slides her tongue into Kevin's mouth at the Night Gallery, it's just by accident" (60). Even on the novel's penultimate page, where conventional fiction promises achieved insight, there is irony aplenty in Carmen's all-too-recognizable self-affirmation (just before she picks up the phone, unenlightened, to try reaching the presumably married and clearly untrustworthy Griffin): "She wasn't so bad in the old days, just a little naïve" (211).[26] In some ways, Carmen's improved insight seems only skin-deep.

It is no accident that, along with Ovid's *Metamorphoses*, *Moon Honey* begins with an epigraph from *The Perfect Wedding Planner*. Ovid is about *change*, the "happy alternative" (113, 125) – although, inevitably with Mayr, irony inheres at times in the latter formulation. By contrast, weddings, in *Moon Honey*, are about *reproduction*, about social sanctions (both authorizing and penalizing), about socially sanctioned heterosexual reproduction. Mabel's father, having used blackmail to get his unruly daughter to the altar, bribes the groom with a job offer tied to the first baby, while her mother joyfully anticipates grandchildren, whom she hopes will be as nasty to Mabel as Mabel has been to her. When Carmen throws her wedding dress and accessories in the garbage, she mentally buries together her wedding day and the cocoa babies she and Griffin would have produced. Renata "knows that by getting married she is making the right decision. This is the normal thing to do, the accepted way; maybe she will even have a baby once she has thoroughly forgotten her own childhood" (156). In *Moon Honey*, weddings are about babies (babies as fantasy, babies as punishment and social disciplining); weddings are about heterosexual gendering; weddings are about ritual and the conspicuousness of one's consumption; weddings are about the reproduction of consumers and consumption through heterosexuality and through discourse; weddings are about babies. Offspring.

> Treating the emergence of a new identity as a discursive event... is to refuse a separation between "experience" and language and to insist instead on the productive quality of discourse. (Scott 409)

In particular, the text represents the degree to which racist, sexist, and homophobic narratives circulate and are reproduced, in the service of order, even when they run counter to the speaker's own history and interests. Note Bedelia's passion in the service of heteronormativity, despite her own happy abdication from those expectations, or Renate's readiness above to set aside her own cautionary experience of childhood. In representing the intractability of stereotype and media representation, even in the face of contrary personal experience, Mayr permits the characters to convict themselves through their own obvious contradictions: "All the coloured women Carmen meets seem so *angry*, not that Carmen's ever met any really" (14). Carmen can sweep over the Winnipeg origins of Rama's parents and commend her accent as just *like* a Canadian's, because popular-culture definitions of "Canadian" override what she has just heard.[27] Luce can insist on the beautiful complexions of "these Pakistani-types" – only belatedly acknowledging the bad skin of her cousin's Black husband, which challenges her generalization about "these coloured people" (13). Through Fran's ability to let caricatured art, golliwogs, and racist clichés about Black women erase Vesta's mothering, and, even more alarmingly, through brown Carmen's "experience" of Black rage in her blood, Mayr complicates experience. In *Moon Honey*, it proves to be as much a reflection of one's assumptions as the basis for or measure of one's conclusions.

Demeter's metamorphosis into an asshole is propelled by her determination to make the putative "happiest day of her life" conform to that prescriptive ideal, even at the cost of increasingly unhappy exertions: "All I want, she whispers, is to have the happiest day of my life be the happiest day of my life" (67).[28] The anxious gap in this apparent tautology is subversive. Demeter's "happiest day," the label, the expectation, the burden, is comically at odds with the emotion it names, as is the case also for the weddings of Fran, Mabel, and Griffin. In this novel, institutionalized heterosexuality and the social ritual that celebrates it seem to have little relationship to the desires they supposedly represent. The formula rules. Or attempts to. Predictably then, the surface is where this novel happens. The cliché is where it happens. And because reflex and unexamined verbal formulas claim such authority, the figurative demonstrates their power, dead metaphors becoming literalized, taking on life.

> Far from being grounded in a mere "recovery" of the past, which is waiting to be found ... identities are the names we give to the different ways we are positioned by, and position ourselves within, the narratives of the past. (Hall 212)

> It [identity] can signal to not only who one is historically and at present, but at its best it can speak to who one can become – it can speak of agencies and political possibilities. (Bannerji 34)

Moon Honey can be read as a novel of passing. And critics have read it that way.[29] Drunk with the empowering elixir of self-affirming brownness, Carmen discovers, on the final page of the novel, "That's what being a white girl turned brown girl is all about. Or a brown girl who was brown all along but nobody knew, not even herself" (212). There is an ambiguity here: is the second sentence an independent, quite different alternative or a correction, a refinement of the first? Does Mayr leave the reader to choose between the two possibilities or does she clarify a process of self-perception that Carmen is undergoing? In the preceding paragraph, Carmen has been described as having "pulled off being white," fooling even herself, and as able now only to think of herself as always having been brown (211). If so, how could such an earlier identity (as brown) mean, separated from any human recognition, known not even to her? (If a tree falls in the forest...?) In a society where social understandings are so powerful, can an unacknowledged identity have any meaning? And how are we to read Carmen's subsequent identity? Is she "now and for the time being a brown girl" or more permanently so? Perhaps, as with Benedict Anderson's documentation of the retrospective longevity projected onto nations to bolster their identities, Carmen's final state is more a representation of how identities get naturalized, come to seem long-standing and inevitable. One thing is clear. She hasn't become a brown woman, still at novel's end self-described as a brown girl.

> No woman is natural without a man. No woman is natural. No woman is. No woman. No.

> Femininity is thus not the product of a choice, but the forcible citation of a norm, one whose complex historicity is indissociable from relations of discipline, regulation, punishment. Indeed, there is no "one" who takes on a gender norm. On the contrary, this citation of the gender norm is necessary in order to qualify as a "one"... (Butler, *Bodies* 232)

Moon Honey doesn't seem to challenge gender in the same way that it challenges essentialist notions of race and sexuality. Or does it? Whereas characters in the novel change their race, their sexual orientation, even their species, sometimes realistically, sometimes surrealistically (or, I would argue, expressionistically), this is not an *Orlando,* by Virginia Woolf, or a *Self,* by Yann Martell, in which characters' sex shifts from male to female (or vice versa) dramatically and provocatively, as Carmen's race changes. I am bemused by this authorial decision. But it doesn't leave the sex/gender system unchallenged. Honour provides just one of several examples of gender destabilizing. As maid of honour at Mabel's wedding, Honour is so ill at ease in that hyper-feminized role as to seem almost in drag. She resists her gendering, fidgeting and fussing, bouquet drooping, hair escaping its comb, stocking seams crooked, hands clumsy and paw-like arranging Mabel's veil. In a more extreme version of transsexuality, Honour's restiveness performing human femininity catapults her not only out of the female gender but also out of the very species that ordains it.

Comedy of manners, with its detailed attention to the stylized mores and conventions of an artificial, dominant society, satirizes the follies and deficiencies of predictable types. *Moon Honey* even includes the convention of pairs of amoral lovers and characters known only as their roles, Maid or The New Boss. The genre allows Mayr to scrutinize the replication of the social order in accumulated detail – although she departs from the genre's ultimate allegiance to social conformity. Hence the tutelary genius of *The Wedding Planner* and *Bride's All New Book of Etiquette.* At the same time, expressionistic techniques, which abandon mimesis and express extreme mental and emotional states through distorted, grotesque, and hyperbolic representations, allow Mayr to rend those surfaces with what cannot be contained. If unimagined spaces are necessary to break out of the familiar, then the novel must move beyond the language of verisimilitude. Hence Ovid's *Metamorphoses.* While the satiric surface of *Moon Honey* shows the power of hegemony to conscript voices and bodies in its task of reiteration, ruptures of reality – through the fantastical – and ruptures of identities signal possibilities of resistance. Even the yoking of these two fairly incompatible genres – comedy of manners and expressionism – itself signals *Moon Honey*'s resistance to the programmatic and coherent, its embrace of the mixed, the "miscegenated," the gender-bending, the sexually ambiguous, the border-blurring, the untidy. The novel's concluding lines, in Carmen's voice, speak with an irony that should by now be familiar to the attentive reader: "The world's a tidy place" (212). The superficial, prescriptive surface of the novel, we have learned, is where tidiness leads.

NOTES

1. Boily has noted the "parallels between the genre of the novel of manners and the popular consumption of racially defined contemporary magazines devoted to fashion, beauty, and notably, wedding planning" (165).
2. Alterations in a formulaic opening ("Back when she was still a girl"), through the tense shift and the radical effect of a single, new adjective, "white," signal the degree to which the novel is going to choose the language of banality for startlingly revisionist ends.
3. Paul Gilroy discusses Franz Fanon's use of the term "epidermalization," in the context of shifts in raciological science from biopolitics (phrenology and physiognomy) to dermo-politics to nano-politics (cellular and molecular explanations) (46).
4. The term "common sense racism" is Erol Lawrence's.
5. Ruth Frankenberg provides useful analysis of the discursive repertoires of racism, race- and power- evasion, and race- and power-cognizance (139, 142–43, 156–58).
6. See, for example, Arun Mukherjee on "Canada" as "a code word for white" (434).
7. A "discourse of deficit" (used somewhat differently, in contrast with a discourse of potential, in her argument) is Linda C. Powell's phrase (4).
8. Compare Omi and Winant's distinction between "equality of opportunity" and the more socially significant "equality of result" (141).
9. Significantly, though, the natural sign, used to cancel a flat or sharp and temporarily alter the pitch of a note, is also termed an accidental.
10. Here the text gestures towards the triumphal and contestatory pairing of its conclusion, signified in its title, the moon honey of Mika and Renata, Asian-Canadian Mika and Renata whose great-great-grandmother was "one slave among many" (177).
11. Theoretically susceptible to a liberatory, postmodern deconstruction that challenges the very notion of gender, Bedelia's formulation, Mayr demonstrates, carries the power simultaneously to incapacitate, on a personal, emotional level: "No woman is natural. Fran is trash" (109).
12. Given the association of "maid" with sexual inexperience, the dropping of "Maid" in favour of "Honour" to designate Mabel's chosen new partner,

mane now bedecked with wedding finery, may subtly suggest and endorse the consummation of their relationship.

13. I was already uncomfortable with this formulation. I knew the arguments about the desexualizing potential of Adrienne Rich's lesbian continuum: "just where on this line do women actually get into bed with one another?" But I knew too the error of narrowly limiting lesbian practice to sexual activity alone.

14. Of course I knew lesbians (and presumed lesbians) in Lethbridge, but their identity was more covert, so that Mayr's representation of eruptive identities may have regional and urban/rural specificity. I thank Robert Gray for raising this issue, at the Canadian Lesbian and Gay Studies Association in Toronto, where I delivered a version of this paper in May 2002.

15. This passage anticipates the TV reality series "Bridezillas" (Life Network), "profiling brides-to-be who turn into monsters while planning their weddings."

16. Too easily, sometimes perhaps. Several of my queer white grad students protested that lesbian erotic practice in the novel is largely closeted or off-stage, noting Renata and Mika's back-room love-making and the speed with which they leave the country and the book. Renata "exits Stage Left forever" – yes, with all the positive political connotations of "Left" and of abandoning an unpromising scene, but an exit nonetheless (185).

17. Note Adrienne Rich, on the dangers of speaking impersonally, in a disembodied, homogenizing way, of "the body" rather than of "my body": "it's also possible to abstract 'the body.' When I write 'the body,' I see nothing in particular. To write 'my body' plunges me into lived experience, particularity: I see scars, disfigurements, discolorations, damages, losses, as well as what pleases me" (*Blood* 215).

18. Even the calculations of orgasm speed – Griffin fifty-eight seconds, Carmen ten minutes – give me pause. If this is duration of orgasm itself, Carmen's seems implausibly generous; if period from arousal through orgasm, Griffin's haste sheds yet more suspicion on physiological explanations of the gender difference.

19. The redness of Renata's wiry hair characteristically disrupts simple figurations of racial phenotypes.

20. If the inherited virus of black irrationality infects Carmen's reactions, are any of her judgements to be trusted, including her biological

reductionism? And if not the latter, then her reliability ceases to be suspect, in a circular unraveling and reknitting, similar to the Paradox of the Liar or Eubulides' Paradox ("This statement is false").

21. Nicole Markotic similarly suggests, "The metamorphosis is not merely superficial, it is deeply historical and social. Carmen absorbs into her body the personal 'essence' (and I employ this word gingerly) of being Black. I don't intend to invoke the term 'essential' which implies a state of being that automatically accompanies skin, but I use this word to indicate that, for Carmen, the transformation includes occupying and assimilating a lived experience of growing up Caribbean-Canadian in a white-dominated racist society" [3–4].

22. Susan Patrick has noted the connection – "*Moon Honey* is a sort of surrealist, whimsical take on *Black Like Me*" (3056) – as has Katie Petersen – "*Moon Honey* draws from two works, Ovid's *Metamorphoses* and John Howard Griffin's *Black Like Me*, both of which deal with transformation, the transgression of boundaries, and the deconstruction of established categories" (73).

23. John Howard Griffin himself was aware of this ironic injustice, later pointing out, "I knew, and every black man there knew, that I, as a man now white once again, could say the things that needed saying but would be rejected if black men said them" (Lagada).

24. Or, more precisely, performativity, to use Judith Butler's distinction: "performance as bounded 'act' is distinguished from performativity insofar as the latter consists in a reiteration of norms which precede, constrain, and exceed the performer and in that sense cannot be taken as the fabrication of the performer's 'will' or 'choice'" (*Bodies* 234).

25. Even skin colour, Paul Gilroy suggests, is not genetically so simple: "Current wisdom seems to suggest that up to six pairs of genes are implicated in the outcome of skin 'color.' They do not constitute a single switch" (49).

26. Note the deep irony, too, in the narrative's ostensible endorsement of Carmen's self-assessment, in her projected conversation with Griffin: "We can be friends, she'll say, her mind sharp, shockingly brilliant" (212).

27. Compare former Prime Minister Jean Chrétien's formulaic parry, "Don't ask me; I'm not a lawyer," when in fact he is one.

28. The insistent, five-fold repetition of this phrase ("the happiest day of my life') and its close pairing with contradictory evidence ("and already

you're trying to ruin things," "I'm going to have to gag down a big log of fruit cake," "lasting out the day is what counted") underline the simultaneous power and complete insufficiency of the formula. Even the apparent resolution of its final application to the happy couple must be read sardonically, at best, with the banality of the "drunken sloppy kisses" of typical newlyweds or, more scathingly, with appreciation of the groom's inability to see that he is (still) dancing with an asshole (65, 67, 69, 71).

29. See Boily 176, and Victor Ramraj, panel chair, commenting on Markotic's MLA paper.

WORKS CITED

ANDERSON, Benedict. *Imagined Communities: Reflections on the Origin and Spread of Nationalism.* 1983. Rev. ed. London: Verso, 1991.

BANNERJI, Himani, *Thinking Through: Essays on Feminism, Marxism, and Anti-Racism.* Toronto: Women's Press, 1995.

BOILY, Lisette. Rev. of *Moon Honey*, by Suzette Mayr. *West Coast Line* 31.1 (Spring/Summer 1997): 164–68.

BRITZMAN, Deborah P. "Difference in a Minor Key: Some Modulations of History, Memory, and Community." Fine, Michelle et al. 29–39.

BUTLER, Judith P. *Bodies That Matter: On the Discursive Limits of "Sex."* New York: Routledge, 1993.

———. *Gender Trouble: Feminism and the Subversion of Identity.* 1990. New York: Routledge, 1999.

———. "Imitation and Gender Insubordination." *Inside/Out: Lesbian Theories, Gay Theories.* Ed. Diana Fuss. New York: Routledge, 1991. 13–31.

DE LAURETIS, Teresa. *Alice Doesn't: Feminism, Semiotics, Cinema.* Bloomington: Indiana University Press, 1984.

DHAIRYAM, Sagri. "Racing the Lesbian, Dodging White Critics." Doan 25–46.

DOAN, Laura, ed. *The Lesbian Postmodern.* New York: Columbia University Press, 1994.

FEE, Margery. "Deploying Identity in the Face of Racism." *In Search of April Raintree.* Critical Edition. Ed. Cheryl Suzack. Winnipeg: Portage and Main, 1999. 211–26.

FINE, Michelle, Lois Weis, Linda C. Powell, and L. Mun Wong, eds. *Off White: Readings on Race, Power, and Society*. New York: Routledge, 1997.

FRANKENBERG, Ruth. *White Women, Race Matters: The Social Construction of Whiteness*. Minneapolis: University of Minnesota Press, 1993.

GAGNIER, Regenia. *Subjectivities: A History of Self-Representation in Britain, 1832–1920*. New York: Oxford University Press, 1991.

GILROY, Paul. *Against Race: Imagining Political Culture Beyond the Color Line*. Cambridge, MA: Belknap Press of Harvard University Press, 2000.

GRIFFIN, John Howard. *Black Like Me*. Boston: Houghton Mifflin, [1961].

HALBERSTAM, Judith. "F2M: The Making of Female Masculinity." *Doan* 210–28.

HALL, Stuart. "Cultural Identity and Cinematic Representation." *Black Cultural Studies: A Reader*. Ed. A. Houston Baker, Jr., Mantia Diawara, and Ruth A. Lindeborg. 1996. 210–22.

HOOKS, bell. *Black Looks: Race and Representation*. Boston, MA: South End Press, 1992.

KING, Thomas. *The Truth About Stories: A Native Narrative*. Toronto: House of Anansi, 2003.

LAGADA, Lili. "*Black Like Me* Celebrates 40th Anniversary." CNN.com.book news. <http://archives.cnn.com/2001/books/01/11/black.like.me/> 18 August 2006.

LAWRENCE, Erol. "Just Plain Common Sense: The 'Roots' of Racism." *The Empire Strikes Back: Racism and Racism in 70s Britain*. London: Centre for Contemporary Cultural Studies, Hutchinson, in association with the Centre for Cultural Studies, University of Birmingham, 1986.

MARKOTIC, Nicole. "The Search for the Perfect Lipstick: Metaphor and Metamorphosis in Suzette Mayr's *Moon Honey*." Modern Language Association conference. Toronto. December 27–30, 1997. Unpublished.

MARTINDALE, Kathleen. *Un/Popular Culture: Lesbian Writing after the Sex Wars*. Albany: State University of New York Press, 1997.

MAYR, Suzette. *Moon Honey*. Edmonton: NeWest, 1995.

———, with Nathaniel G. Moore. "TDR Interview: Suzette Mayr." *TDR: The Danforth Review.* No. page <www.danforthreview.com/features/interviews/suzette_mayr.htm> 7 March 2006.

Mohanty, Chandra Talpade. "On Race and Voice: Challenges for Liberal Education for the 1990s." *Cultural Critique* 14 (Winter 1989–90): 179–208.

Mukherjee, Arun P. "Canadian Nationalism, Canadian Literature and Racial Minority Women." *The Other Woman: Women of Colour in Contemporary Canadian Literature.* Ed. Makeda Silvera. Toronto: Sister Vision, 1994. 421–44.

Omi, Michael and Howard Winant. *Racial Formation in the United States from the 1960s to the 1980s.* New York: Routledge, 1986.

Patrick, Susan. Rev. of *Moon Honey*, by Suzette Mayr. *Canadian Book Review Annual* (1996): 3056.

Perrault, Jeanne. "Writing Whiteness: Linda Griffith's Race Subjectivity in *The Book of Jessica.*" *Essays on Canadian Writing* 60 (Dec.–March 1996): 14–31.

Petersen, Katie, "Defying Categorization: The Work of Suzette Mayr." *Canadian Woman Studies*, 23.2 (Winter 2004): 71–75.

Philip, Marlene Nourbese. *Frontiers: Essays and Writings on Racism and Culture.* Stratford, ON: Mercury, 1992.

Powell, Linda C. "The Achievement (K)not: Whiteness and 'Black Underachievement.'" Fine et al. 3–12.

Report of the Royal Commission on Aboriginal Peoples. Vol. 4. Ottawa: Minister of Supply and Services, 1996.

Rich, Adrienne. "Compulsory Heterosexuality and Lesbian Existence." *Powers of Desire.* Ed. Ann Snitow, Christine Stansell, and Sharon Thompson. New York: Monthly Review, 1983. 177–205.

———. *Blood, Bread, and Poetry: Selected Prose 1979–1985.* New York: Norton, 1986.

Rosenberg, Pearl M. "Underground Discourses: Exploring Whiteness in Teacher Education." Fine et al. 79–89.

Scott, Joan. "The Evidence of Experience." *The Lesbian and Gay Studies Reader.* Ed. Henry Abelove, Michèle Aina Barale, and David M. Halperin. New York: Routledge, 1993. 379–415.

Tihanyi, Eva. "First Novels: Eunuchs and Opiates." Rev of *Moon Honey*, by Suzette Mayr. *Books in Canada* 25.2 (1996): 35.

TYLER, Carole-Anne. "Death Masks." *Rrose Is a Rrose Is a Rrose: Gender Performance in Photography*. By Jennifer Blessing et al. New York: Guggenheim Museum, 1997. 120–33.

VERDECCHIA, Guillermo. Reading at University of Guelph, 25 November 1998.

7

WANDERING HOME IN RUDY WIEBE'S *SWEETER THAN ALL THE WORLD* AND *OF THIS EARTH*

MALIN SIGVARDSON

To concern oneself with Rudy Wiebe's fiction is to concern oneself with movement. In his novels, everything moves! Whether Wiebe writes about a Canadian or about a specifically Mennonite heritage, there is always some dominant spatial, temporal, or spiritual movement going on: the Mennonites of *The Blue Mountains of China* (1970) and *Sweeter Than All the World* (2001) move from place to place and from continent to continent, seeking a place of refuge where they can live and work according to their traditions and convictions. In *Peace Shall Destroy Many* (1962), Wiebe's first novel, the limits of an isolated Canadian Mennonite Prairie community are staged. In *The Temptations of Big Bear* (1973), the Chief's dilemma of accepting or refusing life in a reservation is the end of traditional Cree movement, whereas the continual travel of animals and humans alike in *A Discovery of Strangers* (1994) focus on movement as a necessity for survival in the Arctic. W. J. Keith's assertion in *Epic Fiction: The Art of Rudy Wiebe* that what tends to linger after reading Wiebe is a sense of "movement" is apt indeed (43).

However, geographic movement does not exhaust the complex kinetic reality of Wiebe's fiction. There is a sense of movement also where physical change is not as accentuated as in migration or travel. In the recently published *Of This Earth: A Mennonite Boyhood in the Boreal Forest* (2006), movement is encountered as a constituting factor of its narrator's subjectivity. The memoir gives us a beautifully crafted story of his childhood and early adolescence, but it encompasses much more than that. *Of This Earth* is a mnemonic trace enveloping not only a certain period of this remarkable writer's personal memory, but also what I will call the kinetic-kinaesthetic[1] directedness of his entire fiction. Well-known fictional scenes are reiterated in the memoir, yet they are not entirely familiar. Here, the resemblance to the fictional prototype swerves, as if the light is falling from a slightly different angle. Recognizable events from Wiebe's stories are given different focal points, or the narrative distance to central images may be in- or decreased. One such story is the frequently reiterated tale concerning book-shortage in the small prairie schoolhouse of his childhood. It was encountered first with Thom Wiens in *Peace Shall Destroy Many*, and, more recently, as Adam Wiebe's teacher introduces him to the cupboard of books in *Sweeter Than All the World*. In *Of This Earth*, veteran Wiebe-readers can but share the narrator's consternation at the astonishing realization that no memories at all remain from his first year in school. "That year of begun language, reading, writing, numbers, reading, companions, spelling, traumas, anger, impatience, reading farther and farther ahead is an immense void bottomlessly gone" (118–19). Indeed, coming from a writer who has repeatedly described the immense impact that specific shelf/shelves/cupboard of books had for his continued life of letters, the loss of this particular memory seems unbelievable. Yet, *Of This Earth* reveals, the "residue" of that lost year has itself not vanished, and it is described without anxiety of any meaning the absence of images may have (119). Intriguingly, that residue comes to the Wiebe-narrator through different forms of movement: "like breathing. Words that splashed in my mouth walking home the daily miles from Speedwell School with the crescent moon in the sky opposite the westerly sun, waves of words singing in my head, knowing them by heart" (119). Other movement in the memoir is not residual, but is remembered "exactly" (119). The Boreal aspen poplars, "their countless fingers moved in a canopy of grey on blue: a blue ocean of continuous, circular rhythm… always and continuously moving. They creaked, they groaned, but in summer they would whisper as well. Or shiver. Something too immense to imagine was always breathing over them" (121–22).

Coaldale wind is both precise and endless, but also reversed in its movements: it "could run ice in summer with hailstone, or hot in the depths of winter to lick every flake of snow into mud when Old Man sent the 'snow bitter wind'…, his winter chinook" (387). In the childhood images of Wiebe, life and consciousness in the Boreal forest and on the prairie seem to be constituted by eternal movement.

Saying that, though, Henry Kreisel's long prevailing assertion that all "discussion of the literature produced in the Canadian West must of necessity begin with the impact of the landscape upon the mind" cannot contain the Wiebean enterprise (6). Although he was raised partly on the prairie, there is not much in Wiebe's writing that suggests landscape in general, or prairie in particular, constitutes the human being. In the memoir, the aspens are part of the landscape, but it is the "continuous" motion that is significant for subjectivity rather than the trees or the land per se. Delving deep into Alberta literature, Joy Anne Fehr in "Re-Writing Alberta" suggests a way to look at Prairie literature different from the environmentalist principle long popular in literary criticism.[2] Taking the history of Alberta Prairie writing and Deborah Keahey's discussions of Prairie literature and movement into account, Fehr interestingly asserts that rather than landscape as such, "movement appears as a key feature" of both Prairie and Alberta literature (32). Resisting fixed notions of space, Keahey's *Making it Home: Place in Canadian Prairie Literature* emphasizes the dynamic movements found in literature itself, rather than the assumption that landscape determines human response. In her exposition, Fehr returns to Frederick Jackson Turner's frontier hypothesis, which concerns the process of the frontier and its impact on the American character and culture, but allows the environmentalist notion to merge with Keahey's notion of "home" as a centre of gravity, both pushing away and pulling characters towards it, as well as with Homi Bhaba's conceptions of minority cultures and otherness. Keahey's discussions of Prairie literature reveal many shifting concepts concerning "homeplace," and a "desire for movement" instead of the stable image of home one could expect from a consciousness determined by landscape. At the same time, Bhaba's theoretizations on otherness and on different stages of movement "within the in-between" of postcolonial liminal space bears resemblance to the descriptions of the instabilities of Canadian Prairie home place as discussed by Keahey (qtd. in Fehr 31).

To be sure, such movement between home places is central to the two other contemporary giants of Alberta literature, Robert Kroetsch and

Aritha van Herk. In a 2001 conversation with van Herk, Kroetsch appoints "restlessness" as a defining feature of Western Canadian writing. "I think in the West there was a sense of using up space and moving on.... And that has conditioned us as writers."[3] Keahey similarly conditions van Herk's and Kroetsch's writing in terms of continual dislocations (126), of moving to and from; or, as in the case of van Herk, *from* rather than *to*. Characters in van Herk seem always to be infected by impatient continuation. Arachne Manteia, peddler of women's undergarments in *No Fixed Address* (1986), is kept on the road by the impossibility of remaining or indeed experiencing home. Equally fidgety even by the bare notion of presence, the protagonist of *Restlessness* (1998) seeks the final destination – death, from which there is no return ticket. The referential function or 'pointing' of language sets the mind of both writer and reader along a particular trajectory" (128). This restless aiming as dislocated *betweenness* can itself be discussed in terms of space. Bhaba's conceptualization of movement "within the in-between" is, although bearing a sense of "proximity," still a spatial motion between two positions (qtd. in Fehr 31). As will be shown however, this is not the way movement as kinetic-kinaesthetic directedness manifests itself in Wiebe.

Edmund Husserl's differentiation between distance as *Abstand* and distance as *Entfernung*, conceptualized in the important collection of texts called *Thing and Space* (117–18), will help us elucidate this important distinction further. The former is an objective or subjective distance between one thing and another in the world of measurable spatiality (A to B). It marks a perceivable interval between two phenomena appearing simultaneously "in" objective space (193–94). *Abstand* is the distancing interval or extension between two points given mathematically. The separation is an extensive appearing that *itself* is something tangible, a knowable unit of space. In contrast, *Entfernung* is not a distancing interval. The interval van Herk's suicidal narrator has withdrawn into is a transitional movement, the space between a point of departure and a ditto terminus, in short, an extensional hiatus where not much momentum can be found. Intriguingly, while the protagonist of Wiebe's *Sweeter Than All the World* inhabits that same interval, gaps of restlessness are not constitutive factors of Wiebe's Mennonite fiction as such. Instead, there is in Wiebe's fiction a kinetic reality torn between distance as a separating interval and distance as a remote intimacy materializing as an elision of the span between "moving from" and "moving to." With respect to its evident theological pertinence for Wiebe's Mennonite fiction, dealing with *Sweeter Than All the World* and its preoccupation with Mennonite origins also demand an accentuated concern with the phenomenon of theological directedness and regeneration understood as movement.

The main protagonist in Rudy Wiebe's *Sweeter Than All the World*, the wealthy Edmonton physician Adam Wiebe, experiences a sense of existential angst. He identifies his experienced position in terms of an ethno-theological predicament: the "problem" of "being a semi-demi-secular Lowgerman Mennonite in a massively Nothing society" (170). The sentence calls attention to many things. It highlights a hyphenated sense of postmodernity. It addresses a fall from religion, which is also a distancing of the speaking subject from both Mennonite history and Mennonite tradition. Moreover, it addresses a wound afflicting this particular Mennonite. This wound may be reviewed in terms of what Ihab Hassan has called "the colonial complex," in other words a specific wound, and a specific slit in that wound through which the universe is exclusively viewed (338). For while Adam, as an enlightened individual situated in postmodern society wants to reject all that which so to speak is Mennonite-essential: religion, the traditional way of living, et cetera, from what could be called a postcolonial, or ethnic perspective, he simultaneously wants to embrace his religiously afflicted tradition and history. The dilemma materializes in the feeling of loss and positionlessness inherent in his formulation of the "problem." In this essay, I want to address not the hyphenated, postmodern, cultural and political space that is often said to determine Wiebe's writing, but a primal directedness, the phenomenological intentionality that is fundamental to the Wiebean Mennonite as the force constituting her or him. To broach that problematic, I will foreground the phenomenon of movement.

In alternating chapters of *Sweeter Than All the World*, glimpses of Mennonite history and of Adam Wiebe's ancestors are provided. In those parts, situated in Europe, under and after the time of the Reformation, loss and displacement do not only come to givenness as wound or complex, but also as narrated fact. From the sixteenth century onwards, Mennonites have moved from country to country, from continent to continent, suffering severe hardships and persecution. *The Blue Mountains of China* thoroughly describes the last hundred years of that history of migration. Yet, what is curious in the midst of loss and displacement in the sixteenth century is that with these Mennonite-refugees no feeling of position-loss is present. On the contrary, there is an all-encompassing feeling of being intentionally directed towards *something*. The Mennonites are driven not by an urge within themselves – by any Mennonite subjectivity – but by a sense of God as immanent reality.

Migratory movements are an issue for the early Mennonites as well as for a contemporary Mennonite like Adam, who, while no immigrant himself, was born on a tiny farmstead in Canada to immigrant parents. However, these differently directed Mennonites move differently, and their migratory movements come to presentation on two separate strata of the text. The first one, the geophysical, kinetic stratum, has already been mentioned. Here, migration takes place in a schematic A-to-B movement, in which the Mennonite is the *moving being*, travelling, as Adam Wiebe does, from Edmonton to Prague in order to visit the grave of Franz Kafka. The restlessness described by Kroetsch and van Herk is understood in terms of this interval. The second stratum is the condition of possibility for Mennonite migration as such. It is the theological stratum of "being moved," or being impelled by the Holy Spirit.

I want to elucidate the workings of these different strata of geophysical and theological movement by means of Husserl's phenomenological distinction between self-movement and being-moved (134). A body can move kinetically, physically, but it can also *be* moved kinaesthetically. Kinaesthesia is the perception of, or the sensation of movement, the feeling of being touched rather than the touching per se. In a penetrating investigation of the nature of movement and self-movement, Maxine Sheets-Johnstone extends the Husserlian project of understanding movement as a *constituting* source of time and space. "The crucial role of kinesthetic experience to the experience or sense of a spatio-temporal dynamic strongly suggests how the constitution of space and time have their genesis in self-movement, and why the consciousness of animate forms... is in the most fundamental sense just such a spatio-temporal dynamic" (146). With Husserl, she stresses how, broadly speaking, movement is the primal kinetic-kinaesthetic core of life, "the very source of our being in the world" (148). "Everything cognitive," Sheets-Johnstone argues, "leads back" to movement: "Insofar as our primal animatedness is the bedrock of... kinetically- and kinesthetically-rooted conceptual understandings, our primal animatedness is, to borrow (and singularize) a phrase from Husserl, 'the mother of all cognition'" (137). Species-specific acts of movement that we "simply 'do' in coming into the world.... happen to us before *we* make them happen," that is, before any cognitive comprehension has made a self-conscious movement-decision (137). In a more determinate sense, however, movement is an activity that comprehends itself as aiming, that closes an interval. This difference is highlighted in the eighteenth-century philosophic writings of James Beattie: "Action implies motion; but there may be motion, as in a clock, where, *properly* speaking, there is no agent. Many motions necessary to life are continually going on in the human body; as those of the heart, lungs, and arteries: but there [sic] are not human actions, because man is not the cause of them" (194).

For Wiebean Mennonites, movement, understood theologically, *constitutes* consciousness and regeneration. Sheets-Johnstone points out that primal movement "*forms the I that moves before the I that moves forms movement*" (138). In Mennonite religious life, analogously, something that is not a human agent is at the root of existence as a force already moving it. It comes to givenness as regeneration, but also, in Adam Wiebe's predicament, as persecution. Here I utilize this phenomenological finding to explicate the status of the Mennonite as a literary figure in Wiebe's fiction.

Within the agrarian communities of, for example, *The Blue Mountains of China*, displacement is materialized *less* as migration than as an eternal de-positioning of non-nomadic farmers. For those Mennonites, and for Frieda Friesen in particular, the pull towards the Creator has affective priority over all other movement. Truly non-itinerant at heart, Wiebean Mennonites laconically assert that they "moved more than most" (13). However, no felt starting point ever appears, nor any conception of a teleological journey's end. Such an end is for the Mennonite eschatological – that is, theologically directed towards an ideal paradisiac end of movement. Instead, Mennonite migration comes to givenness as a multiple infinity of displacements where movement lacks extensionality altogether. Between one displacement and the next in Wiebe, there is not primarily a "between," a liminal space, but the kinaesthetic nothingness of movement as such. I would suggest that there is movement rather than a distancing interval.

In reviewing the Mennonite novels, and especially their foregrounding of language, one cannot conveniently overlook the circumstance that, for Christian fundamentalists, movement dwells in the Word itself. In *Sweeter Than All the World*, Trijntjen Pieters, the sixteenth-century narrator of the third chapter of *Sweeter Than All the World*, "Flour and Yeast," tells us of how her mother Weynken remembered:

> when a priest named Ulrich Zwingli began teaching in Zurich far away. He taught that, according to the Scriptures, the Pope himself had no more power to forgive sins than any true Christian

> believer did. She heard that Melchior Hoffman was travelling across Europe saying the Holy Spirit was poured out on every living person, you must listen to God's Word in the Bible and you would feel the Spirit *move* in your heart, all men and women too, it made no difference! She heard the New Testament read aloud, first in Martin Luther's German translation, and then the reader translated it on the spot into Dutch. (34; emphasis added)

The decisive word here is *move*. When Mennonites move between continents, deserts, prairies, steppes, and grasslands the ultimate underlying factor is not the politico-theological intolerance driving them from land to land but the sense of God as prime mover and source of regeneration. The basic Mennonite movement-affect is not theirs, in that it is not felt to be instigated by any activity originating in them. That movement chiefly lies in the Word means, theologically speaking, that it is not primarily viewed as a property of human life. Protestant fundamentalists are by definition open to *the movement that is in the Word itself* (Klassen 24-25). Its momentum comes to expression as already given as such, as already "poured out" on women and men alike (34).

Because movement as primal directedness is felt to be centred in the Word rather than in the human ego or religious cogito, the Mennonite refugee is largely passive vis-à-vis the movement s/he is drawn, or "being moved," into. When harassed Mennonites *move*, the intrinsically different versions of submission – the submission to the movement of the Word's call and the submission to authority – cannot be visually externally distinguished from each other. Through flight, submission to the regenerating movement of the Spirit, furnished in free access to the written and printed Word, has taken on the appearance of subjection to ecclesiastical and secular authority. In the Mennonite predicament, these two quite different forms of movement have phenomenally (though not phenomenologically) become indistinguishable, and movement is thus made intriguingly ambiguous. Through hardships, regenerative movement has come to assume the external form of expulsion from Europe instigated by Catholic, Lutheran, or Calvinistic rulers. In the last analysis, the movement into exile does not have its source in theo-political force ("recant from heresy, or die") or in submission to worldly authority ("let us move on: this governor does not want Mennonites to live here"), but in Mennonite ideology – in the refutation of secular society as ultimate authority over human life. Since this refutation goes hand in hand with quietism, the tension between movement in the most theologically radical sense (being moved by the Spirit) and geographic world-movement is obscured.

This stratum of regeneration-movement is quite distinct from the stratum of territorial-extensional movement. The tension between the two strata is of primary constructional importance in the text. Body-movement is in the last analysis other than religious movement. Even the most physically immobile person may share the movement that is accomplished by the Word. Without physically moving an inch, anyone could be moved by the Word. But in the shadow of such movement-differences, confusion materializes, for us and for the Wiebean Mennonites. While the regenerated Mennonite moves in the attempt at sustaining a way of life that seems somehow "truer" than the non-Mennonite alternative, somewhere along the line, for some people, the Mennonite fashion of moving around as such becomes a kinetic-kinesthetic substitute for being moved by God. The different phenomenological movements become complexly intertwined. A being-moved that for the believer is theologically necessary – regeneration – turns into a being-moved that is theologically unnecessary: namely, travel. Travel-movement could of course also be viewed theologically, as exodus within a covenant,[4] but even then, it contains an extensional element that is distinguishable from the movement of regeneration and grace. Faith is not reducible to migration.

The longer the temporal-spatial journeys of the Mennonite-refugees become, the greater is the likelihood that being-on-the-road becomes a simulacrum of regeneration, faith, and devotion. Being-moved turns into a sacred phenomenon in itself, and in the hands of the implied Mennonite writer, it gradually emerges as an object of worship and veneration. Displacement becomes a cult. In a strange substantiation, the event of being-moved by the Spirit has become the habit of moving about on the earth as pious refugee, and there is a slight but significant sense that moving-always-as-refugee has settled down into being an idol, a travel talisman, that progressively replaces regeneration. A refuge-romanticism, an idealization of pain and position-loss, almost presents itself as a means to salvation. By such slippage, the way of the Mennonite turns into a tourism-spirituality: we are not regenerated to be moved; we move, and that *per se* is regeneration.

If this line of suspicion is pursued to the final analysis, one might even argue that Adam Wiebe, the nomadic postmodern male narrator has fallen victim to a theological backsliding or a religious slippage. In the polyphony of the text's voices, those who seem to have lost religion altogether

– e.g., Adam Wiebe, or, which will be shown presently, his father-in-law, Bud Lyons – at the same time as they have been in total abstention from any trace of inner regeneration, have nurtured a pseudo-theological sense of noble exodus. These descendants of truly non-itinerant, non-nomadic, farmers devote themselves to a self-reflective vagabondage that has the appearance but not the reality of an authentic devotion to God.

Sweeter Than All the World simultaneously exhibits and conceals the structural discrepancy between religious and geographical movement. The text encourages us to understand – but also to forget – the difference between conversion and displacement, between being regenerated and feeling persecuted. Yet for Protestants giving priority to faith over merit, the hardships of wandering in themselves can obviously never themselves furnish justification. In a bedside talk of Abraham Loewen and his eponymous grandfather, being-on-the-road in terms of a sense of regeneration, and in terms of a sense of being persecuted have been mixed up. The meeting between the two Abrahams takes place during a few hours in an Idaho hospital, in 1941. In this hospital, the elderly Abraham Loewen's bodily extensionality is severely diminished by a stroke. Confined to his bed, the old man's "mind wanders" far beyond the parameters of that confinement (180). During the talk and silences of their brief meeting, the status of the phenomenon of being-on-the-road comes to the fore.

Being-on-the-road implies a certain aimlessness, an absence of predetermined goal. Yet the aimlessness does not lack directedness. Although there is no *particular* aim, there is a generalised sense of moving-towards. Restricted to a hospital bed, immovable but for his face, right arm, and leg, Abraham Loewen "wanders" in a wandering without wandering-aim (180). His eyes "sink" into a "distant bemusement" as he recalls the event of somehow surviving a dangerous Mennonite migration into Turkistan (181).[5] The "wilderness" into which old Abraham Loewen had "moved" as a boy is still with him as the permanentized sense of being stranded in an idealization of suffering (181).

Abraham Loewen's secularized grandson also drifts, but his roving is born out of a firm decision *not* to wander with the Mennonites. "'Mennonites move all the time.' I have heard this from him forever; it is what I got away from by *removing myself*" (181; emphasis added). Feeling alienated from his grandfather's unabated belief, he attempts to eliminate himself from his Mennonite background by eradicating "Abraham Loewen" and becoming "Bud Lyons" (183). In a double removal, in a getting away by removing himself, he is doing exactly what he intended not to do: he "wanders." Perplexingly, what for Abraham the elder is a sense of being moved by God, is to his grandson nothing but hypocritical, moralistic displacement. Afraid that the hardships of the disastrous Asian wandering may have clouded his grandfather's mind into celebrating suffering rather than God, Abraham justifies his own removal by means of feeling persecuted. The getting away in this passage is not only a change of address, but also an affective getting away from his grandparents, and from that which is Mennonite in general. Abraham's striving to protect himself from feeling persecuted amounts to a transformation of that effort into feeling regenerated – "saved" from Mennonite affinity.

However, no matter how fiercely decisive the removal is experienced to be, it is evident that the intended partition failed. Bud's reaction to well-known sayings is instinctive and violent: "Abruptly it sounded so much like what I once hated, and still hate, that I jerk away from him rigid as half a log, I'm outta here!" (183). The final move of consciously willing *not* to be Abraham Loewen is affectively and kinaesthetically impossible to effectuate. Kinesthetically, neither the removing-motion, nor the getting-away-movement will ever come to an end, and the intention to leave the Mennonites forever cements the bond he wishes to dissolve.

I have described a backsliding occurring in the text, from accentuation of regeneration as a feature of Mennonite life to an un-sought for form of Mennonite ethnicity as a phenomenon coinciding with the intricacies of Mennonite migration. Adam Wiebe's ethno-theological complex, the double and conflicting feeling of being that "semi-demi-secular Low-German Mennonite" amounts to a conflict between a feeling of ethnic belonging and theological doctrine which beforehand disintegrates any such movement.

Perhaps coincidentally, the strange void brought about by the theological slip may be hinted at in old Abraham Loewen's Samarkand story of the lily feet. As old Abraham and his sister, during the tragic Epp-trek already mentioned, encounter a Chinese girl selling silk, the ancient Chinese necessity for female beauty is suddenly revealed. Their horror at finding that the Chinese girl's feet were practically missing is perfectly understandable, as is the implied critique against such means of female suppression, yet the scene reverberates with additional implications – namely with the sense that the event of being deprived of one's feet is especially traumatic for the Mennonite whose faith has taken on the permanent form of walking.

> Susannah's hand was holding the Chinese girl's foot. But there was no foot. Below her folded knee, at her ankle, her leg ended in layers of wound cloth coiled and tied tight around a square stub. I couldn't understand: where was her foot? I looked at her face: her eyes were stretched shut now in a tight line clenched across her face, a slit where pain shrieked, where it would never be let out. (192)

If the neo-normative means of salvation for the Mennonite feeling-persecuted is suffering through wandering, the Chinese girl, by lacking feet to walk with, is beyond salvation. From the point of view of the slipped Mennonite, the physical-existential suffering of the Chinese girl has neither meaning nor support, since her suffering – unlike the suffering on the road – seems unlikely to reap any divine reward. Because the foot is missing, it leads nowhere, *walks* nowhere, and lacks the perambulatory virtuousness of the Mennonite in search of salvation.

As has been shown, in *Sweeter Than All the World* certain characters slip from a celebration of the Word into a celebration of Mennonite travel-suffering, where the suffering of God gives way to the suffering of the worshipper. This move seems justified according to its own ability to remember itself not primarily as movement of the Word, but as movement of suffering, of feet treading alien deserts.

Returning to the memoir and to the notion of Prairie movement, one recognizes that in Wiebe's powerful writing about childhood, family, community, and landscape, there is hardship but no suffering on the road. Although the Wiebes – like the fictional Mennonites – moved around a bit, wandering is not itself an issue in *Of This Earth*: Wiebe is truly "home" in the memoir. But of what does "home" consist? One can see the Speedwell homesteads in Saskatchewan; the temporary home with relatives in Vancouver; the new house on the Alberta Prairie – but the sense of "being home" is itself not *at* home in those places. The homesteads are described seemingly from a distancing interval, as if by a spectator rather than by a participator. The idea of a geographic *home place* that is "singular and locatable – pinpointable – in space" clearly does not suffice for Wiebe's sense of home (Keahey 3).

In fact, much of the memoir is mediated through something, notably family photographs and diaries kept by Wiebe's sisters. Inevitably then, *Abstand* appears between the narrator's struggles with those "facts" and what he can actually remember. If there is a danger of any slippage in *Of This Earth*, it concerns a fall from authentic memory to what the "accidentally retained" pictures allows the narrator to create memories around (333). One such preserved photograph shows a team of horses and a sled, as well as Rudy and his older brother dressed for church. On the back of the photo, the words "*abgenommen den 28 März 1947*" are written (334). "I cannot doubt my mother's handwriting," the Wiebe-narrator says, but "where were Dan and I going in our Sunday clothes on a winter Friday morning?" (335). In the background of another photo is Dan's car: an "absolute uniqueness in our Speedwell life" (333). Yet the narrator cannot recollect any of the times he must have ridden in it.

What he never doubts, however, are words, story, and presence; in moments of doubtless textual immediacy, memory suddenly comes alive. Those instances are not about any "home place." Just as Keahey argues concerning the Prairie literature, so *home* is in Wiebe found less in "place" than in writing. The sense of "being home" is found in the parts where the struggle to remember and to communicate gives way to the movement of story. As the narrator abandons his spectator position and weaves word into the memories, the memoir too dares to abandon its pretence to truth and become story. In one of the earliest memories presented, the children are in a tent because the house is being cleansed from lice by smoke. The oldest sister is telling the little ones a fairy tale. The breathing movement of the aspens, "too immense to imagine" (122), is again emphasised and the narrative nudges us to remember the Word and the home, which are not at all "other," but always intimately remote in the Wiebean oeuvre. The moment is kinetic as well as kinaesthetic: "The poplar leaves shiver like fear in the wind, their branches groan above us in the moonlight. And *it comes to me now* that Helen and I, and Liz as well, yes, we are in a tent under the trees in the hollow behind our log house" (43). The event, says the narrator, is "as sharp a memory as I have of our first homestead: ducklings, a fox, the tent in the hollow under poplars, our house sealed thick with poison gas, the bush vermin my mother detested: Waunztje" (48). Yet the fact of the children and the story under the trees is not a distant memory in the narrator's mind, but something that is near. It "comes" to the narrator and to the reader alike, and although the workings of memory are "fathomless to the looking eye," it is indeed "touchable by words" (387).

NOTES

1. Kinaesthesia is the perception or the sensation of movement, the sense of "muscular effort that accompanies a voluntary motion of the body" – as well as the "sense or faculty by which such sensations are perceived" (*OED* 2nd ed., s.v. "kinaesthesis").

2. Fehr discusses the writings of Edward McCourt, Laurence Ricou, Dick Harrison, and Henry Kreisel as environmentalist criticism.

3. Sellery 30–31.

4. Movement of course defines radical discipleship: "spreading the Word." In his book *The Politics of Jesus,* Mennonite theologian J. H. Yoder sees Jesus as having called his disciples to radical social reform, rather than to an apolitical life. Yoder argued for movement rather than stagnation: "The community of disciples must be constantly 'on the road' in search of 'restitutions'" that will come in forms that are simultaneously unexpected and familiar (133).

5. In the 1880s, a group of some six hundred Mennonites followed the millenialist Claus Epp on a journey east. They experienced severe hardships. Many died, especially children; others returned to the Ukraine, or, aided by Mennonites in America, went to the US (Dyck 181).

WORKS CITED

Beattie, James. *Elements of Moral Science.* 1790. Delmar, New York: Scholars' Facsimiles and Reprints, 1976.

Dyck, Cornelius J. *An Introduction to Mennonite History.* 1967. Scottdale, PA: Herald Press, 1993.

Fehr, Joy Anne. "(Re)Writing Alberta." Diss. University of Calgary, 2005.

Hassan, Ihab. "Queries for Postcolonial Studies." *Philosophy and Literature* 22.2 (1998): 328–342.

Keahey, Deborah. *Making it Home: Place in Canadian Prairie Literature.* Winnipeg: University of Manitoba Press, 1998.

Keith, W. J. *Epic Fiction: The Art of Rudy Wiebe.* Edmonton: University of Alberta Press, 1981.

Klassen, Walter, ed. *Anabaptism in Outline: Selected Primary Sources.* Waterloo, ON: Herald Press, 1981.

KREISEL, Henry. "The Prairie: A State of Mind." *Trace: Prairie Writers on Writing.* Ed. Birk Sproxton. Winnipeg: Turnstone Press, 1986.

HUSSERL, Edmund. *Ideas III* (*Ideas Pertaining to a Pure Phenomenology and to a Phenomenological Philosophy: Third Book*). Trans. Ted E. Klein and William E. Pohl. The Hague: Martinus Nijhoff, 1980. First German edition 1952 (*Husserliana* V).

———. *Thing and Space: Lectures of 1907.* Trans. Richard Rojcewicz. Dordrecht: Kluwer, 1997. First German edition 1973 (*Husserliana* XVI).

SELLERY, J'nan Morse. "Robert Kroetsch and Aritha van Herk on Writing & Reading Gender and Genres: An Interview." *Canadian Literature,* Autumn–Winter 170–171, 2001: 21–55.

SHEETS-JOHNSTON, Maxine. *The Primacy of Movement.* Philadelphia: John Benjamins, 1999.

VAN BRAGHT, Thieleman J. *The Bloody Theater or Martyrs Mirror of the Defenceless Christians Who Baptized Only upon Confession of Faith, and Who Suffered and Died for the Testimony of Jesus, Their Saviour, from the Time of Christ to the Year A.D. 1660.* Trans. Joseph F. Sohm. Scottdale: Herald Press, 2001. First Dutch edition 1660; first English edition 1837.

VAN HERK, Aritha. *No Fixed Address.* Red Deer, AB: Red Deer College Press, 1986.

———. *Restlessness.* Red Deer, AB: Red Deer College Press, 1998.

WIEBE, Rudy. *A Discovery of Strangers.* Toronto: Knopf, 1994.

———. *Of This Earth: A Mennonite Boyhood in the Boreal Forest.* Toronto: Knopf, 2006.

———. *Peace Shall Destroy Many.* 1962. Toronto: McClelland & Stewart, 1972.

———. *Playing Dead: Essays Concerning the Arctic.* Edmonton: NeWest Publishers, 1989.

———. *Sweeter Than All the World.* Toronto: Knopf, 2001.

———. *The Blue Mountains of China.* 1970. Toronto: McClelland & Stewart, 1995.

———. *The Temptation of Big Bear.* 1973. Toronto: Vintage, 1999.

YODER, J. H. *The Politics of Jesus.* Grand Rapids, MI: Eerdmans, 1972.

8

RICHARD WAGAMESE – AN OJIBWAY IN ALBERTA

FRANCES W. KAYE

When he walked into a shabby basement room in Calgary in the fall of 1994, the quality of light vivified. He had the whole audience at that long soiree up on our feet and singing a Susan Aglukark song before he read from his first novel, *Keeper 'n Me.* I had never seen anybody so alive.

Richard Wagamese is an Ojibway writer from Ontario who has lived in and written of Alberta – as well as other parts of Canada. His career to date provides a window into an Alberta that is still invisible, or at least hazy, to most non-Native Albertans and other mainstream readers. Wagamese also writes of his own struggle – and the struggle of many Native people raised in the 1950s and 1960s – with the demons of anomie caused by the shattering effects of the widespread "scoop-up" that saw unbearable percentages, in some reserves "almost a generation" (Johnston, quoted in Bensen 12) of Native children taken from their families of origin and placed in foster and adoptive care, the attempts of the criminal justice system to contain the pathologies, and the ever-beckoning false friends of alcohol and street drugs.

Wagamese is particularly effective at depicting the search for and the at least momentary achievement of balance and healing. Richard Wagamese's career also shows his self-education through intensive reading, personal contact with Aboriginal communities in Alberta, the practice of journalism, and the widespread discussion of Indigenous arts provided by the newspaper *Windspeaker.*

Wagamese began his Alberta working life as a journalist. In 1988, *Windspeaker* was one of several federally funded Native newspapers. Published in Edmonton, it was well established and had a history of winning awards, particularly for some of its feature stories. Wagamese, a self-educated thirty-three-year-old with some experience in Native radio, began contributing a column. As he commented in a 2006 radio interview, these columns, like all his writings, were concerned with introducing non-Natives to the day-to-day lives of the Native neighbours (CBC). Eclectic and comprehensive, *Windspeaker* was an excellent venue for stimulating a writer to consider all facets of Indigenous communities in Alberta, in Canada, and even internationally. Its front page and first few succeeding pages usually dealt with political matters including, during the years Wagamese wrote for the paper, the Manitoba Justice Inquiry, Elijah Harper's successful opposition to the Meech Lake Accord, and the "Oka Crisis." Alberta news included the Lubicon Lake Crees' use of the "Spirit Sings" art exhibition during the 1988 Calgary Winter Olympics to draw attention to their land claims and Peigan Lonefighter opposition to the Oldman Dam in southern Alberta. Wagamese's columns ran in the opinion section, approximately page five, usually under Bill MacKay's political cartoons. *Windspeaker*'s long feature articles, on almost every issue of interest – including economic development, education from pre-school up, the lives of successful Native individuals from teenagers to elders, issues involving health, incarceration, childcare, and so on – usually ran after the editorial pages, sometimes before or sometimes in the middle of stories on the arts and extensive coverage of Native rodeo, reserve hockey teams, and other sports. Feature stories often covered well-known Native artists including Jane Ash Poitras and Joane Cardinal-Schubert as well as new and rising artists. The journal gave generous space to reviews of Native books, videos, art exhibitions, theatre, and any other art that came to their attention. Special editions dealt with issues of health, substance abuse rehabilitation, justice concerns, and other large topics of general interest. Sometimes other columnists, including Drew Hayden Taylor, shared Wagamese's space and Taylor gradually took over when Wagamese moved primarily to the *Calgary Herald.*

In March of 1990, the Mulroney government slashed the budgets of Native media organizations, including *Windspeaker*, which immediately cut its weekly production schedule in half, becoming a bi-weekly, laid off some staff members, and began to cultivate other revenue sources. That *Windspeaker* still survives as one of North America's predominant Native newspapers speaks to the strength of its leaders and the excellence of its material. Both before and after the cuts, it was an outstanding venue for an aspiring writer who wanted to cover the daily lives of Native people and especially the ways they were portrayed in the arts. The blend of major national and Alberta stories with the "local colour" of sports and school activities and an active "Letters" section gave (and gives) *Windspeaker* a distinctive power of representation.

Perhaps even more important for an aspiring novelist was *Windspeaker*'s focus on the arts. Almost every issue of the paper included serious reviews of everything from children's books to the most harrowing documentaries about suicide or AIDS awareness. For instance on August 11, 1989, after news stories on CSIS investigations of some bands' NATO-like mutual defence pact and the opening of a northern Alberta chopstick factory, *Windspeaker* ran two reviews of art exhibitions, a feature story on Edmonton artist Kim McLain, and a long article by Gary Gee with the headline "Debate over 'Native art' engages art community." Artists explained that they did not want to be stereotyped as "Native" artists – a theme that Joane Cardinal-Schubert in particular has developed – but did want to use images that were significant to them. Artist and curator Gerald McMaster was given the last word, pointing out that Native art had been shaped by more than 10,000 years of history on this land that is now called Canada. While such reviews and discussions are by no means absent in whitestream media, they are, not unreasonably, less dense and less concentrated. Land and the connection to land is one of Wagamese's continuing themes. Certainly he did not need Gerald McMaster to inform him of its significance – he had already devoted a column to the subject on March 17 of the same year – but the quality of the conversation inherent in participating in *Windspeaker* provided an active background for Wagamese's development of his own aesthetic as an Ojibway male writing in the late twentieth and early twenty-first centuries.

The success of Wagamese's *Windspeaker* columns attracted the attention of Gillian Steward, managing editor of the *Calgary Herald*, who asked him to contribute a weekly column to the *Herald* (*Terrible Summer* 9). Although some columns appeared in both papers, the *Herald*, with its much larger circulation and daily publication, became the main venue for Wagamese's columns from August 1989 to May 1992, and the *Herald* columns were the ones that won a National Newspaper Award in 1991 (*Terrible Summer* 10) and were re-published in Wagamese's second book, *The Terrible Summer* (1996). As he described the columns, all are political, some are personal, some are historical, and some are primarily analytical (9). All end with "Eagle Feathers" (a mark of respect or accomplishment) to individuals or organizations Wagamese wishes to recognize for their efforts to improve the lives of Aboriginal people or Native/non-Native relations. "These columns, I believe, represent the essence of the people and make recognizable and valid the lives of people most Canadians have never seen before – their Aboriginal neighbours," wrote Wagamese in his Foreword (*Terrible Summer* 9).

Yet essays, no matter how fresh and personal, do not have the ability of a "story" to awaken an emotional response from a reader, so it is not surprising that Wagamese would turn to the novel as a vehicle for "most Canadians" to recognize and care about the lives of "their Aboriginal neighbours." *Keeper 'n Me* (1994) is a limpid story about a young man, Garnet Raven, who, like Wagamese himself, was taken from his family of origin and lost in foster and adoptive childcare, only to reach adulthood with no sense of identity or origins. Through Garnet's older brother's patient detective work, he reunites with his family. Their small Ojibway reserve, he discovers, is genuinely his home, and he begins to learn from Keeper the healing ways of the Anishinabeg people. This gentle, humorous book is a study in retribalization, primarily for Aboriginal people who have been distanced by generations of residential schools, foster and adoptive practices, and the wholesale attack on North American Aboriginal cultures, but, like all of Wagamese's writings, it is for non-Native readers, too, because, as Wagamese often says, we are all tribal people a few generations back, and we are all in need of healing. (See, for instance, *A Quality of Light* 291.)

While *Keeper 'n Me* is set almost entirely in Ontario, Wagamese's second and most ambitious novel, *A Quality of Light* (1997), moves back and forth between Ontario and Alberta, where the climax takes place. Unlike most other twenty-first century Canadian Native writers, including Thomas King, Eden Robinson, and Richard Van Camp, who have honed their craft at universities and in creative writing programs, Richard Wagamese is essentially self-educated, having left high school long before graduation and having learned to write from libraries, from oral storytelling, and from journalism. His voice is utterly distinctive, and he shows, through the reading habits and experiences of his characters, how he began developing that voice.

Reading is the first requisite, and the books that Wagamese reports himself or his characters reading are primarily polemical, including *Black Elk Speaks* (John G. Neihardt), *A Century of Dishonor* (Helen Hunt Jackson), *The Long Death* (Ralph K. Andrist), *Akwesasne Note[s]* (a newspaper published on the Akwesasne Reserve) *The New Indians* (Stan Steiner),[1] *Bury My Heart at Wounded Knee* (Dee Brown),[2] *God Is Red* (Vine Deloria, Jr.), *Prisoners [Prison] of Grass* (Howard Adams), *The Diaries of Louis Riel*, Harold Cardinal's *[The Unjust Society:] The Tragedy of Canada's Indians*, and other revolutionary books from Mao to the Black Panthers.[3] No fiction or poetry or even memoirs or plays appear in the list. While there is not room to look at all these works, *Black Elk Speaks*, the first one mentioned, *Bury My Heart at Wounded Knee*, the one the main character and narrator describes as most pivotal and that Wagamese refers to again in *for Joshua*, and *The Unjust Society*, the only book where we are given the author, may show how Wagamese has learned from his readings and how their polemical style shapes his novels.

Black Elk Speaks is a study of one Lakota Holy Man and his immediate family and colleagues, and, like *Bury My Heart at Wounded Knee*, ends with images of destruction and defeat at Wounded Knee, South Dakota, where hundreds of Lakota people, mostly unarmed women and children, were gunned down by the Seventh Cavalry just after Christmas 1890. *Bury My Heart* is a long litany of defeats, beginning with Columbus. Both books come through non-Native American authors, and while Brown keens for the loss of life and freedom of Native Americans and the duplicity of non-Natives, Neihardt, for all his strong sympathy with Black Elk and traditional Lakota ways, writes within the context of a "fortunate fall," whereby the defeat of the Lakotas led to the creation of the American Republic, just as the fall of Troy led to the founding of Rome. Vine Deloria has rightly called *Black Elk Speaks* "the central core of a North American Indian theological canon" (xiv), and it is this quality, rather than the remnants of Manifest Destiny, that Wagamese prizes in the book.

Unlike stories collected by anthropologists, such as Julie Cruikshank's stories of three Yukon elders in *Life Lived Like a Story* or Wendy Wickwire's collection of Harry Robinson's stories in *Write It on Your Heart*, *Black Elk Speaks* is heavily edited by Neihardt, who introduces didactic elements that do not seem to have appeared in the original telling. For many people within an oral culture, such as Annie Ned, Angela Sidney, and Kitty Smith, Cruikshank's storytellers, the story *is* the explanation, something it took Cruikshank some time to understand and that she carefully explains to non-Native readers.

Neihardt, however, writing primarily for a non-Lakota, English-speaking audience, glossed references to the circle, gave the moral of the story of White Buffalo Calf Woman, and explained the significance of courtship traditions, all in Black Elk's voice. *Bury My Heart at Wounded Knee,* like *A Century of Dishonor*, is constructed to point to the moral – that European and American policies toward Indigenous North Americans were genocidal from the point of contact on. It is a litany of massacre, betrayal, and general duplicity – truly an eye-opener, especially for people who have been brought up with images of benevolent little Pilgrims and happy little Indians at some stylized "First Thanksgiving," or even for Canadians raised with images of benevolent red-coated Mounties protecting Indians from evil American whiskey traders. We can see why *Black Elk* and *Bury My Heart* would incite Wagamese's radical warrior figure, Johnny, to anger, defiance, and finally a symbolic act of simulated terrorism.

Cardinal's *The Unjust Society: The Tragedy of Canada's Indians,* like *Prison of Grass* and *God Is Red,* is no less eye opening but far less apocalyptic. It points out where Canadian Indian policy has gone wrong and shows how destructive and stupid it has been, but it does not dwell on victimhood and ending. Instead of a massacre and people dying in the bloody snow, Cardinal ends with a reiteration of the need for Canada's Indians to organize and for non-Indians to respect Native self-determination (162). While Cardinal decries other Canadians who pity Indians as more of a problem than those who hate or ignore Indians (165), Neihardt and Brown deliberately end with pitiful images. Not surprisingly, Joshua Kane, Wagamese's protagonist, sounds a great deal more like Cardinal than like the white American authors who lead the list of readings. Victimhood deals with content, but in terms of style, particularly in the need to explain the moral of the story, all three of these source books have more in common with each other and with Wagamese's own practice than they do with the oral tales recorded by Cruikshank and Wickwire. Neihardt and Cardinal are particularly willing to tell stories and then to gloss them for both Native and non-Native readers who have no practice in "reading" the story itself as the gloss of the story.

Unlike novelists like Ruby Slipperjack, who do not explain and who expect readers to learn by observation, Wagamese uses the stories as hooks for the lessons he wants to impart. But he is not merely writing from the library books. As someone raised in ignorance of Ojibway traditional ways of learning that privilege observation over explanation, Wagamese sought out explanations, and those are what he provides his readers. Especially in

A Quality of Light, whose narrator is an ordained Christian minister as well as an Ojibway healer, Wagamese presents oral stories as if they were parables, with definite paraphrasable messages. His stories are mostly animal creation stories, not necessarily Ojibway ones, especially as many come from Johnny and are either pan-Indian or vaguely Lakota. Like the rest of the book, they are luminous, unlike the humorously twisted Coyote stories of Thomas King or the omnivorous Nanabush's appearances in Tomson Highway's plays. Yet Johnny's "Indian name," given to him by Joshua when they are both still boys, is Laughing Dog, which certainly suggests Coyote, and Johnny plays several Trickster roles. As a white boy, he shape shifts into an AIM (American Indian Movement) radical, and his hostage-taking with make-believe weapons is a trickster act that, although it does not seem to succeed in unbalancing Canadian society, does unbalance Joshua and enable him to attain a more profound understanding of his own beliefs and values. He is forced out of his comfortable role as Ojibway and pastor and becomes the bridge for healing both non-Native and especially Native people of the wounds of the five hundred years of dishonour inflicted by wounded Europeans who have lost contact with the land. Thus the carefully explicated animal parables are balanced by the unglossed and understated Coyote possibilities inherent in the novel. In addition to retelling oral tales directly, Wagamese alludes to Coyote and the function of the trickster in oral literature.

Wagamese's fabulistic writing and his unabashed references to tribal peoples and the power of the land distance him from more academic writers, such as Eden Robinson or Richard Van Camp, as well as from American Ojibway writers such as Gerald Vizenor and David Treuer. Wagamese uses land as synecdoche for the people. In *A Quality of Light*, his main character, Joshua, thinks,

> As I flew over the undulating conversation of Ontario and then the eloquent hush of prairie, I thought about how very much our lives are like the land. The lives of the wounded are scant, stark and remorseless – the barrens almost. While the lives of the saved are lush, arable and gratifying – a heartland. The wounded are nomads, moving like ghosts, incorporeal, ethereal, leaving no sign on the territories they cross.... The saved in their plenty dream of travel, and the wounded in their barrens carry dreams of permanence. (185)

But Wagamese immediately goes on to complicate this either/or scenario with a letter from Joshua's best friend and antagonist, Johnny:

> *That's what white trash is – a motley collection existing without the life-enhancing benefits of background. No cultural, historical anchor. No rich emotional homeland. Nomads willing to settle anywhere the grass looks greener or else latching on to some scrabbly semblance of order and squatting there, hoping boards and bricks can heal them, flesh them out, give them detail. Life without detail is life without edges, borders, perspective. I hated it.* (201, italics in original)

Land here is abstract and exists as words rather than specific images. But it is also the measure of a people. Both boys have been displaced, but Joshua has been saved, both by his adoptive farmer parents' love of the land they till and by his connections with his birth Ojibway people. Johnny remains the displaced European, displaced again by his father's drinking and the broken, wandering life it creates.

Robinson's *Monkey Beach* shows people on the land, berrying, or more characteristically, on the water, fishing for many different creatures in an unselfconscious combination of traditional resource harvesting with contemporary outboards and commercial vessels, but the reader is left to draw the "moral" of the story. In Van Camp's *Lesser Blessed* there are animal fables, all right, but they are literally "Indian" – about the Blue Monkeys of India. The land is the place where the protagonist and his stepfather fail at hunting or where his stepfather miserably dispatches the burned and dying animals left after a forest fire. Gerald Vizenor hails the Trickster in many guises, while David Treuer both uses Trickster and nature images and sees Trickster and nature images as dangerous "short cuts" to Native fiction that can be played effectively even by such arrant racists as "Forest Carter," the KKK leader who wrote the hoax Cherokee memoir *The Education of Little Tree* (lecture). Wagamese, on the other hand, reminds us that many clichés started as wisdom and resuscitates them through his powers of belief and language. Drew Hayden Taylor, who inherited some of Wagamese's duties at *Windspeaker*, can be a similarly didactic writer, as in *Toronto at Dreamer's Rock*, for instance, but he usually uses humour to undercut any lurking sentimentality or clichés. Wagamese relies simply upon his emotional intensity and the power of the stories he tells, a power that is often embedded in the neighbours' lives recorded in his journalism.

The columns he wrote for *Windspeaker* and the *Calgary Herald* gave him the chance to examine and discuss what was happening in Canada's (and Alberta's) Native communities, and some of the material he directly reworks for *A Quality of Light*. For instance, essay 19, "Mole Tale Mines Spiritual Depths" from *The Terrible Summer* establishes the small, almost sightless mole as the most respected of all animals, because mole lives always in contact with earth and "always investigates what he feels" (48) as he hears the steps of the other animals overhead. In the novel Wagamese retells the story in one of Johnny's letters to Joshua, detailing his own spiritual journey. Here, because the mole "was always in contact with Mother Earth," he "possessed great wisdom. And because he had lost the use of his eyes the mole had developed true spiritual insight" (222). The Eagle Feathers in the mole essay Wagamese awards "To all the Indian playwrights, writers, and storytellers keeping those old teachings alive and vibrant" (49). In the novel, he joined their number.

Some of Wagamese's more strictly journalistic pieces also play a part in the novel. For instance, his eulogy of Nelson Small Legs is transformed into a eulogy for Johnny's friend and mentor, Staatz. Both the real Peigan man and the fictional Six Nations character were leaders rooted in traditional life who fought for the rights and dignity of Native peoples in Canada and across North America. Both committed suicide in frustration and despair. Of Nelson Small Legs, Jr., Wagamese writes, "He shot himself through the heart because that's where all the pain was" (*Terrible Summer* 65) Similarly Johnny writes of Staatz, "'He'd put a bullet through his heart because that's where all the pain was'" (271). Many of the observations and analyses in the journalistic essays are similarly reprised and developed in the novel.

A Quality of Light is currently out of print and seems to be the least appreciated of Wagamese's novels, perhaps because it is the most complex. It tells the tale of two boys, Joshua Kane, born Ojibway, adopted by a particularly admirable and loving farm couple, and grown to be a Christian pastor who has reconnected with an Ojibway community; and Johnny Gebhardt, blue-eyed child of an alcoholic father, who falls in love with the idea of being an Indian, improbably apprentices himself to a militant young Six Nations friend, and, in the present of the book, has staged a hostage-taking at the Harry Hays Canadian government building in Calgary. He tells police he will only negotiate through Joshua. The novel proceeds through Joshua's recollections of their shared boyhoods, Johnny's letters detailing his education as a militant and his scorn at Joshua's non-militant, Christian life choices, and the present of the hostage crisis. In an epilogue, we see how the crisis has moved Joshua back to the reserve and out of the church.

The lyricism of the book and the initially confusing role reversal of white militant and Ojibway Christian have puzzled some readers, but allow Wagamese to produce a profound effect with a simple story. As we have seen, Wagamese adopts a polemic strategy in his fiction, telling more than he shows and laying out "the moral" of the book as if he were Dee Brown or Harold Cardinal or Vine Deloria rather than following the conventions of oral storytelling or of university creative writing courses. Like Stuart McLean or Garrison Keillor, he creates relationships that are sentimental without tipping over into sentimentality. The first half of the book contains a parable about the failures of the justice system and Canada and the possibilities of restorative justice (see Kaye). The book as a whole is about the ways in which all humans – in even the most "First World" circumstances – are tribal people, in need of songs and stories around the campfire, in need of strong bonds with the earth. Like many other Native writers, such as Maria Campbell, Simon Ortiz, and Leslie Silko, Wagamese sees people of European descent as the most dispossessed because they were the first ones to be disinherited and because they have been brought up to think that they are thus superior to everyone else. Wagamese never discounts the wisdom and land traditions that Amer-Europeans have had, but he is acutely aware of where they are failing. As Joshua tells the policeman who mediates his role as negotiator with Johnny,

> History is about dissolution… unless we're willing… to save and preserve the hereditary truths we're born in, we all become the disappeared…. It happened to the white races first and I think that's what colonization… is all about. (241)

Joshua has read *Bury My Heart* and the other books that Johnny has recommended, the books that Wagamese reports himself as reading in *for Joshua*, but unlike Johnny or Wagamese himself, the fictional Joshua Kane does not become a radical or join AIM. Instead, he decides

> I would preach *choice.* I would preach about my own disinherited past, my own journey to my identity, the tools of both cultures that I used to get me to my Ojibway-ness, my Indian-ness, and my faith. You don't need to kill or fight to reclaim yourself… (241)

Knowing history, for Joshua, gives one the ability "to avoid recreating its vices in our own worlds" (246). And when he goes inside to negotiate with

Johnny, he discovers that Johnny has learned what he already knew. The weapons and explosives (if not the fear felt by the hostages) are all fake. The hostage taking is based on lies, not force; something that Johnny suggests sounds more than a little like the land taking in Canada (288). Johnny has staged the crisis to get the attention of the politicians and the media and all other Canadians who "won't listen to politics any more." Or to "human rights and moral obligation" (290). Johnny is writing – by enacting – a story that people will remember and that will make a point, at least to the people…

> …who understand intuitively that surviving isn't about going back, it's about learning to pull out the arrows and heal. Everybody needs to heal, Josh. Not just the Indians. (291)

But Johnny's plans go awry when, through his own accidental but tragic lapse, he is shot and killed by police snipers after the hostages have been released, leaving Joshua alone to read to the television cameras the statement that the two of them have written. Johnny will never get to Germany and Austria to explore his own tribal heritage. Although Wagamese telegraphs the outcome to the attentive reader, anyone caught up in the story is likely to miss it, so Johnny's death hits us as hard as it does Joshua, who missed the same clue and is therefore complicit with Johnny in the shooting. To calm down, then, and to listen to the message is hard. What Wagamese calls for is a recognition of the facts of Indian North America – massacres, lies, rapes, dispossession on all sides. Like the Truth and Reconciliation process adopted by South Africa, he stipulates a recognition that will then allow for a moving on and healing. Perhaps because *A Quality of Light* has not registered as clearly as some of his other work, in *Dream Wheels* (set in British Columbia) Wagamese drops the call for recognition, and his attractive cast of Native, white, and black characters move directly forward to healing through physical contact with the land, with rodeo bulls, and with an old pickup truck.

Wagamese's third Alberta book is the haunting memoir *for Joshua: An Ojibway Father Teaches His Son,* written in the form of a letter to his then six-year-old son, from whom he is separated.

> Drinking is why we are separated. …Booze owned me…. I drank out of the fears I'd carried all my life, the fears I could never tell anyone about, the fears that ate away at me constantly, even in the happiest moments of my life, and your mother did the only

> thing that she knew to do and that was to take you away where you could be safe. I don't blame her for that. I'm thankful in fact. (7–8)

The book, he says, is an attempt to live up to the responsibility that he felt to his son when he finally sobered up.

In *for Joshua,* Alberta is the site of a private ceremony – that might be named, in popular culture terms, a vision quest – that Wagamese successfully undertakes in the foothills near Calgary, as well as of the teachings and reflections that give value to this four-day interlude. As in *The Terrible Summer* and the other newspaper columns, Alberta shows itself as having a large, diverse, and successful collection of Native communities that work with non-Natives for healing across cultures. It is also very far from Toronto, the place Wagamese associates with his son because that is where they had briefly lived together as part of a family. This distance seems to add clarity, and with the help of a knowledgeable older friend, Richard Wagamese picks a place to perform a ceremony that will return him to his own centre:

> There was a hill where I had been going for a month or so to watch sunsets. The hill faced the Rocky Mountains, which were only about twenty miles away. (23)

It reminds him of the cliffs in Ojibway territory and feels "right" to him. He walks to a place with

> a small copse of trees where there was an outcropping of rock with a ledge from which I could dangle my feet. The drop from that ledge to the road was more than two hundred feet and I had seen eagles and hawks soar between me and the road below. It's an eerie feeling when you see great birds from above, and eerier still when they make their silent passes against a backdrop of coyote howls from the hoodoos and hills all around you. (24)

For four days, Wagamese stays in this place without food or shelter, and the body of the narrative shifts back and forth between his thoughts on the cliff and his recollections of his life – in foster care, on the streets, as an AIM militant, and as a writer. Like Johnny in *A Quality of Light,* he talks about the books he has read: *Bury My Heart at Wounded Knee* again and Vine Deloria's *God Is Red* and [*Custer Died for Your Sins: An] Indian Manifesto* (127). And he talks about other experiences, including an evening at an improvised youth hostel in Nipigon where young travellers from all over Canada sang songs and told stories around a campfire, giving him a complex and personalized sense of the people of the country (105–10). Wagamese sees no technicolour visions, but focussing on the rain, a little tree, and other inhabitants of his ledge induces a kind of introspection. He explains to his sponsor, his son, and all his other readers that

> ...if I want love, security, trust, friendship, and all those good things in life, then I need to give away those things to the people around me. *All* people, all the time. Not just Native people, but all people. (201)

The lesson Wagamese builds from the ceremony is that neighbours of Native people must come to see that Native people are "not angry. We're sad" (222). Tribal people are haunted by the land and the losses that it represents. Neighbours need to know that "every land claim, treaty negotiation, blockade and court case is born out of... a spiritual hunger, not a physical greed" (223). Native people cannot bring back the past, but

> [w]e can recreate the spirit of community we had, of kinship, or relationship to all things, of union with the land, harmony with the universe, balance in living, humility, honesty, truth, and wisdom in all of our dealings with each other. (224)

Between the death of Pauline Johnson in 1913 and the publication of Beatrice Culleton [Mosionier]'s *In Search of April Raintree* and Jeannette Armstrong's *Slash* in the mid 1980s, published fiction and poetry by Indigenous Canadians virtually disappeared. While Alberta in the 1970s displayed great interest in Native characters and situations developed by non-Native writers, including Robert Kroetsch's Anna Yellowbird, W. O. Mitchell's Archie Nicotine, W. P. Kinsella's Silas Ermineskin, and Rudy Wiebe's Big Bear and others, Alberta Native writers were also developing their voices. Harold Cardinal's *Unjust Society* (1969) we have already mentioned. Maria Campbell's extraordinary memoir *Halfbreed* (1973) is set partly in Alberta, and her clear voice has been crucial to Canada's Native literary renaissance. When *Windspeaker* began publication in 1982, Alberta's distinguished Native arts community was beginning to come into prominence, and *Windspeaker*, as we have seen, promoted the work of such important artists as painter Jane Ash Poitras, internationally known architect Douglas Cardinal, and painter and installation artist Joane Cardinal-Schubert. When Richard Wagamese joined *Windspeaker* in 1988, he was tapping into a vibrant literary and artistic journal and its surrounding community, a good place to practice his writing and to develop the themes that would occupy his fiction and memoir.

In its deeply political news columns and its endlessly optimistic articles about the arts, education, sports, and other upbeat stories, *Windspeaker* itself was a kind of truth and reconciliation committee, a function that Wagamese builds upon. *A Quality of Light* is a book of healing that overrides any concerns about the Alberta Advantage and the economic boom and bust cycles of an extractive economy that usually define Alberta – especially in the rest of Canada. Wagamese offers all readers the beginning of a dialogue that can encompass the relentless, destructive assault on Indigenous people and culture waged by taking children from their families of origin. It can deal with Red Power and alienation, with the rising rate of incarceration of Native people in Western Canada and the substance abuse that serves as an anodyne for the persistent feeling of being defective that Wagamese describes as coming from the continuing disruption of the foster and adoptive systems, from unthinking racism, and from the fear of being a child in an uncertain world – the condition of being human. While this anomie is not distinctive to Native people, it is particularly pronounced in Native communities for the historical reasons sketched above. Wagamese never asks for pity nor embraces the vanishing and doomed images of *Bury My Heart at Wounded Knee* or *Black Elk Speaks.* He asks his readers to acknowledge that we are all wounded in a society that takes all of us away from our tribal roots and our life-giving contact with the earth.

Middle-class readers – who are, of course, most readers – may like to complain or feel entitled and hard done by, but they do not have practice in seeing themselves with a "plight," in the same shoes as Native people. Thus *A Quality of Light,* with its white militant who comes from a dysfunctional and alcoholic family and claims the dispossession of Native people, and its serene and gentle Native protagonist, can be an uncomfortable text to read. And, as is the case with many uncomfortable texts, it challenges and heals readers.

Alberta's Native heritage is proudly on display in the province, from the Calgary Stampede to Head-Smashed-In Buffalo Jump to the many little museums of the Peace country and in many local powwows and celebrations of National Aboriginal Day. Joane Cardinal-Schubert is among the artists showcased at the Calgary airport, the Banff Centre supports vital international Indigenous performing arts, and the huge tar sands operation near Fort McMurray provide Indigenous job-training programs and include Indigenous artists in their beautification projects. Thomas King taught for many years at the University of Lethbridge, Eden Robinson was writer-in-residence at the University of Calgary, while Richard Van Camp hails from just across the border in the Northwest Territories. In the context of this vast cultural wealth, Richard Wagamese's openness, his generosity, his determination to create reconciliation, and the luminosity of his words make him a writer to whom we may always return.

NOTES

1. All mentioned in Light 213.
2. Light 233.
3. Light 242.

WORKS CITED

BENSEN, Robert, ed. *Children of the Dragonfly: Native American Voices on Child Custody and Education.* Tucson: University of Arizona Press, 2001.

CARDINAL, Harold. *The Unjust Society: The Tragedy of Canada's Indians.* Edmonton: Hurtig, 1969.

DELORIA, Vine, Jr. "Introduction." *Black Elk Speaks.* Neihardt, John G. Lincoln: University of Nebraska Press, 1979.

JOHNSTON, Patrick. *Native Children and the Child Welfare System,* 1983, quoted in Bensen.

KAYE, Frances W. "The Children of Someone Else's History: Reading for Restorative Justice." *The American Review of Canadian Studies* (Spring/Summer 2001): 225–39.

NEIHARDT, John G. *Black Elk Speaks: Being the Life Story of a Holy Man of the Oglala Sioux.* 1932; rpt. Lincoln: University of Nebraska Press, 1979.

TREUER, David. Lecture, Lincoln, NE, November 2006; see also *Native American Fiction: A User's Manual.* Minneapolis: Greywolf, 2006.

WAGAMESE, Richard. *Keeper 'n Me.* Toronto: Doubleday Canada, 1994.

———. *The Terrible Summer.* Toronto: Warwick, 1996.

———. *A Quality of Light.* Toronto: Doubleday Canada, 1997.

———. *for Joshua: An Ojibway Father Teaches His Son.* Toronto: Vintage, 2002.

———. *Dream Wheels.* Toronto: Doubleday Canada, 2006.

———. Interview, "The Homestretch," CBC Calgary, 16 August 2006.

Windspeaker, 1988–1989.

PART FOUR
NONFICTION

9

FROM *GRIZZLY COUNTRY TO GRIZZLY HEART*: THE GRAMMAR OF BEAR-HUMAN INTERACTIONS IN THE WORK OF ANDY RUSSELL AND CHARLIE RUSSELL

PAMELA BANTING

> Never was there an animal so fond of peace – he loves to laze and loaf in the wild places, where the sky is his roof, the mountain lakes his bathtub, the wind his newspaper, and few things are too small for him to smell or taste.
>
> – Andy Russell (*Grizzly Country* 258)

In the Western philosophical tradition, debates about animal language and the ability of animals and humans to communicate across species dates back at least as far as Aristotle, whose opinion it was that man is the only animal to possess the gift of speech. From Aristotle onward, including Descartes, who depicted animals as soulless automata, animals have, for the most part, been said to lack – variously – voice, speech, the necessary organs for speech, the ability to produce both consonants and vowels, the ability to use conventional signs, inner speech, syntax, reason, and abstraction, and sanctions, sometimes severe, have been placed on those who thought to the contrary. In his article "The Passions and Animal Language, 1540–1700," R. W.

Serjeantson notes, for example, that "Lawyers held that belief in animal language was sufficient evidence of idiocy" (426).[1]

Notably, however, and somewhat surprisingly, many of the philosophers, linguists, and academics of various stripes who have debated the issue of animal language have had a relatively insignificant amount of contact with animals, especially wild ones. In the case of bears, even many of the biologists who have had a great deal of physical contact with them have been occupied with and thoroughly invested in the accepted scientific methods of darting with a tranquilizer gun, and then ear-tagging, weighing, hair sampling, tooth removal, and general handling of unconscious bears[2] and have not attempted to observe bears' communicative strategies from a position of non-intrusive, peaceful co-existence. Ideal language-learning situations do not involve trapping, tranquillizing, rendering comatose, and removing a swatch of hair and a tooth from one's language instructor.

Members of the Andy and Kay Russell family, on the other hand, have lived their entire lives in relation to wild animals. Andy Russell (1915–2005) was for more than two decades a professional big-game guide and outfitter in southern Alberta and British Columbia, Canada, and is the author of a dozen creative nonfiction books about his experiences while guiding, conservation issues such as the Oldman River Dam, the lives of wild animals, and back-country incidents and anecdotes including, to mention just a few, *The Life of a River, Memoirs of a Mountain Man, Trails of a Wilderness Wanderer, Horns in the High Country,* and *The Canadian Cowboy,* most of which are still in print.[3] In the early sixties,[4] Andy turned from guiding for a living to photography, slide show presentations, wildlife documentary filmmaking, and writing. *Grizzly Country* (1967), his first book, draws upon more than four decades of his own back-country experience; anecdotes from family, friends, park wardens, trappers, fellow guides, and clients; as well as his experiences between 1961 to 1963 in Alberta, British Columbia, the Yukon, and Alaska while shooting the footage that became their documentary film *Grizzly Country.* Russell and his two eldest sons, Dick and Charlie,[5] share the distinction of having made the first documentary ever of grizzly bears in the wild (completed in 1963). For about eight decades then (or more if we consider Andy's father- and mother-in-law, Bert and Dora Riggall, the original owners of the guiding and outfitting business, as forerunners of the Russell clan) members of the Russell family have been and continue to be pioneers in documenting bear-human interactions through film, photographs, audio, and text.[6]

In his book *The Literary History of Alberta, Vol. 2,* George Melnyk astutely notes that Andy Russell's first book, *Grizzly Country,* "had gone through its thirteenth printing in hardcover by the mid-1980s.... Russell's work links a nineteenth-century sportsman's sense of conservation with today's more demanding environmentalism" (129). In this essay, I shall compare the discourse of the sportsman-cum-conservationist Andy Russell with the discourse of ethics and etiquette of his son Charlie Russell and begin the process of charting the Russell family's ongoing development of a grammar (including language, sound, tone, and bodily gesture) in which both to conduct and to portray their relationships with grizzly bears in the wild.

Given his historical placement (b. 1915) and literary influences, it is not surprising that in *Grizzly Country* Andy Russell blends devices associated with the realistic wild animal story,[7] the guiding/campfire storytelling tradition, and natural history with techniques such as interviews, an informative question-and-answer format, anecdotes, a metaphor-rich Western-Canadian ranch-country vernacular prose, and what is commonly called anthropomorphism. Particularly in the earlier chapters of the book, he refers to bears in fairly standard language as "the living symbol of the mountain wilderness, one giving an impression of power and royalty matched by no other" (5). He describes a large female grizzly as having "the bearing of a monarch" (5), the grizzly as the "king of all animals" (6) and its territory as its "kingdom" (5). A particular male bear is depicted as possessing royal "arrogance" (7) and "dignity" (8),[8] though Russell notes that the same bear will switch without ceremony to the role of clown, sitting down on his rump and sliding down-slope on the snow (8).[9] A ragged-looking bear with remnant tatters of his winter coat has "the look of a king burlesquing as a beggar" (15). Sometimes Russell describes a grizzly as having almost mythic – "colossal" (7) – physical proportions. In these early chapters, in the tradition of the sportsman, he uses this regal and mythic terminology – borrowed both from the tradition of the hunting guide, elevating the animal's status in order to make the hunter's kill that much more significant, and also perhaps from the tradition of the sublime[10] – supporting it by supplying the reader with weight and height measurements or sometimes length once skinned.[11]

However, Russell's bear descriptions are as many and as varied as the individuals he encounters among the species. The fifth chapter of *Grizzly Country* is entitled "In the *Society* of Grizzlies" (emphasis added), and here and elsewhere in the book bears are referred to as "associates." The *American Heritage Dictionary of the English Language,* Third edition, defines associate as

"1. A person united with another or others in an act, an enterprise, or a business; a partner or colleague. 2. A companion; a comrade. 3. One that habitually accompanies or is associated with another; an attendant circumstance." All of these meanings of "associate" apply to Russell's use of the term as applied to bears.[12] While he does not attribute "personhood" as such to bears (as in the first definition), and whereas some individual bears' association with him during his big-game guiding career would have been relatively "short-lived," nevertheless while engaged in his film enterprise he suggests that the bears are not just objects to be captured on film but subjects and even partners in an enterprise that will, he hopes, earn Andy a living to replace that lost from the closure of his guiding business and awaken society to the dangers of our excessive incursion into and destruction of grizzly country.[13] He also uses the word "associate" to describe other inter-species relationships – those between bears and tuna, caribou, Dall sheep, wolves, and coyotes – as well as co-operative inter-species relationships as "a sort of liaison" and "partnership" (86). In two or three spots in *Grizzly Country* and in interviews, Andy Russell places himself and grizzly bears in the same category – as those displaced from their home range (or in his case, from wilderness, from "grizzly country," and his guiding business) by the intrusion of oil and gas roads and activities into wilderness and wilder places (xii).

In Andy Russell's metaphors, while relationships between humans and bears are intermixed with the language of sociality and even business partnership,[14] nevertheless his conception of social and ecological relations between bears and humans is also thoroughly imbricated with the language of ethics. In one passage, he writes that a bear moving off a kill may be "honoring the wolf's desire to feed," postulating that not only do older or injured animals sometimes form partnerships for mutual survival but that there may be a sort of code of ethics and social practices among them as well. Russell comments wryly, "Man, being civilized and having highly cultivated ethics, not to say the last word in principles, has always had difficulty recognizing the ethics of others. Grizzlies also have ethics and very definite ideas of proper protocol, wherein lies the crux of the dispute" (62–63).

Breaches of etiquette and ethics are always socially dangerous situations. On one occasion, Russell tries to run bears off because they are feeding within full view of the highway and he knows someone will come along and may try to shoot them. He fires a shot into the ground near the female grizzly with cubs to get them to move away from the road. Her reaction, as he describes it, is as follows: she "swiveled on her feet and stared at me long and hard, as though to say, 'What the hell did you do a thing like that for?'" (92). According to Russell (and many other bear experts), unannounced intrusion into their terrain is regarded by bears as at best both a serious breach of etiquette and a source of embarrassment. One bear Russell accidentally surprised first ran away and then returned and charged him and his horse twice before heading up over a mountaintop. When Russell rode up to see where the bear had gone, he saw him "fleeing in the distance as though pursued by devils, and I knew this to be a proud animal not wishing to lose face by instant flight" (81). Russell draws the reader's attention to aspens scarred by bears "who have escaped the embarrassment of sudden contact or perhaps are practicing in anticipation of it" (81).

After Russell closed his big-game guiding business and turned full time to writing, photography, and filmmaking, the most significant "grammatical" change in the Russells' approaches to grizzlies during their three seasons of filming from 1961–63 was the abandonment of their guns. As long as the trio was armed, throughout their entire first season in the field they simply could not get near enough to any bear to shoot decent footage with the cameras then available. As soon as they decided midway through their second season of filming that they must leave their guns at home, access to the bears improved dramatically, as if the bears could sense the corresponding change in their attitude toward them. Andy writes:

> Reviewing our experiences, we had become more and more convinced that carrying arms was not only unnecessary in most grizzly country but was certainly no good for the desired atmosphere and proper protocol in obtaining good film records. If we were to obtain such film and fraternize successfully with the big bears, it would be better to go unarmed in most places. The mere fact of having a gun within reach, cached somewhere in a pack or a hidden holster, causes a man to act with unconscious arrogance and thus maybe to smell different or to transmit some kind of signal objectionable to bears. The armed man does not assume his proper role in association with the wild ones, a fact of which they seem instantly aware at some distance. He, being wilder than they, whether he likes to admit it or not, is instantly under more suspicion than he would encounter if unarmed. (267–68)

Not only does Russell attribute to bears characteristics many would consider anthropomorphic, he goes so far as to speculate that they also have a kind of extrasensory perception. He writes, "But as I have often suspected, animals have keen extrasensory perception, which is only latent in man through lack of use. Many times while wandering the wilds, it has seemed that animals can tell if a man is of a killing or a friendly frame of mind. It is something I have strongly sensed, but of course it is almost impossible to prove" (96). Twenty-five years later, in a 1992 interview Russell says, "I think that the animals are more sensitive to that sort of thing [people's mental attitude toward them] than we give them any credit for. I believe that there can be a mental hook-up between different kinds of animals and that of course includes people and grizzly bears" (Searle 9). Although their personal history with guiding and the respective bear projects of father and son differ significantly,[15] Charlie Russell and Maureen Enns's project in Kamchatka, Russia, the subject of *Grizzly Heart,* is prefigured in Andy Russell's 1967 *Grizzly Country.*[16] Andy writes:

> One would have to keep captive grizzlies – or better yet, tame ones running free, as did "Grizzly" Adams in the early days of California – to learn things more positive of their language. If a man could learn some of their terms, it would be possible to exchange signals with them and understand them much better. What would happen if some insult was accidentally uttered is anyone's guess. (35)

Indeed in chapter one of his second book, *Grizzly Heart: Living Without Fear Among the Brown Bears of Kamchatka* (2002), Charlie Russell comments that in order to write *his* books about bears (first the white kermode bears who live on Princess Royal Island off the West Coast of Canada, and then the grizzlies of the Russian Far East) he almost had to invent another language in which to describe human-bear interactions:[17]

> I was working on *Spirit Bear,* trying to find words for the Eden-like experience I had enjoyed on Princess Royal Island. That kind of connection with bears was something I'd dreamt of since childhood. Now that it had happened, I wanted to tell people about it in hopes of changing the relationship between humans and bears to something less hostile and rigid. I had to almost invent a new language to describe the human-wild animal relationship in ways that were not about conflict and fear. (12)

Charlie points to two particular problems with regard to the obstacles posed by the English language and its inheritance: 1) the definition of "wild" and 2) strictures against anthropomorphism:

> By definition, a wild animal is one that is fearful of humans. Simply by enjoying the company of a human, a wild animal becomes something that can no longer be accurately described that way. I struggled with this anthropocentric view because of the negative twist it put on the possibility of kinship with wild animals. Humankind believes it no longer fits into the wild, or even needs to fit. We have spent centuries perfecting a rhetoric that distances us from the idea that we are also animals, a rhetoric that closes the door to understanding what we have in common with our fellow mammals and other fauna. (12–13)

North American definitions of wild and wilderness, the residual ideology associated with the medieval concept of the Great Chain of Being, fear of insulting the gods, and other linguistic taboos associated with anthropomorphism effectively block considerations of any similarity or potential contact points between human and non-human animals.[18] While none of the Russells set out to anthropomorphize bears – that is, they did not set out to discover that bears and humans are alike, nor is that the conclusion they have reached – their sustained close contact with grizzlies spanning decades has given them the right to have their interpretations considered carefully and seriously and in some detail.

In the Prologue to *Grizzly Heart,* Charlie describes a situation in which bear-human communication hinges on mutual readings of body language and tone of voice. He opens the book with a description of a life-changing experience he had with a bear he had gotten to know very well during five years of guiding in eco-tourism in the Khutzeymateen. One day the bear started down a log toward him and Charlie decided to let her come as close as she wanted (1). This adult bear, dubbed the Mouse Creek bear after her range, was uncommonly friendly toward people, liked to entertain the eco-tourists with her antics, and had made herself into, in Charlie's words, "one of the main attractions." As she walked toward him, Charlie, "looking into her eyes," read her intention as wanting to push the frontiers of her experience with humans:

> As she made her way down the log, she moved with a swaying nonchalance. I am certain she was trying to set me at ease. I tried to accomplish the same thing in reverse by talking to her in the calmest voice I could muster. There was an uncertain look on the bear's face, and a similar look must have been on my own.
>
> Finally, she sat down beside me. After a time, she moved her paw along the log towards my hand and touched it very gently. (1–2)

Although his father also reads bears' intentions and emotions in a broad sense (anger, fury, comedy, playfulness, predatoriness), in his role first as a hunting guide and then even as a filmmaker, he is usually in a relationship with bears in which he wants something from them – head and hide for a wealthy client, the bear's photograph or representations of normal bear activity for his film. By contrast, as an eco-guide in the Khutzeymateen, Charlie is in a position both to ask less than his father of any bear (not its life certainly) and, in the scene described above, much more – namely, a shared desire to push the boundaries of bear-human relationships. Similarly, as he is able to get that much closer to bears (with not even a camera and tripod between them, and without having to watch through a lens or view-finder),[19] he is also in a position to interpret refinements of their general attitudes, emotions and moods. In the above passage, he interprets the Mouse Creek bear's swaying motion as deliberate "nonchalance" intended to set him at ease (which implies several things including a knowledge of her power relative to his). He reads her facial expression as one of uncertainty, matched by his own.[20] In a gesture reminiscent of Michelangelo's "Creation of Adam," the painting of man and God touching fingers, the Mouse Creek bear initiates gentle, curious contact with the man. Just as God animates Adam in the Michelangelo, the Mouse Creek bear animates Charlie with the desire and determination to build on that moment. If he could "prove that it [the moment of extreme trust between a bear and a man] was not a fluke… a huge shift in perception [about bears] might flow from it.… I also knew in that moment that I could not back away. What was happening was something my life had been moving towards for decades, and from which I must not swerve" (2).

This "metaphor," if that is what it is and I am not suggesting it is only a metaphor, of ethics, etiquette and protocol is one that runs through both Andy's and Charlie's work with bears (and it may have been part of Bert Riggall's thinking as well). Although anthropomorphism is often regarded with great suspicion, Andy Russell's frequent use of anthropomorphism is very complex, serving among other things to point both to zones of animality in humans and those of subjectivity in grizzly bears. That is to say, his metaphors work in both directions. Just as he uses an extended metaphor to compare a grizzly still wearing parts of his winter hide to a hobo, so too Andy metaphorizes himself as an elder in the environmentalist movement as "still rarin' up," for example. Often within the same general area of the text in which he attributes to bears emotions we like to think of as ours alone, he will flip his metaphors around and attribute to humans bear-like behaviour to the point that after a while it becomes difficult to maintain the normally strict demarcation line between our species and theirs.

In conclusion, Andy Russell, his wife Kay and their five children grew up in such proximity to wilderness and animals that they have, through habituation, taken on some aspects of the animal Others. The title of Kevin Van Tighem's article on Andy is "Still Rarin' Up" (rearing up) and Mike Gibeau, a bear scientist with Banff National Park, says that Charlie "thinks like a bear. He acts like a bear. He fundamentally understands bears" (quoted in Stevenson 2). Both Andy and Charlie have observed in bears not personhood but subjectivity, both species-based and individual, along with reasoning, curiosity, learning, play and game, adaptation and historical change,[21] character, psychosis, a sense of humour, and the desire and ability to communicate with people. Their prolonged contact with and studies of bears strongly suggest that, in the words of poet Gary Snyder, we need a new "rhetoric of ecological relationships" in order even to begin to account for grizzly ontology and epistemology.[22]

NOTES

I gratefully acknowledge the financial support and encouragement for the larger project, of which this essay is a part, of both the Canada Council for the Arts and the Banff Centre for Mountain Culture, Banff, Alberta.

1. See Christopher Manes's wonderful essay "Nature and Silence" for amplification on how humans have largely silenced the rest of nature.
2. I wonder if all this "mauling" by humans of bears is not the acting out of some profound unconscious need or desire to touch the bear, to know the bear.
3. According to Kevin Van Tighem, *Grizzly Country* "sold tens of thousands of copies and was translated into more than a dozen languages. It is still in print, more than 30 years after it first came out" (17).
4. Andy closed his guiding and outfitting business in 1960 (Van Tighem 16).
5. Andy and Kay Russell had five children: Richard (Dick), Charlie, Gordon, John, and Anne.
6. In addition to the books by Andy and Charlie, Dick Russell is a zoologist and John Russell a biologist.
7. For a list of the characteristics of the realistic wild animal story, see Ralph Lutts's article.
8. Russell does not use these metaphors pertaining to royalty only in the early part of the book. See page 266 as well. Moreover, it is worth noting Maureen Enns's remarks in *GH* that during her own bear project, initiated before she met Charlie, she encountered a female grizzly whom she found to be both beautiful and triumphant and promptly dubbed her "Queen of the Rockies" (11).
9. It is interesting to speculate what the play *King Lear* might be like had its titular character been able to switch roles so easily.
10. Here is a brief passage of Burke on the sublime as it relates to animals: "SUBLIMITY includes, besides the idea of danger, the idea of danger [sic], the idea of power also. Pleasure follows the will, and we are generally affected with it by many things of a force inferior to our own; but pain is always inflicted by a power in some way superior. Strength, violence, pain, and terror are therefore ideas that occupy the mind together. The sublimity of wild animals is due to their power; and the power of princes is not unmixed with terror, so that we address them as

"dread majesty'" (www.publicbookshelf.com/public_html/Outline_of_Great_Books_Volume_I/edmundbur_bhi.html).

11. Charlie Russell writes that "Hunting guides describe bears as ferocious, unpredictable, and savage predators. They tell one horrifying story after another about people being torn apart. The victims are always those who approached the encounter poorly armed. Then the guides move on to recount countless acts of sportsman bravery: tales of real men stopping huge angry bears just short of the barrel of their guns. They keep it up until their clients are shaking in their boots, barely able to muster the courage to face the dreadful foe. I suppose when these hunting clients actually do kill a bear, they feel tremendously powerful, as if they have collected all the formidable power of the bear into themselves" (8).

12. Additional research will be needed to discover whether Russell applied the term "associate" to bears while he was still in the sport hunting business or whether he adopted the term only after he discovered common cause with the bears in being forced out of grizzly country by the oil and gas industry. Nevertheless, what I am examining here is the book he published in 1967, seven years after he stopped guiding, not his use of the term throughout his life.

13. Andy writes, "To kill an animal that has stood for pictures is more than unjustified: it is the mark of ignorance, lack of appreciation, and a most unforgivable breech of ethics" (*Grizzly Country* 210).

14. Russell himself was in partnership with his father-in-law Bert Riggall in the guiding business. Andy went to work for Bert as bronc-buster, wrangler, and packer at the age of 19 in 1935. In 1938, he married one of the boss's two daughters, Kay Riggall, and in 1946 when Bert retired, Kay and Andy took over the guiding business and stayed in it until 1960. The notion of intermingling business and the environment is these days, justifiably, a suspect one, and yet at the same time such ecotheorists as Paul Hawken have written extensively about the potential implicit in blending the two.

15. For instance, although he became a professional guide very early in his life, after one year Charlie Russell gave it up: "In my late teens I became a hunting guide for so-called 'big game.' The first clue that I wasn't cut out for it was when I started wondering how my clients would like the chase if they were the ones being hunted. I told Dad that I liked animals more than wealthy hunters, and ended my career as a professional guide after one year" (*Grizzly Heart* 8).

16. As this essay focuses on the work of a father and son (who therefore share the same surname), please note that the book by the father, Andy Russell, is *Grizzly Country*, which is also the name of the documentary film made by both of them together with another son, Dick Russell, and the book by Charlie Russell, is *Grizzly Heart*. At some points in the essay, I refer to them by their first names for the sake of clarity.

17. In *Grizzly Heart,* Charlie alludes briefly to his childhood "wars" and "tug-of-war" with school, where his self-confidence about his intelligence and abilities was seriously eroded. Ironically or not, this man who struggled with Language Arts in junior high school went on to become an expert in interspecies communication.

18. For an excellent analysis of and critique of scientific strictures against anthropomorphism, see Pamela J. Asquith and Emanuela Cenami Spada.

19. Credit is also due to the unique personality and life history of the Mouse Creek bear.

20. It is important to note that not everyone with an intimate knowledge of bears shares Charlie's belief that one can read the expressions on bears' faces. For instance, in his essay "Black Bears, Poem Bears," former park warden Sid Marty writes, "It takes a lot of field study to read the body language of a bear. His face is a mask, as writer Edward Hoagland has pointed out, that tells you little about his inner emotions, though if he (or she) bristles up, flattens the ears, and runs at you – watch out" (162). The paragraph continues with a brief grammar of bears' vocalizations, gestures and other signs. Later in the same essay, Marty writes, poetically, "A bear is like a wild man of the woods, his expression frozen from facing into solitude" (174).

21. Charlie Russell states that "Vitaly Nikolaenko, the veteran bear expert up at Kronotskiy Preserve, had told me that bears can pass down their fears to cubs for several generations as a way of keeping them from having to learn the fear first-hand in the face of actual danger" (*Grizzly Heart* 100).

22 In his book *Grateful Prey* Robert Brightman writes, "Bears are understood by many Crees as exceptional animals possessing intelligence equaling or exceeding that of humans. It is said that bears, for example, understand spoken Cree, a competence not conventionally generalized to other animals. Consequently, the behavior of bears is likely to be interpreted by Crees as manifesting this intelligence in ways that are not salient to non-Cree observers. Crees are likelier than whites to ascribe a studied

deliberateness to the doings of bears. Anything that bears do is likely to be apprehended as a particular token occurrence of a conventional type of ursine acumen" (32).

WORKS CITED

ASQUITH, Pamela J. "Why Anthropomorphism Is *Not* Metaphor: Crossing Concepts and Cultures in Animal Behavior Studies." *Anthropormorphism, Anecdotes, and Animals.* Ed. Robert W. Mitchell, Nicholas S. Thompson, H. Lyn Miles. SUNY series in Philosophy and Biology. General ed. David Edward Shaner. Albany, NY: State University of New York Press, 1997. 22–34.

BRIGHTMAN, Robert. *Grateful Prey: Rock Cree Human-Animal Relationships.* Regina: Canadian Plains Research Center, 2002.

CENAMI Spada, Emanuela. "Amorphism, Mechanomorphism, and Anthropomorphism." *Anthropormorphism, Anecdotes, and Animals.* Ed. Robert W. Mitchell, Nicholas S. Thompson, H. Lyn Miles. SUNY series in Philosophy and Biology. General ed. David Edward Shaner. Albany, NY: State University of New York Press, 1997. 37–49.

LUTTS, Ralph H. "The Realistic Wild Animal Story." *Literature of Nature: An International Sourcebook.* Ed. Patrick Murphy. Contributing eds. Terry Gifford and Katsunori Yamazoto. Chicago and London: Fitzroy Dearborn, 1998. 109–15.

MANES, Christopher. "Nature and Silence." *The Ecocriticism Reader: Landmarks in Literary Ecology.* Ed. Cheryll Glotfelty and Harold Fromm. Athens and London: University of Georgia Press, 1996. 15–29.

MARTY, Sid. *Switchbacks: True Stories from the Canadian Rockies.* Toronto: McClelland & Stewart, 1999.

MELNYK, George. *The Literary History of Alberta,* Vol. 1. Edmonton: University of Alberta Press, 1998.

———. *The Literary History of Alberta,* Vol. 2. Edmonton: University of Alberta Press, 1999.

RUSSELL, Andy. *Grizzly Country.* New York: Lyons Press, 1967.

RUSSELL, Charlie, and Maureen Enns, with Fred Stenson. *Grizzly Heart: Living Without Fear Among the Brown Bears of Kamchatka.* Toronto: Random House, 2002.

SEARLE, R., and T. Tanaka. "Interview with Andy Russell." Interview conducted while filming Andy Russell, Sept. 1992. Unpublished typescript. RUSSELL FONDS M153/554.

SERJEANTSON, R. W. "The Passions and Animal Language, 1540–1700." *Journal of the History of Ideas* 62.3 (2001): 425–44.

SNYDER, Gary. "Tawny Grammar." *The Practice of the Wild: Essays by Gary Snyder.* San Francisco: North Point Press, 1990. 48–77.

STEVENSON, Mark. "The Bear Whisperer: The Relationship Between Humans and Bears is Marked by Fear: That's the problem, says naturalist Charlie Russell, who spends much of his time walking, swimming and rubbing noses..." *Globe and Mail* [Toronto] 5 Oct. 2002: 1–2.

VAN TIGHEM, Kevin. "Still Rarin' Up." *Outdoor Canada* 28.5 (2000): 12–17, 72, 74.

10

THE DOOMED GENRE: MYRNA KOSTASH AND THE LIMITS OF NON-FICTION

LISA GREKUL

In an article that appeared in a recent issue of *Quill and Quire* – "In praise of journalism: Why the 'creative non-fiction' label obscures the real value of true stories about the world" (2005) – Myrna Kostash makes a surprising about-face with regard to "creative non-fiction," repudiating the value of the genre that she has spent the better part of her career defending. Readers who are familiar with Kostash's work know her as an overtly politicized voice in Canadian Prairie literature, outspoken in her views as a third-generation Ukrainian Canadian, a feminist, and a New Left socialist. But for years, "whenever [she] could," she also "championed the cause of 'creative non-fiction'" (Kostash, "In Praise" 14). Many of the books that comprise her oeuvre – including *All of Baba's Children* (1977), *Long Way From Home: The Story of the Sixties Generation in Canada* (1980), *The Doomed Bridegroom: A Memoir* (1998), and *The Next Canada: In Search of the Future Nation* (2000) – could be, and indeed have been, termed "creative non-fiction." In lectures, articles, and workshops, moreover, she has persistently argued for the value of the "creative non-fiction" genre.[1]

Not alone[2] in practicing and promoting a craft that is inherently slippery – though not without defining characteristics – Kostash admits that settling on a single term is no easy task. "Creative non-fiction," she says, can also be classified as "literary non-fiction, literary journalism, [or] creative documentary" ("In Praise" 14). In her introduction to *Going Some Place: Creative Non-fiction Across Canada* (2002), Lynne Van Luven concurs, arguing that "the genre includes poetic personal journals, meditations, memoirs, activist personal reportage, autobiography, personal essays on being an outsider, historical and literary travelogues, tributes to a particular person, celebrations of a distinctive place, and explorations of the past" (ii). Clearly, "creative non-fiction" is complexly hybrid – and yet there is ample evidence to suggest that it has become the accepted term for a recognizable literary tradition. Consider, for example, the Edna Staebler Award for Creative Non-fiction (aimed at texts that are "literary rather than journalistic," by writers who "[do] not merely give information, but intimately shar[e] an experience with the reader by telling a factual story with the devices of fiction, original research, well-crafted interpretive writing, personal discovery or experience, the creative use of language or approach to the subject matter, dialogue, and narrative") or the Pittsburgh-based journal *Creative Nonfiction* (which publishes work by writers who "employ the diligence of a reporter, the shifting voices and viewpoints of a novelist, the refined wordplay of a poet and the analytical modes of the essayist") or the recent special issue of *Women's Studies* devoted to "creative nonfiction."[3]

But despite the fact that "creative non-fiction" has been embraced in some circles, the extent to which it has been marginalized in the Canadian literary mainstream is amply evinced by the genre's long list of institutional slightings, outlined by Kostash in an earlier article, "The crisis of non-fiction," published in *Canadian Issues* (2003). As she points out, with the "glamourization of Can Lit and the Celebrity Novel," fiction has come to dominate "the literary festivals, creative writing programs and schools, the sexy prizes, the book clubs, translation grants, [and] international Canadian Studies conferences" (25).[4] Forums, she says, that one might expect to have a "lively curiosity" in creative non-fiction, such as "the book review sections of newspapers and journals," are "vastly more interested in the cult of the novel" (25). Part of the problem, well illustrated by the dearth of critical work on her own writing,[5] is that genres of non-fiction are rarely taught, studied, or written about by literary scholars (25). The "real crisis," though – at least according to Kostash – lies in the "apparent indifference of the large majority of readers... to the national discourses on society that circulate" in creative non-fiction (25). "How many times," she asks, "have I heard otherwise thoughtful people, literate citizens, claim never to read non-fiction as a matter of some principle: they find it too 'depressing' or 'fatiguing' to read at the end of a stressful day" (25).

In her 2005 *Quill and Quire* article, then, acknowledging that writers of "creative non-fiction" have made at least a few inroads in the Canadian literary institution ("[w]riting programs have opened up to non-fiction... substantial prizes are distributed to its writers, literary journals regularly feature 'creative non-fiction'" ["In praise" 14]), Kostash nonetheless finds herself reconsidering the genre's nomenclature. For her, CanLit's partial and reluctant embrace of her craft is a case of "too little, too late." Midway through the article – after she explains that, "since the literary establishment turned up its nose at non-fiction, we could only establish our right to be treated as equal to fiction writers and poets if we called ourselves *creative* non-fiction writers" – she unceremoniously drops the first part of the label. Fed up with having to "play" to the literary mainstream's love of fiction, she says,

> I now believe that "creative non-fiction" is an overused term for writing that is essentially narrative prose (magazine writers have been writing the stuff for generations), and when we use it we exhibit the "cultural cringe" of non-fiction writers who are ashamed their roots are showing. The genre of non-fiction books began in journalism, with the writer as witness to his or her world, and it's time we reclaimed our origins. (14)

And so the genre Kostash once referred to as "creative non-fiction" becomes, for her, "'non-fiction,' without any qualification or tarting up" (14).

What are we to make of Kostash's change of heart? Do generic labels really matter, and can they be decided on once and for all, when we are talking about an inherently hybrid genre? What is at stake for writers, and for readers, in Kostash's call for "non-fiction" to be recognized as such? When we, as readers, identify a text as "non-fiction," *tout court*, what expectations do we bring to our interpretation of it? Are they different from those we would bring to an ostensibly more "creative" genre? And, most importantly (for this discussion at least), how do we approach a "non-fiction" text that explores the complexities of diasporic subjectivity – itself a largely imagined state?

Bloodlines: A Journey Into Eastern Europe, her 1993 work, can be examined in light of both Kostash's *Quill and Quire* recantation article and recent genre-based life writing scholarship. The primary goal of this paper is to explore how Kostash's identity may change when we categorize the text as "non-fiction," and how her diasporic identity is informed by the genre in which she writes.[6] *Bloodlines*, the first of the two books she has written about her travels to Central and Eastern Europe (*The Doomed Bridegroom: A Memoir* was published five years later, in 1998), closely "fits" the description of "non-fiction,"[7] and I want to focus on a text about this "other" part of the world that most clearly supports Kostash's claims about "non-fiction" (that it is "narrative prose"; that the genre "began in journalism, with the writer as witness to his or her world"; that it involves "lobbing arguments into the public square" ["In praise" 14]).

As Laurie McNeill explains, in her introduction to the 2005 issue of *Life Writing* devoted to "Reconsidering Genre," the burgeoning of life writing scholarship in the 1970s and 1980s produced "genre-based definitions" that allowed writers and critics not only to justify life writing as "literary texts worthy of study" but also to "make clear how [the] texts should be read" (McNeill xii). Referring to Carolyn Miller's theorization of genres as "social actions" – as "recognizable responses," that is, "to recurring situations" – McNeill notes that genre has come to be seen by many scholars as an integral tool for "understanding the actions people imagine performing when they create texts based on their lives" (McNeill xiii).[8] Genre, within this model, teaches us how to recognize a text's function; how to detect the social "work" that its writer has set out to do. Given that generic "fuzziness" is, as Peter Medway suggests, a hallmark of life writing ("[p]erhaps," he says, "there are degrees of genreness, from tightly defined... to baggy and indeterminate" [Medway quoted in McNeill xiv]),[9] sifting through a text in search of formal properties that will justify the affixing of a generic label seems unproductive unless we give concentrated thought to the *purpose* of that label. Though "genres are still expected to display characteristic textual forms... [i]dentifying patterns of text format, syntactical and lexical choice, and discursive ordering [...] is no longer considered sufficient for pinning down the genre" (Medway quoted in McNeill xiii).[10] Rather, each "fuzzy" form of life writing fulfills its unique function ("at particular places and times, for particular authors" [McNeill xiii]) because readers can and do "identify 'genreness,' and all the expectations and cultural freight attached to specific forms, without forcing a text into one labeled box" (McNeill xv). "The point," according to G. Thomas Couser, "is to interrogate [the text's] *form* as a means of understanding its *function* and its *force*: how particular genres encode or reinforce particular values in ways that may shape culture and history" (Couser 129–30). Form matters, in short, only insofar as its function is understood and agreed upon between writer and reader.

In terms of subject matter, *Bloodlines* explores Kostash's complex engagements with the people, the politics, and the histories of various countries in Eastern Europe. The text grows out of six separate trips she made to this part of the world over an eleven-year period, beginning in 1982 and ending in 1991. Divided into four chapters, each focused on a single country to which she made repeat visits (Czechoslovakia, Yugoslavia, Poland, and Ukraine), the narrative is not without structure, but it follows no linear chronology of her travels, nor does it cohere around a clearly discernible plot. As Kostash explains in her introduction, "I did not travel haphazardly. I had a plan" (1).

> Initially, my idea was to interview writers of my generation, bred by the events of the 1960s, who were writing from within the opposition in their respective societies. I was most interested in how they coped, as creative people, with the political demands of their situation. [...] I limited myself to Slavic Central and Eastern Europe (excluding, therefore, Rumania, Hungary, and Bulgaria) as I felt, in some still unformulated way, that my project was "about" ethnicity. My third traveller's hat was that of the New Left socialist. [...] I wanted to see for myself how "actually existing socialism" looked and wondered how this might affect my own political beliefs. (1–2)

And yet, even as she admits that "[t]his all sounds neat and tidy," Kostash is upfront about the extent to which she "lost control" of her plan (2). Forced to question her existing assumptions about Eastern Europe, to do a "prodigious amount of reading," and to learn new languages (she "learned to speak Ukrainian" [2] and became fluent in a "generic Slav speech" that included "a little bit of everything – Serbo-Croat, Slovene, Slovak, Polish and Ukrainian" [3]), she found that, "each time [she] traveled [she] was turned inside out again" (2). Not surprisingly, the chaotic structure of the text – its constant temporal and geographical movement – reflects the "turbulent" and "upsetting" nature of her travels (2).

Given the subject matter of the text, *Bloodlines* most transparently belongs to the travelogue genre, though critics who have worked on the text quibble about this label. Eva-Marie Kröller, for example, broadly describes the text as a "travel book" but then qualifies her statement by specifying that *Bloodlines* is a work of "leftist tourism" (354). Smaro Kamboureli, acknowledging that the text resembles travelogue, cautions that it "[does] not fit *neatly* into the tradition of travelogues" (at least not those by authors who unselfconsciously occupy the position of the privileged traveler) because Kostash is rarely unaware of the politics of her foreign-ness (Kamboureli 167, my emphasis). And yet there are many points in the text where the author plays the unmistakable part of the apolitical tourist, observing her surroundings for the sheer delight of it ("we pass… bare-footed youths whacking at the weeds in the field-strips of corn, wheat and beans, the crops gaily broadcast with red poppies" [Kostash, *Bloodlines* 74]; "[t]ypical of European cemeteries, Lychakivsky is a very pleasant place for a stroll" [178]). And given that the narrative opens with a scene that is "normative" to travel writing, it clearly borrows some conventions from the travelogue genre. The first chapter, focused on Czechoslovakia, begins with the foreigner being initiated into her journey (Kamboureli 172) as Kostash receives advice from Zdena, a Czech-in-exile: "I am to telephone her from the continent. I am to ask her how the weather is. If she tells me it is cold and wet, I am not to go to Prague or attempt any contacts there. If she tells me the weather is fine, I may proceed" (Kostash, *Bloodlines* 6). This conversation marks the point at which Kostash, a "Westerner" unaccustomed to the need for such secrecy, faces the threshold to the foreign and repressive "East," but the scene also hints at her determination to cross over, regardless of risk. When she calls her friend Zdena from Prague, and when Zdena's son answers the phone, giving her the ambiguous news that the weather is "[n]ot bad," Kostash's response is unequivocal: "I decide I will go to Prague" (6). Kostash's decision to proceed, despite the ambiguity of the son's weather report and the possible danger it foreshadows, sets the stage for the rest of the book. From the get-go, just as her plans are disrupted and she is consequently forced to improvise alternatives so too does the narrative of her travels proceed without an apparent chronological or geographical logic. But while the travelogue aspects of *Bloodlines* are neither "neat" nor "tidy," they are nonetheless present in the text.

Travelogue it may resemble; but *Bloodlines* also has much in common with academic writing – historical scholarship, more specifically. The text is rife with moments, for instance, in which Kostash draws attention to the fact that she is well-versed in traditions of travel writing about Eastern Europe ("Prague," she writes, "is the Paris of the East – so say travel guides and travelers before me" [6]; "Kalemegdan Park, approached from town centre along the old Stamboul road, was observed by Rebecca West in 1937 to be 'the special glory of Belgrade'" [56]). The entire book, moreover, is framed by devices that construct Kostash as an authority on the histories, political structures, and cultural nuances of the countries that she visits. *Bloodlines* is prefaced by a map of Eastern Europe (n.p.)[11] and it concludes with some seven pages' worth of "notes" in which the author lists the scholarly sources she consulted and provides detailed comments on their usefulness. Additionally, each chapter begins with a "snapshot" of major historical events that took place in the country during the period following the Second World War. ("Czechoslovakia" opens, for example, with "1946: *Communists win 38 per cent of popular vote in free elections* 1948: *taking advantage of trade union support during political crisis, Communists seize power* 1949–52: *show trials of Communist 'renegades'*" [5]). Reinforcing her authoritative position vis-à-vis the subject matter of her book, Kostash textures every chapter with historical references, background information on local politics, explanations of major movements, figures, and events. The places she visits and the conversations she has with locals are always burdened for Kostash by the history that precedes them. To visit an Orthodox church is to be reminded that "[t]his church, and all the nations that have embraced it, have been 'eastern' since 285 A.D. when Diocletian, himself a Dalmatian, divided the Roman Empire into two administrative units, the western part governed from Rome, the eastern one from Constantinople" (80). To chat with Zdenek about his childhood summer holidays in Uzhhorod is to recall that "[i]n Slovakia during the war, the Nazis recruited local Ukrainians into a special brigade formed for the purpose of assaulting the local Slovak villages" (30). As readers, we have the sense that, through these and countless other "informative" moments, we are reading history lessons with Kostash as teacher. She wants to learn, and teach readers, about the first-hand experience of living in this part of the world. As a result, *Bloodlines* contains countless journalistic interviews and excerpts of reported conversations between Kostash and the people she meets. Each chapter offers a veritable litany of names (she usually uses first names only and sometimes changes names to protect individuals' identities). But her brief and superficial "reports" of the individuals she meets achieve an important objective in the text: they illustrate the extent to which she travels as a journalist, gathering as much information as she can in a short period of time, writing concise "stories," much like a newspaper reporter, that hinge on key, pithy quotations.

In part a travelogue, then, in part a history "textbook," in part a work of journalism, *Bloodlines* is also autobiographical, since the only consistently recurring, multi-dimensional "character" in the book is Kostash herself. As she takes on the roles of traveler, observer, recorder, and translator, everything we learn in *Bloodlines* about Eastern Europe is not only filtered through her (raising questions about the reliability of her observations) but also, ultimately, *about* her. The loose structure of the narrative allows Kostash to insert herself into her observations of Eastern Europe as well as her discussions of its history and its people. Throughout the text, we find examples of what Kamboureli calls "circuitous" narration (178): the chapter focused on Poland, for instance, opens not in Poland at all but in "Nafplion, Greece, 1981" (Kostash, *Bloodlines* 110), with Kostash watching Polish demonstrations on the television news. Then, reporting from "Gdansk, 1984" (112), she reflects on the strike that took place four years prior, during which "a wooden cross was embedded in the ground on the spot where four striking workers had died in December 1970" (112). And in the next section of the chapter, she is "at Harvard University" (when, she does not say) interviewing a professor of Polish literature who was involved in "clandestine publishing in pre-Solidarity Poland" (115). The disjointed pattern, marked by Kostash's movement in time and place, opens textual spaces for Kostash to embed diary-like reports of her travels with her personal memories of the recent or relatively distant past, as well as interior ruminations on the situations she finds herself in. In Prague, as she attends synagogue with Jiri and notices a large number of Americans in the congregation, she interrupts her account of the service to reflect on "*relatives*" in the diaspora, the "*ones who got away*" and "*saved the bloodlines*" (16). Later, as she and Jiri eat lunch in the Jewish hall, she again interrupts the account with recollections of her grandmother's cooking: "I ache with the familiarity of this soup, ladled out into a flat-bottomed basin, the pattern of the china washed by the clear, yellowish, fatty brother, thin egg noodles afloat like a water plant. It is my baba's chicken soup" (17). Just as her experiences are always burdened by the history preceding them, so too are they evocative of personal memory.

But it is in the Ukraine portion of the narrative that the autobiographical nature of *Bloodlines* becomes most pronounced: the eastern-most country she visits, it is also the country in which she is most personally invested.[12] Fittingly, Ukraine represents the furthest point that she reaches, both literally and emotionally, during her journeys "into" Eastern Europe. Admitting that "for a Ukrainian Canadian Ukraine is not a country like other countries" because "[e]verything about it is 'loaded,' freighted with meaning" (168), Kostash is not unaware of the shift in attitude that her ancestral homeland brings about in her. Family stories and childhood memories appear more frequently in this chapter than in any other: writing about Cossack history, she remembers being ten years old and seeing pictures of "*these funny men*" who "*live in some never-never land, east of the sunrise, without children, without women... in an exotic summer camp that is both dangerous (all those swords) and entertaining (the belly laughs)*" (224). Later, still riffing on the Cossack motif, she recalls folk dancing in a church basement: "*girls in a line at the very back, mincing girlishly with little pointy steps and holding our hands coquettishly; the boys doing a Cossack dance*" (229). And as she prepares to meet her family members in Ukraine, reflections on Taras Shevchenko, national poet of Ukraine, become entwined with thoughts about family history ("when Taras imagined a free Ukraine, he never imagined someone like me: granddaughter of a Ukrainian peon upended from the 'eternal' village and cast upon the North American plain to breed a second generation of Anglophones practising professions in the cities" [233]). Importantly, too, Kostash leaves readers with a description of her final trip to Ukraine that includes images of wheat and bread, both sacred in Ukrainian culture, which are linked to the future and invoked as symbols of optimism. She notes that the "Ukrainian lands seen from the air in June are green, green, and green again"; from the country's black loam spring "the beginnings of bread" (249). Less an ending than a new beginning – and very much in keeping with the autobiographical nature of the text (since, of course, the author's "life story" is far from complete) – *Bloodlines'* conclusion suggests that Kostash has at last, in Ukraine, planted the seeds for an ongoing relationship with and connection to Eastern Europe.

Ultimately, because *Bloodlines* borrows conventions from the travelogue tradition, historical scholarship, journalistic writing, and autobiography, the genre of the text can be labelled (for lack of a more precise phrase) as "mostly non-fiction": that is to say, while its form is clearly hybrid, the book exclusively hybridizes non-fictional genres and therefore presents itself as a representation of reality. To be sure, readers cannot ignore the active, not to mention artful, role that Kostash plays in shaping the narrative; trained as we are to recognize that the author always mediates between the "real" world and her construction of it, we are necessarily skeptical about the fullness, accuracy, and reliability of Kostash's writing. But at the same time, as Laurie McNeill argues, "life writing requires a level of generic buy-in" (McNeill xv). By omitting elements that we would recognize as belonging to the realm of fiction (an invented and clearly discernible plot, an invented and fully developed cast of characters), Kostash asks and expects us to "buy into" *Bloodlines* as a "true" story, or a series of "true" stories. This, for her – if we revisit the subtitle of her *Quill and Quire* article ("Why the 'creative non-fiction' label obscures the real value of true stories about the world") – is both the function and value of "non-fiction": it tells the "truth" in a way that a more fictional genre cannot. If we recall, too, Kostash's suggestion that "non-fiction" involves "lobbing arguments into the public square" ("In Praise" 14), we begin to see that all of her generic choices are intended to support a single "argument" about the relation between her "self," as a second-generation Ukrainian Canadian especially, and the "other" world from which her grandparents emigrated. Kostash wants to show readers that, despite being born and raised in Canada and despite continuing to make her home there as an adult, she also belongs in Eastern Europe

At a glance, this reading of the text might appear to contradict arguments advanced by other scholars. Kamboureli, for example, says that "the trope of self-representation is employed in order to... question authenticity" (167); *Bloodlines,* she says, "does not posit the history it examines in the shape of a historical continuum that has an identifiable origin" (169). Because Kostash "approaches the sites of her study not as stable historical grounds that will easily fit within the ideological matrix of her values, but as spaces that are inherently fluid and therefore capable of challenging her assumptions about them as well as about her own subjectivity," *Bloodlines* "lacks a thesis that has to be proven true" (169). In a similar vein, Kröller notes that the text "constantly challenges its own assertions" as Kostash "frequently questions her own readings" of her experiences in Eastern Europe (358). And in a previous analysis of the book I suggest that *Bloodlines* is less about finding or coming home than about the "open-ended, perpetual search for home" (Grekul 201). We all conclude, in other words, that after journeying "into" Eastern Europe, Kostash feels no less ambivalent about her relation to this part of the world, no less confused about why she is attached to it or whether she has a right to call it "home."

Vijay Agnew argues in her introduction to *Diaspora, Memory, and Identity: A Search for Home* (2005) that "the individual living in the diaspora experiences a dynamic tension every day between living 'here' and remembering 'there,' between memories of places of origin and entanglements with places of residence, and between the metaphorical and physical home" (Agnew 4). Salman Rushdie, in *Imaginary Homelands* (1991), argues that diasporic writers are "haunted by some sense of loss, some urge to reclaim, to look back, even at the risk of being mutated into pillars of salt" (10). But he insists too that "if we do look back, we must also do so in the knowledge – which gives rise to profound uncertainties – that our physical alienation from [the homeland] almost inevitably means that we will not be capable of reclaiming precisely the thing that was lost": we will, in short, "create fictions, not actual cities or village, but invisible ones, imaginary homelands" (10).[13] Stuart Hall makes a similar point in "Cultural Identity and Diaspora" (2003) when he says that the past is "always constructed through memory, fantasy, narrative, and myth" (237). In diasporic texts, according to Hall, images of "*imaginary* reunification" offer a "way of imposing an *imaginary* coherence on the experience of dispersal and fragmentation, which is the history of all enforced diasporas" (235, my emphasis). The imagination, in other words, is a necessary component of the diasporic writer's repertoire.

Kostash's desire to impose "imaginary coherence" on her experience of diaspora is nowhere more evident than at a turning point, late in the text, where she recognizes and embraces her origins. The revelation happens during a conversation that she has with Ukrainian dissident Leonid Pliushch (Kostash, *Bloodlines* 189). After listening to him speak at a public meeting in Edmonton, Kostash asks Pliushch, "How is it that, although we come from opposite ends of the world and we do not speak each other's language and I cannot begin to imagine your experience, still I feel close to you?" Pliushch replies, "Because, in the end, we come from the same village" (190). Looking back on his words, midway through her chapter on Ukraine, Kostash says, "[s]o there it finally was: the Ukrainians and I: kin" (190) – and, near the end of the book, returning the metaphor of "the village," she says, "I've been to the village. It lives, and it is ours" (233). A place that cannot be found on a map and that exists outside of time, "the village" becomes the originary site at which all of Ukraine's history collapses. For Kostash to identify "the village" as the point of common origins for all Ukrainians is not only to lay claim to the collective past of the Ukrainian people but to reconstruct her "self" as part of Ukraine's present and future (since the village "*lives*," not *lived*, and it is "*ours*," not *theirs*). And yet because this epiphany hinges entirely on Kostash's ability to *imagine* the village, it reinforces the notion that diasporic identity is just that – a function of the imagination.

The epiphany further underscores the fictional function of Kostash's narrative about her journey "into" Eastern Europe. Although she actually heard Pliushch speak in 1977, long before she began traveling to Eastern Europe, she waits until her chapter on "Ukraine" to share her thoughts on "the village," framing the better portion of the text as build-up to this important moment. So *Bloodlines*, from the start, takes the shape of a quest whose details are, in a sense, irrelevant. Where she actually travels matters little, since – long before she set out – she had an imaginary destination in mind. The experiences she chooses to narrate in the text matter even less, given that the outcome of her journey "into" Eastern Europe was determined some fifteen years before she published the text ("the Ukrainians and I: kin" [190]). And so the "true" story of Kostash's experiences in Eastern Europe both begins and ends with a fiction: in choosing not to narrate her return to Canada in the final pages of *Bloodlines* – remaining instead, narratively speaking, in Ukraine – Kostash asks readers to believe that she continues to reside in the village, a place that no longer exists, if it ever did. The village "lives" only in her imagination; to believe that she has found the village, readers must acknowledge the inherently creative aspects of her diasporic identity.

It is how she expresses here ethnicity within the genre that offers an answer to how that genre may be categorized. That genre matters to Kostash is obvious from her rallying cry to other "non-fiction" writers ("it's time we reclaimed our origins" ["In praise" 14]), and genre should matter to readers too because, as McNeill argues, we "need to 'pin down,' to name, what we read or watch or hear, in order to comprehend the work these texts do" (xiii). But Kostash's call for her work to be categorized as "non-fiction" ultimately says as much about her desire to reclaim *ethnic* origins than it does about the journalistic roots of her craft. Referring to *Bloodlines* as "non-fiction" becomes, for the author, an act of wish-fulfillment; as readers, however, we need a different generic label, one that helps us gain firmer interpretive ground in terms of understanding the actual function and the real value of the text. Kostash was right the first time – right, that is, when she championed "*creative* non-fiction," a term whose "fuzziness" more accurately describes the "fuzzy" and fraught nature of living, literally, in one world and, figuratively, between two. Her story, as she tells it in *Bloodlines*, is at once "true" and not true, "real" and not real: to call it "non-fiction" is to miss the ways in which its creative elements enable Kostash to redefine identity, reconstitute community, and re-imagine home. To inhabit "the village," she must first invent it; to transcend the limitations of reality, she must – and does – embrace the transformative power of the fictional.

NOTES

1. On March 11, 2004, for example, at the University of Calgary (Nickle Arts Museum), Kostash gave a public reading entitled "From Two Hills to Byzantium: A Journey in Creative Non-fiction." In 2004, at the Banff Centre, and in 2005, at the University of Alberta, she taught workshops focused on creative non-fiction.

2. Her cohort of like-minded creative non-fiction writers includes Erna Paris, Susan Crean, Marni Jackson, Gordon Laird, Stan Persky, and Brian Fawcett, to name a few (Kostash "Crisis" 25).

3. See the following website for more information on the Edna Staebler Award: <library.wlu. ca/internet/prizes/staebler.html>. See, too, Creative Nonfiction's website at <http://www.creativenonfiction.org/thejournal/whatiscnf.htm>. The special issue of *Women's Studies* is 33:6 (2004).

4. In "Genreing: A Personal, Autocritical, Confessional essay" (2005), Helen M. Buss refers to creative non-fiction writers as "almost an oppressed minority given the dominance of the NOVEL as the most honoured art form in [Canada]" (144).

5. While Kostash's books are often reviewed, little scholarly work has been done on them. For example, only three scholars (Smaro Kamboureli, Eva-Marie Kröller, and I) have worked on *Bloodlines*, though it was published almost fifteen years ago.

6. Jana Evans Braziel and Anita Mannur point out that, "[i]n the last decade, theorizations of diaspora have emerged in area studies, ethnic studies, and cultural studies as a major site of contestation." They caution against using the term as a "catch-all phrase to speak of and for all movements, however privileged, and for all dislocations, even symbolic ones," because "some forms of travel are tourism" (3). My assumption is that Kostash explores her diasporic identity in *Bloodlines*: she does not travel as a tourist but rather as a member of an ethnic community whose history has been shaped by "reluctant scattering" (Gilroy 123). As a Ukrainian Canadian, Kostash shares with other diasporic Ukrainians "a history of dispersal, myths/memories of the homeland... desire for eventual return... and a collective identity importantly defined by this relationship" (Safran, paraphrased in Clifford 247). James Clifford's relatively broad definition of diaspora is instructive here: he suggests that the term encompasses "a whole range of phenomena that encourage multi-locale attachments, and dwelling and traveling within and across nations" (249).

7. As I have argued in *Leaving Shadows* (169–92), *The Doomed Bridegroom* radically blurs the distinction between what is "real" and what is "imagined," making it easy (too easy) prey for the critic who wants to resist categorizing it as "non-fiction." In this text, I have said, "Kostash allows herself the freedom to explore – formally as well as thematically – how her long-term obsession with Eastern and Southern Europe has been defined by the inextricability of reality and fantasy" (172). Indeed, as she narrates her affairs with six "lovers" (one of whom she never met), Kostash embraces "the role of the storyteller, whose imagination is as limitless as it is lively" (172).
8. The original citation, in McNeill's essay, is Miller 151.
9. The original citation is Medway 141.
10. The original citation is Medway 123.
11. Kröller argues that "[u]p-to-date maps are indispensable in travel books about Eastern Europe, given the numerous and extensive territorial changes in the area" (359), so the map that Kostash provides can be read not only as a device that lends scholarly weight to the text but also as a convention of the travelogue genre.
12. See my discussion of *Bloodlines* in *Leaving Shadows: Literature in English by Canada's Ukrainians* (2005).
13. The original reads "our physical alienation from India," as Rushdie is writing specifically about diasporic Indian writers, but because his point is applicable to all diasporic writers, I have replaced "India" with "homeland."

WORKS CITED

AGNEW, Vijay. "Introduction." *Diaspora, Memory, and Identity: A Search for Home.* Ed. Vijay Agnew. Toronto: University of Toronto Press, 2005. 3–17.

BRAZIEL, Jana Evans, and Anita Mannur. "Nation, Migration, Globalization: Points of Contention in Diaspora Studies." *Theorizing Diaspora.* Ed. Jana Evans Braziel and Anita Mannur. Oxford: Blackwell, 2003. 1–22.

BUSS, Helen M. "Genreing: a personal, autocritical, confessional essay." *Life Writing* 2:2 (2005): 143–54.

CLIFFORD, James. *Routes: Travel and Translation in the Late Twentieth Century.* Cambridge: Harvard University Press, 1997.

COUSER, G. Thomas. "Genre Matters: Form, Force, and Filiation." *Life Writing* 2:2 (2005): 123–40.

GILROY, Paul. *Against Race: Imagining Political Culture Beyond the Color Line.* Cambridge: Harvard University Press, 2000.

HALL, Stuart. "Cultural Identity and Diaspora." *Theorizing Diaspora.* Ed. Jana Evans Braziel and Anita Mannur. Oxford: Blackwell, 2003. 233–46.

GREKUL, Lisa. *Leaving Shadows: Literature in English by Canada's Ukrainians.* Edmonton: University of Alberta Press, 2005.

KAMBOURELI, Smaro. "Staging Cultural Criticism: Michael Ignatieff's *Blood and Belonging* and Myrna Kostash's *Bloodlines.*" *Journal of Canadian Studies* 31:3 (1996): 166–86.

KOSTASH, Myrna. *Bloodlines: A Journey Into Eastern Europe.* Vancouver: Douglas & McIntyre, 1993.

———. "The Crisis of Non-fiction." *Canadian Issues* Dec. 2003: 25.

———. *The Doomed Bridegroom: A Memoir.* Edmonton: NeWest Press, 1998.

———. "In Praise of Journalism: Why the 'creative non-fiction' label obscures the real value of true stories about the world." *Quill & Quire* 71:6 (2005): 14.

KRÖLLER, Eva-Marie. "The Journey Home: Myrna Kostash's *Bloodlines* and Other Journeys into Eastern Europe." *Images of Central Europe in Travelogues and Fiction by North American Writers.* Ed. Waldemar Zacharasiewicz. Tübingen: Stauffenburg-Verlag, 1995. 353–62.

MCNEILL, Laurie. "Labelling our Selves: Genres and Life Writing." *Life Writing* 2:2 (2005): xi–xxii.

MEDWAY, Peter. "Fuzzy Genres and Community Identities: The Case of Architecture Students' Sketchbooks." *The Rhetoric and Ideology of Genre: Strategies for Stability and Change.* Ed. Richard Coe, Lorelei Lingard, and Tatiana Teslenko. Cresskill, NJ: Hampton, 2002. 123–53.

MILLER, Carolyn. "Genre as Social Action." *Quarterly Journal of Speech* 70 (1984): 151–67.

RUSHDIE, Salman. *Imaginary Homelands.* London: Granta, 1991.

SAFRAN, William. "Diasporas in Modern Societies: Myths of Homeland and Return." *Diaspora* 1:1 (1991): 83–99.

VAN LUVEN, Lynne. *Going Some Place: Creative Non-fiction Across Canada.* Regina: Coteau, 2000.

AFTERWORD

WRITING IN ALBERTA – UP, DOWN, OR SIDEWAYS?

FRED STENSON

In 1967, when I was fifteen years old and living on a farm in Twin Butte, Alberta, I wanted to be a writer. About the only thing I knew about becoming a writer was that, if successful, I would not be the first one in my community. Andy Russell, who lived near Waterton and occasionally bought grain from us, had written the book *Grizzly Country*, which was a major success. I had attended a film-talk by Andy at the Twin Butte Hall, where he described speaking to the Explorers' Club in New York – and how much easier it was to impress the New Yorkers than the Twin Butte locals who were so much more inclined to argue on the subject of bears.

Besides Andy, there was Scotty Freebairn, a tiny bald man with a white fringe above his ears, who in my childhood used to visit his way around the clothing stores where he had formerly worked as a sales clerk. Scotty had moved to Pincher Creek from Scotland around 1900 and had written two books of poetry. He also wrote a memoir of Pincher Creek's early days, which his family published under the title *60 Years in an Old Cow Town.*

There were still more writers. Across the Waterton River were the Mormon villages of Hillspring and Glenwood. Herbert Harker, author of the novels *Goldenrod* and *Turn Again Home,* was born in Glenwood.

Though my own ambition to be a writer was tied to 1960s pop culture, and was excited into being by authors like Leonard Cohen, Ken Kesey, and J. D. Salinger, I was still aware, from the evidence of my own community, that writing was a possible career for a rural southern Albertan. Without the local practitioners, I may have felt I had to leave Alberta. Maybe I would have moved on to a different dream.

While pursuing a Bachelor of Arts at the University of Calgary, I was not shy about telling people I planned to be a writer. I had already, during high school, penned my first novel, a not unfaithful facsimile of *Catcher in the Rye.* My hero Ben Hollinger had been sent to a boarding school by indifferent parents, just like Holden Caulfield. I had seen one boarding school, the St. Mary's Catholic Residential School on the Blood Reserve. My friend Charlie Weaselhead of the St. Mary's Warriors had given me a tour during a basketball tournament. But, for my novel, Charlie's school did not seem right. I created one that was in a city. It had cruel prefects (whatever those were) and a girls' boarding school conveniently just across a park, so you could sneak over at night.

In 1972, when I graduated from the University of Calgary with a BA in economics, I still intended to be a writer and saved money for the backpack journey to Europe that I was sure would turn me into one. Less than a month before leaving, I went to a library in Lethbridge to look at travel books. I saw a poster advertising the Search-for-an-Alberta-Novelist Competition put on by the Alberta Government. I decided to enter it.

The existence of that contest was remarkable – in ways I did not understand at the time. I knew the Social Credit Party of Alberta had been defeated by Peter Lougheed's Progressive Conservatives in 1971, but I did not know how the look and content of government had changed. Lougheed's Conservatives created Canada's first provincial environment and culture ministries. In the culture ministry was a Literary Arts Branch under the direction of John Patrick Gillese. Mr. Gillese had raised a large family in Edmonton as a short story specialist in the era before television. The novelist competition was John Patrick's idea. Macmillan of Canada would publish the winner if they thought it good enough.

I did write the novel – a new one after the *Catcher in the Rye* one struck me as, well, unoriginal. I wrote *Lonesome Hero,* on trains, in youth hostels, and in pubs. Understanding the impossibility of going further on my own, I bundled up the mass of scribblers and airmailed them home, begging my family to get it typed. Amazingly, heroically, they did.

Six months later, I received the news that my novel had not won the competition, but was one of two finalists out of 98 entrants. Jan Truss's *Bird at the Window* was the winner. Cecelia Frey's *Breakaway* was one finalist; *Lonesome Hero* was the other. The three novels were to be published by Macmillan in 1974.

When I returned to Canada in the summer of 1973, I heard that the Literary Arts Branch was putting on a weekend writers' workshop at Lethbridge. Of course I went. I met John Patrick Gillese and his assistants, and a nice fuss was made over me. I made another discovery that was not so much to my liking. In the first room full of people I entered, I was the youngest by two decades. However age-ist that may sound, any 21-year-old would have felt the same. I was hoping to make new friends who were writers; maybe even writer girlfriends. I did meet two people near my age: Donaleen Saul, an Edmonton film writer, and the playwright, Gordon Pengilly, from Stirling.

Over the next few years, I saw many of these weekend workshops. They had a style that no longer exists: patriotic, monarchist, always positive and hopeful. John Patrick Gillese's generation of writing friends were the speakers. They introduced one another flatteringly and at great length. For a budding satirist, it was a bit too nice, a bit square – like a fowl supper or a silver wedding anniversary.

But I *was* amazed by what the speakers at these workshop weekends had done in their lives. Dr. George Hardy, a U of A professor emeritus, had written popular historical novels about Ancient Rome. I was blown away to discover that Dr. Hardy had been with Sir Arthur Evans when Evans excavated the palace of Knossos on Crete in the 1920s.

Another writer I met was Lovat Dickson, former publisher of Macmillan UK. Dickson had published my childhood hero Grey Owl in England and had introduced Grey Owl to the Queen.

I met Rudy Wiebe in Red Deer. Rudy had just caused a fuss by breaking the positivism rule. He had told a packed house that, out of the whole bunch of them, maybe one would publish a book. He invited me to visit him at the University of Alberta English Department. A nice coincidence was that, when I did visit Rudy at U of A, he had just received the phone call telling him that his novel *Temptations of Big Bear* had won the Governor General's Award for Fiction. It was a novel I would soon read and love, and be changed by.

These meetings were the best part of my experiences at the Literary Arts Branch writing workshops. But I was also growing irritated and frustrated by them. The lack of current examples was a problem; the absence of reference to Margaret Laurence, Margaret Atwood, Alice Munro, Robertson Davies, Robert Kroetsch. The advice on how to write emphasized something called the family short story: Christian values and likeable characters. Meanwhile, I was reading *The Ginger Man*, George Macdonald Fraser's Harry Flashman series, *The Alexandria Quartet*. I wanted bawdy stories and unreasonable madmen in lead roles. I wanted black-humorous laughs and wrenching unfair sadness.

Lonesome Hero was published by Macmillan in 1974. Toronto was about the only place in Canada that an Alberta writer could be published in 1974. Macmillan of Canada and McClelland and Stewart were the giants of Canadian publishing, followed by a handful of branch plants and small experimental presses. But the big time was M&S: the domestic superstar upon whose list everyone wanted to be. Macmillan was almost as good, but Jack McClelland's company was always more in the news because of his flamboyance.

Even in 1974, the power of these two English-Canadian giants was under threat. M&S was losing money. The Canada Council was propping it up and getting annoyed. Canadian presses were under pressure to be more viable, which meant safer and more commercial publishing. A good reader of tea leaves could have seen that publishing new writers from the regions was something they were likely to lop off. I had arrived at the height of the good times, about a moment before the decline.

Our Alberta trio of contest books was reviewed all across Canada. Fool that I was, I thought that was normal. Kildare Dobbs said nice things about *Lonesome Hero* in the *Globe and Mail*. The novelty of the competition caused this interest. When the Seal Books first book award came along a few years later, the Alberta contest looked instantly puny. It would be a very long time before I had a *Globe and Mail* review again.

After 1974, I wrote like mad. I taught creative writing at Drumheller and Bowden prisons and tried to squeeze a novel out of it. When I came to Macmillan with the novel, it was declined. Douglas Gibson, who was with Macmillan back then, said something indicative of the state of change. The time when big Canadian publishers could nurture baby careers at a loss was over. My kind would have to go away and learn to write finished books before they could be published. I went away and continued to try, but it was a time of darkness and despair. The better part was that I shifted gears and became a freelance writer of documentary and educational films: a living that would support me for decades.

It was also a time of meeting writers. In 1976, I received a letter from Robert Kroetsch, inviting me to join The Writers Union of Canada. Soon, I was attending TWUC AGMs in Ontario. All around me were Canada's finest writers: Atwood, Lawrence, Berton, Shields, Matt Cohen, Alistair MacLeod, Jane Rule. I probably made a social gaffe an hour, but the benefits outweighed making a fool of myself. I met Alberta writers there too: Merna Summers, Robert Kroetsch, and, after a couple of years in the union, Aritha van Herk. Aritha and Robert Sherrin were the first TWUC members to come along who were younger than I was. Aritha had recently won the SEAL award for *Judith*, with its astounding $50,000 prize. I was no doubt envious, but also pleased that an Albertan had taken the plum.

By meeting these fellow Albertans, I discovered that there was a process in the works to see that Alberta's government presence in the literary arts became more literary. I heard about plans for publishing companies in western Canada. The feeling was that the federal publishing structure was holding us back, slowing us down, defining Western Canadian literature by the process of publish or reject. If we had our own presses, the future could be different.

An early result was NeWest Press, founded in 1977 by George Melnyk. NeWest Press was part of the NeWest Institute. This family of cultural vehicles sought to bring Western writing and thought more into visibility, with more independence from central Canadian editorializing of our content. Saskatchewan and Manitoba were ahead of Alberta. Coteau Books of Regina and Manitoba's Turnstone Press had started in 1975. These presses, along with Thistledown, Red Deer College Press, and Queenston House, were destined to give a new vitality and freedom to writing and publishing in Western Canada. They were important reasons why a powerful surge of literary activity took place.

In 1980, the Writers Guild of Alberta was founded. The founding meeting was in Calgary, in October. That summer, thirty-five Alberta writers had met in Edmonton to hammer out the concept of the guild. They donated the money that allowed the founding meeting to happen. Those involved included Robert Kroetsch, Rudy Wiebe, Merna Summers, Jan Truss, Miriam

Mandel, Chris Wiseman, Ted Blodgett, Edna Alford, Doug Barbour, Monty Reid, Aritha van Herk, Warren Graves, and Larry Pratt. My apologies to the rest, whose names elude me now.

There were 150 writers at the guild's founding meeting in October 1980. Rudy Wiebe was elected first president. It was a time of excitement and wild fun. That weekend I completed the circle of friends I had long been looking for. Among others, I met Wade Bell, Diane Schoemperlen, Mary Riskin, Joan Clark, Monty Reid, Candas Dorsey, Reg Silvester, and Rhona McAdam.

One of the first projects of the guild was "The Travelling Nude." The name was that of a Henry Kriesel story about a woman who travels from town to town to pose nude for art classes. Our traveling nude would be a roving writer-in-residence. The first one was Gloria Sawai and she went to the town of Killam.

The guild was a force: a blend of senior, mid-career, and beginning writers, all committed to community and improvement of our literature and our lives as writers. From the first, we wanted an Alberta literary foundation at arm's length from government, where writing grants could be decided by peer juries. The idea began its grudging progress through government.

I was on the second board of the guild when Edmonton poet Ted Blodgett was president. It was the year the WGA awards program was initiated. It was Ted's idea to name the awards after famous literary pioneers. It was humbling that Ted, an immigrant from the U.S., had names in mind for every award: Stephan Stephansson, Ross Annett, Howard O'Hagen, George Bugnet, and Wilfred Eggleston. The first four presidents of the guild were Rudy Wiebe, Ted Blodgett, Joan Clark, and Chris Wiseman. The first executive director was Mary Riskin (now Mary Walters) who many credit with enabling the guild to survive its early years.

The Alberta Foundation for the Literary Arts was founded in 1984. Culture Minister Mary LeMessurier had created a steering committee to work on the foundation concept and many guild members sat on that committee. I was on it for a short while, with Rudy Wiebe and Doug Barbour. John Patrick Gillese was present at the meetings, and it was clear that his vision of Alberta literature and his power over Alberta literature were being curtailed. Much as I liked John Patrick, and much as I had benefited from his arts branch programs, this was a necessary change. The founding of AFLA was a revolution, and like all revolutions was at times messy, unkind, and gloating. John Patrick's fondness for digging in the rural lands for writers was an important counterbalance to the university-based approach to building our literature. But the guild was better at understanding that literary writing was the respected writing of the world, not some pointy-headed closet activity. The guild brought everyone together; respected everyone; listened to everyone.

The first executive director of the Alberta Foundation for the Literary Arts was George Melnyk. Based on lottery funds, the foundation was almost everything we wanted. It was well funded. It would decide grants by peer jury. Was it arm's length? About as arm's length as such a body can be. The composition of the board was determined by government, but we did manage to get poet Chris Wiseman appointed to the board in its early years. Eventually, in 1991, the government wanted and took tighter control. AFLA was rolled into one big arts foundation called AFA (Alberta Foundation for the Arts). There would be an erosion of the literary arts budget and an absence of writers on the board. But the basic peer jury principle has survived, albeit through many challenges.

This thirty-year story has made it only as far as year ten. But, from my vantage, those first ten years do seem to have been the crucial ones. The WGA, AFLA, and the first prairie presses were the institutions that allowed us to grow. My life as a writer has been an Alberta career first, a Canadian career second. The Alberta writing institutions, government and civil, have nourished me more than federal and central Canadian ones. The Writers' Union of Canada has been an important factor in my life, but no more so than the Writers Guild of Alberta.

When I did start publishing again after my first novel, the next four books of fiction were published in Alberta and Saskatchewan. I edited two anthologies of Alberta writing: *Alberta Bound* and *The Road Home* (both published by Alberta presses).

I remained active with TWUC and the WGA. I have over the years served on three TWUC councils and four WGA boards. I was president of the WGA in 1996. The popularity of the provincial guilds was occasionally seen as a threat and impediment to federal writing institutions, and I remember a tremendous argument I had in the Toronto airport with an Ontario TWUC person who felt something should be done about that. I remember saying, "You leave the prairie guilds alone. It's none of your damn business if we prefer them and feel better served by them." It still makes me mad. A whole literature was flowering out of our regionalism: Sawai, Summers, Hollingshead, Walters, Dorsey, Bell, Bishop, McAdam, Silvester, Jakober, Alford, Wiseman,

Clark. I could go on for several lines more and not run out of names. Saskatchewan had, if anything, a longer list of writers that its provincial guild had fostered. To have all that perceived as anti-national, un-Canadian was truly infuriating – as if we were to blame for the fact that the rest of Canada wasn't as interested in reading us as we were.

But if writing careers were being fostered regionally in Alberta and on the prairies generally, it begs the question, "What kind of writing careers?" It did seem at times that we were doomed to small careers and readerships, but that too began to change with the years. Robert Kroetsch and Rudy Wiebe had led the way for Albertans into the winners' circle of national awards in the 1970s. In the 1990s, the parade resumed and lengthened. Looking at the Governor General's Awards for Literature, Rudy Wiebe and Robert Hilles won in fiction and poetry in 1994; Greg Hollingshead won for fiction in 1995; Ted Blodgett won for poetry in 1996; Gloria Sawai won for fiction in 2002. All of those people were living in Alberta at the time of their awards.

In the year 2000, my own novel *The Trade,* fifteen years in the works, was nominated for the Giller Prize and won three Alberta awards. *The Trade* was my eleventh book. In 2008, my novel *The Great Karoo* was nominated for the Governor-General's Literary Award.

The current generation of Alberta writers and artists has a different sense of identity. The young writers I work with at the Banff Centre, where I direct the Wired Writing Studio, write about their adventures and work in places like Thailand, Guatemala, and the Hindu Kush. They wish to be global writers, and I wish them well even if I will never perceive of myself that way. Writing about my region, past and present, is what works for me.

Finally, on a note of humility, I recognize that this history must be rather like the ones I listened to at the Alberta Literary Arts Branch weekend workshops of the early seventies, the ones I found so pointlessly autobiographical and square. Maybe all I really have to say to younger writers, critics, and theorists is that tradition is important. Whether the tradition you choose is local, regional, national, continental, or global is up to you.

CONTRIBUTOR BIOGRAPHIES

Jars Balan is an Edmonton author, poet, editor, and literary translator. He is the administrative coordinator of the Kule Ukrainian Canadian Studies Centre for the Canadian Institute of Ukrainian Studies at the University of Alberta. A specialist in the history of Ukrainians in Canada, he has written and published extensively on Ukrainian Canadian literature and drama.

Pamela Banting is the author of *Body Inc.: A Theory of Translation Poetics* and the editor of the anthology *Fresh Tracks: Writing the Western Landscape.* She teaches creative nonfiction, nature writing and environmental literature, literary theory, and North American literature in the English Department, University of Calgary. She is the inaugural president of the Association for Literature, Environment, and Culture in Canada (www.alecc.ca).

Douglas Barbour is the winner of the Stephan Stephansson Award for Poetry and the author of many books of poetry, including *Visible Visions: The Selected Poems of Douglas Barbour* (NeWest Press 1984), *Story for a Saskatchewan Night* (rdc press 1990), *Fragmenting Body etc.* (NeWest Press/SALT Publishing 2000), *Breath Takes* (Wolsak & Wynn 2001), and, most recently, with Sheila E. Murphy, *Continuations* (University of Alberta Press 2006). His critical works include *Michael Ondaatje* (Twayne Publishers 1993), and *Lyric/Anti-lyric: Essays on Contemporary Poetry* (NeWest Press 2001). He is Professor Emeritus in the Department of English, University of Alberta, Edmonton.

Donna Coates teaches Canadian and Australian literatures in the Department of English, University of Calgary. She has published numerous essays and book chapters on Canadian, Australian, and New Zealand women's responses (fiction and drama) to the First World War, and Australian and Canadian women's responses (fiction and drama) to the Second World War, and Australian women's responses (fiction) to the Vietnam War. With Sherrill Grace, she is co-editor of *Canada and the Theatre of War: Eight Plays* (2008).

Sherrill Grace is Professor of English and Distinguished University Scholar at the University of British Columbia where she teaches Canadian Literature. Her most recent books include *Theatre and Autobiography* (Talonbooks 2006), co-edited with Jerry Wasserman, and *Inventing Tom Thomson* (McGill-Queen's 2004). Her biography of Sharon Pollock, *Making Theatre: A Life of Sharon Pollock* (Talonbooks) was published in the spring of 2008.

Lisa Grekul is a creative writer and a literary scholar whose research focuses on Canadian literature (minority/diasporic writers, in particular). Her first novel, *Kalyna's Song*, published by Coteau in 2003, was shortlisted for the Amazon.ca/Books in Canada Best First Book Award and her second book, *Leaving Shadows: Literature in English by Canada's Ukrainians* (University of Alberta, 2005), for the Kobzar Literary Award. Grekul teaches Canadian literature in the Department of Critical Studies at the University of British Columbia's Okanagan campus in Kelowna.

Helen Hoy teaches English and Women's Studies at the University of Guelph. She has published *Modern English-Canadian Prose* (Gale 1983), *The Native in Literature* (ECW 1987), co-edited with Thomas King and Cheryl Calver, and published articles on Canadian fiction, Hugh MacLennan, Gabrielle Roy, Robertson Davies, Henry James, and Alice Munro. Her latest book, *How Should I Read These? Native Women Writers in Canada* (University of Toronto Press 2001), examines reading and teaching First Nations writing by cultural outsiders.

Frances Kaye teaches Native Studies, Canadian Studies, and Great Plains Studies at the University of Nebraska-Lincoln and occasionally at the University of Calgary. Her study of arts audiences on the Prairies, *Hiding the Audience*, was published by the University of Alberta Press in 2003. She also considers the streets and jails to be her classrooms.

George Melnyk is Associate Professor, Canadian Studies and Film Studies, Faculty of Communication and Culture, University of Calgary. He is a cultural historian specializing in two distinct areas: Alberta's literary identity and Canadian cinema. In the area of Alberta literature, he is the author of the two-volume, *Literary History of Alberta* (1998–99) and co-editor of *The Wild Rose Anthology of Alberta Prose* (2003).

Anne Nothof is Professor of English at Athabasca University. She has published critical essays in journals such as *Theatre Research in Canada*, *Modern Drama*, *Mosaic*, and the *International Journal of Canadian Studies*, and in two texts on postmodern theatre: *Siting the Other*, and *Crucible of Cultures*. She has edited a collection of essays on Canadian playwright Sharon Pollock for Guernica Press, a collection of essays on Alberta theatre for Playwrights Canada Press, and an issue of *Canadian Theatre Review* on Alberta theatre. She is a board member and editor for NeWest Press, board member for AU Press, and past president of the Canadian Association for Theatre Research. She is also editor for the *Canadian Theatre Encyclopedia* (www.canadiantheatre.com).

Christian Riegel is Associate Professor and Head of English at Campion College, University of Regina. He teaches Canadian literature and has published *Twenty-First Century Canadian Writers* (Thomson-Gale 2007); *Response to Death: The Literary Work of Mourning* (University of Alberta Press 2005); *Writing Grief: Margaret Laurence and the Work of Mourning* (University of Manitoba Press 2003); *A Sense of Place: Re-evaluating Regionalism in Canadian and American Writing* (University of Alberta Press 1998); and *Challenging Territory: The Writing of Margaret Laurence* (University of Alberta Press 1997). He is currently working on a monograph on mourning and memorial in the works of Robert Kroetsch, Eli Mandel, and Birk Sproxton.

Malin Sigvardson is Visiting Assistant Professor at the English Department, Stockholm University, Sweden, and at the Centre for Modern Languages at Stockholm School of Economics. Her PhD thesis "The Constitution of Movement in Rudy Wiebe's Fiction: A Phenomenological Study of Three Mennonite Novels" (Stockholm University) was accepted in 2006.

Fred Stenson has written fifteen books (eight fiction, seven non-fiction). His historical novels *The Trade* and *Lightning* won the Grant MacEwan Author's Prize. *The Trade* also won the Writers Guild of Alberta George Bugnet Novel Prize and the City of Edmonton Book Prize, and was nominated for the Giller Prize. He is director of the Wired Writing Studio at the Banff Centre and has been a regular columnist for *AlbertaViews* Magazine since its inception in 1999. He is a former president of the Writers Guild of Alberta and a current board member of the Writers Union of Canada. His third historical novel *The Great Karoo* was short-listed for the Governor-General's Award for Fiction, and was published by Doubleday Canada in 2008.

Aritha van Herk is a University Professor and Professor of English at the University of Calgary. She is a novelist, writer, teacher, and public intellectual. Her first novel, *Judith,* received the Seal First Novel Award in 1978. Her second novel, *The Tent Peg,* appeared in 1981, and her third novel, *No Fixed Address,* was nominated for the Governor General's Award for fiction in 1986. Her most recent novel is *Restlessness* (1998). She is the author of hundreds of reviews and articles on contemporary literature and history. Her nonfiction *Mavericks: An Incorrigible History of Alberta,* won the Grant MacEwan Author's Award for Alberta Writing in 2002. *Audacious and Adamant: The Story of Maverick Alberta* accompanies a permanent exhibit, inspired by her earlier book, which was recently installed at the Glenbow Museum in Calgary. She is a Fellow of the Royal Society of Canada and active in the literary and cultural life of the West, the nation, and the world.

MARQUIS

Marquis Book Printing Inc.

Québec, Canada

2009